THE BOOK OF THE SAVIOUR

BLESSING CHRIST
Hans Memling
In the collection of Dr. A. Hamilton Rice, New York

THE BOOK
OF THE
SAVIOUR

✠

Assembled by

F. J. SHEED

✠

Sheed & Ward : New York

1952

Nihil Obstat
John J. Consodine
Diocesan Censor

Imprimatur
✠ Richard J. Cushing
Archbishop of Boston

May 12, 1952

The Nihil Obstat and the Imprimatur are ecclesiastical declarations that a publication is free of doctrinal or moral error, not a statement of the positive worth, nor an implication that the contents have the Archbishop's approval or recommendation.

Assembler's Note

All the selections here included, except G. K. Chesterton's "The God in the Cave" and "Riddles of the Gospel" are from books we have published in England or America or both, though some of the poems are of our publication only in the sense that they appeared in anthologies published by us.

For the reader's convenience I have provided Narratives at the beginning of each Part and Theological Appendices at the end of Parts I and III. These last might be omitted on a first reading. Where there is uncertainty about the order in which things happened, I have followed Père Lagrange, O.P.

F.J.S.

CONTENTS

III. FROM PALM SUNDAY TO PENTECOST

ILLUSTRATIONS

[xi]

Acknowledgments

We wish to acknowledge the courtesy of the following in permitting us to include reproductions in this book:

W. F. Mansell for THE RAISING OF LAZARUS, THE ENTRY INTO JERUSALEM, THE CRUCIFIXION, and THE RESURRECTION.

The Frick Museum for THE PRESENTATION IN THE TEMPLE.

CHRIST BEFORE PILATE, from The Art Museum, Princeton University, is reproduced from a photograph by Reuben Goldberg.

PROLOGUE

I

❧ FROM THE FIRST MAN, Adam, we are all sprung; in him the whole human race was incorporated, since there is no one of us that does not come from him; he *was* the whole human race when God made him. Adam had the natural life that made him man—the union of spiritual soul and material body which constituted his nature as man, without which he would not have been man: and this natural life he had in a state of perfection, all his powers and faculties rightly ordered, body subordinate to soul, soul ruled by reason. He also had the Supernatural Life—the life above nature—that whereby he would be able to live the life of Heaven hereafter, whereby even in this life his whole soul was "supernaturalized," capable of a relationship with God altogether higher and holier than anything that could take its rise in man's merely natural endowments. The highest and holiest point of this relationship and the very condition of the Supernatural Life was for Adam, as it is for all men, the union of the soul with God by love. And while he had the Supernatural Life, God also exempted his nature from the law of death—from the separation of soul and body which is the natural termination of man's life on this earth.

For Adam the simplest elements of the road of human life were two, not three—his entry into life was at one end and Heaven was at the other: death did not lie in between. That, simply

and directly, was God's scheme. And man wrecked the scheme.
Adam sinned, rebelled against God; and thereby lost the Supernatural Life, for this Life cannot exist where the love of God
is not, and love of Him cannot exist where there is rebellion
against Him. Scripture represents the sinful action as the eating
of the fruit of the forbidden tree. There is some mystery here.
But two things about it we know. The first is that it was a sin
of disobedience to God. The second is that the Devil played
a part in it.

It is important to understand Adam's new condition. He had
lost the Supernatural Life: he retained the natural life, or the
union of body and soul; the soul retained the natural powers
of intellect and will. Supernaturally he was dead, for the loss
of life is death; naturally he still lived. But even his nature did
not emerge from the disaster unimpaired. It lost the privilege
of exemption from death; henceforth man must pass through
the gateway of death to reach his eternal destiny. More serious
still was that man's nature lost its *direction*. Adam had sinned
because he had chosen his own will instead of God's—he had
swung his nature out of its true Godward direction, and had
introduced war into the very inmost part of his nature, into the
union of body and spirit—body warring against spirit, spirit torn
by war in its own powers.

Thus then stood Adam, the *individual* man—the Supernatural Life lost, the natural life impaired because given a wrong
direction; but still knowing the purpose of his being and the
laws set by God for the governance of his life. But Adam was
also, by God's dispensation, the *representative* man, and the
effect of this catastrophe upon the whole human race is meas-
ureless. As a mere physical consequence the nature he had to
hand on to his descendants was an impaired nature, strongly
attracted to sin. Worse than that: in Adam the race lost the
Supernatural Life: so that men thereafter (with one glorious
exception) were to enter this world with the natural life of soul

and body but without the Supernatural Life: the right relationship of oneness between God and the human race was broken
and Heaven was closed to man.

The problem for the human race was precisely the restoration
of the broken oneness with God: it was the problem of at-one-
ment, which we disguise by the pronunciation *atonement*. God
knew how He would solve the problem: how the human race
might be re-united with Him. And it can hardly be for nothing
that the first statement God made of what He would do, He
made not to Adam, but to the Devil, and He made it in terms
of victory over the Devil: his head was to be crushed.

II

In God's plan for the re-establishment of the whole race, a
special part was to be acted by one race, the Jews, and because
of this God brought them into a special relation with Himself.
This special relation of one people with God begins at a time
and a place—the time roughly 2000 B.C., the place Haran in the
land of Chanaan. There had come Abram, with his father and
his brothers, from the Chaldean town of Ur. And God said to
Abram (Gen. xi): "I will make of thee a great nation, and I
will bless thee and magnify thy name: and thou shalt be blessed.
I will bless them that bless thee and curse them that curse thee;
and in thee shall all the kindred of the earth be blessed." In the
years that followed, God renewed the promises many times:
but it was twenty-five years later that the great covenant was
made which constituted the Jews God's people (Gen. xvii):
"God said to him: *I am*. And my covenant is with thee; and
thou shalt be a father of many nations . . . And I will establish
my covenant between me and thee, and between thy seed after
thee in their generations, by a perpetual covenant: to be a God
to thee, and to thy seed after thee." God changed Abram's name
to Abraham, which means "father of nations" and gave the
command of circumcision "as a sign of the covenant."

God then had singled out a particular family which was to grow into a nation: not for their own sake but for the sake of all mankind: they were chosen not simply for a favour but for a function, something God was to do through them for the whole race. This God makes clear again (Gen. xxii): "In thy seed shall all the nations of the earth be blessed."

These promises were repeated to Abraham's second son Isaac (he had already had a son Ishmael by a bondwoman) and to Isaac's second son Jacob (for the elder, Esau, had foresworn his birthright). In all this we see the hint of Redemption—all mankind is to be blessed through the seed of Abraham. And soon comes the hint of a Redeemer, and even of the mode of the Redemption—Jacob, dying, prophesies one who is to come from his fourth son Juda: "The sceptre shall not be taken away from Juda, nor a ruler from his thigh, till he come that is to be sent: and he shall be the expectation of nations. Tying his foal to the vineyard, and his ass, O my son, to the vine: He shall wash his robe in wine and his garment in the blood of the grape." (Gen. xlix, 10–11).

By now the children of Jacob, to whom God had given the new name of Israel, were in Egypt, and there they were to be for four hundred years. The last part of that time they were fiercely oppressed, until God brought them out of Egypt under the leader Moses, whom he had appointed to them. The last act of their time in Egypt was spectacular. The angel of God visited the houses of the Egyptians slaying the first-born, but he passed over the houses of the children of Israel, who had marked their door-posts with the blood of a lamb sacrificed by God's ordinance. And God ordered that this passing over (pasch is the Hebrew word) should be celebrated each year by the sacrifice and eating of a lamb.

So the Israelites went from Egypt, crossed the Red Sea and came into the Arabian Desert: and there, upon Mt. Sinai, the Covenant was renewed and the Law was given. God gave the

Jews, through Moses, the Ten Commandments and a great mass of moral, ritual and legal precepts covering every detail of their lives. Sacrifices were offered and Moses "taking the book of the covenant" read it in the hearing of all the people: and they said, "All things that the Lord hath spoken, we will do. We will be obedient. And he took the blood and sprinkled it upon the people, and he said: *This is the blood of the covenant* which the Lord has made with you concerning all these words" (Ex. xxiv).

Let us repeat that the Jews were chosen because of something God meant to accomplish through them for the whole world. The essence of their function lay in this—that from them was to come the Redeemer, who should redeem all mankind. Meanwhile, they were to bear witness to truths which were in danger of perishing, which indeed seemed to have perished utterly: the truth that there is but one God, the truth that God will send a Redeemer of mankind.

Observe that the Jews showed no great natural aptitude for, or any very tenacious hold upon, either truth. Monotheism, for instance, made no more appeal to them than to all that ocean of polytheistic people which surrounded them. All their instincts ran to strange gods and to idols: the thing seems to have been a craving as strong as a man might feel for alcohol. They were forever going after the ways of the heathen, and God forever restoring them to right ways. God's pedagogy was of two sorts: He allowed their enemies to work their will upon them as a reminder that they were in the hand of the one God and could achieve nothing without Him: He sent them the Prophets to bear glowing and glorious witness to the same truth. If the Jews found monotheism difficult, they found not much easier the doctrine as to the nature of the Messias, the Anointed One, who was to come, and of the Kingdom He was to found. Here again the Prophets were their instructors, and as the centuries pass the picture of the Messias grows in detail and in clarity.

Yet we should be mistaken if we exaggerated the clarity.
There is a vast mass of prophecy and a magnificence over all
of it. But much of it is obscure even to us who have seen its
fulfilment; certain elements which now seem most wonderfully
fulfilled appear buried in their context, not emphasized as
prophetical or especially likely to catch the ear or the eye. The
Prophets did not provide a blackboard diagram and then proceed to lecture on it. Indeed our modern use of the word
prophet may give us a wrong notion of their office. To prophesy
does not mean to foretell but to speak out. They were not there
primarily to foretell the future but to utter the eternal and
judge the present by it. The Jews not unnaturally found morality
harder even than monotheism: the Law had imposed on them
a morality stricter than any known to men, and they fell from
it. The Prophets thundered against this as against strange gods.
For here too they must judge the present by the eternal.

But precisely because that was their function they did speak
much of Him who was to come. Consider how the picture builds
up. We have already seen that One who was to be the expectation of nations should come from Juda. From the Psalms (e.g.,
Ps. cxxxi, 11) we gather the further detail that He was to be
a descendant of David the King, and this is confirmed by the
statement of Isaias (xi, 1) that he is to be "a rod out of the root
of Jesse," for Jesse was David's father: "In that day, the root
of Jesse, who standeth for an ensign of the people, him the
Gentiles shall beseech: and his sepulchre shall be glorious."
There is no explicit statement that this is the Messias: but St.
Paul takes it for granted (Rom. xv, 12), and in any event no Jew
doubted that the Messias was to be sprung from David.

In the seventh chapter of Isaias we read "Behold a virgin shall
conceive and bear a son: and his name shall be called Emmanuel."
From St. Matthew (i, 23) we know that this is a prophecy of
the virgin birth of Christ; yet in the context, one might well
think that the prophecy referred to an event immediately ex-

pected and actually described in the next chapter of Isaias, the eighth, as having happened. In the light of our new knowledge, we can re-read the eighth chapter and see that though there is some sort of fulfilment there and then, yet some mightier thing is involved: the language used is of a grandeur too great for the actual episode.

The fifth chapter of Micheas tells us that the Messias is to be born in Bethlehem: "And thou, Bethlehem Ephrata, art a little one among the thousands of Juda: out of thee shall he come forth unto me that is to be the ruler in Israel: and his going forth is from the beginning, from the days of eternity. . . . And this man shall be our peace."

There are other details which we see fulfilled, but which could hardly have meant so much to their first hearers: thus Zacharias (ix, 9) writes: "Rejoice greatly, O daughter of Sion, shout for joy, O daughter of Jerusalem: Behold thy King will come to thee, the just and saviour. He is poor and riding upon an ass, upon a colt, the foal of an ass."

Such details as we have been considering—that the Messias was to be of the tribe of Juda, of the family of David, born of a virgin and in Bethlehem—are not the primary things about Him. Two things that matter far more are Himself and what He was to do. Upon both, the prophecies are fuller and clearer.

As to what He was; there is a central stream of teaching which shows Him a man triumphant, and two parallel streams, one showing Him as more than a man, the other showing Him as less than triumphant. It would seem that the Jews concentrated on the central stream, and made little of either of the others. Yet these others are of such vast importance, that missing them one hardly sees Him at all.

That He was to be more than man, not simply the greatest of men, is indicated again and again. We have already seen the phrase of Micheas—"his going forth is from the beginning, from the days of eternity." The same truth is to be found in Psalm cix—"before the day star, I begot thee." But it is not only by pre-existence that the Messias seems to be more than man. The hints are everywhere—as for instance in the suggestion that He is to be son to God in a special way. (It is hard to see how they could be more than hints: the truth about the divinity of the Messias could not well be conveyed to a nation that did not know the doctrine of the Trinity.)

The reverse of the medal is the even clearer stream of prophecy that the Messias is to be poor and suffering. The greatest passages are in Psalm xxi and in Chapter liii of Isaias. The Psalm and the Chapter should be read most carefully. Here note a few verses from the Chapter, summing all up: "Despised and the most abject of men, a man of sorrows and acquainted with infirmity. . . .

"He shall be led as a sheep to the slaughter and shall be dumb as a lamb before his shearer. . . .

"And the Lord was pleased to bruise him in infirmity. If he shall lay down his life for sin, he shall see a long-lived seed. . . ."

To say that the Jews ignored a good deal of all this is not to accuse them of any startling malignity. The assertion of the Messias's pre-existence, for example, was difficult to reconcile with the certainty that he was to be a descendant of David: one gets the impression that the Jews, faced with two elements difficult to reconcile, simply took the intellectual line of least resistance, concentrated upon the clearer one and left the other in its mysteriousness. Similarly it is hard to see how anything short of what did in fact happen to Christ Our Lord could have shown the fulfilment both of the splendour and the suffering: lacking that clue, they concentrated on the more obvious.

But if their intellect followed the line of least resistance in the picture they formed of the Messias in Himself, their will seems to have followed the line of greatest complacency in the picture they formed of the Kingdom He was to found. They saw it as a Kingdom of Israel in which the Gentiles, if they came into it at all, should be very much in a subordinate place; and they saw it as an earthly and not as a spiritual Kingdom. The Prophets, properly read, supply correctives for both.

Thus they assert that the Messias is coming for a light to the Gentiles and that the Gentiles are to share in the joy of his Kingdom. When Psalm lxxi says: "In him shall all the tribes of the earth be blessed: all nations shall magnify him," it simply reasserts what God said to Abram in the first of the promises. Isaias is filled with the same teaching: and he indicates the possibility that there may be Jews excluded from the Kingdom and Gentiles admitted. So St. Paul (Rom. x, 20) explains the contrast (Isaias lxv) between what God says of the Gentiles: "Those who never looked for me have found me: I have made myself known to those who never asked for word of me," and what He says of the Jews: "I stretch out my hand all day to a people that refuses obedience and cries out against me." But if we find from the Prophets that the Gentiles were to have a place, and a place of joy in the Kingdom, it was left for St. Paul to utter in plain words the intimate secret of the total equality of Jew and Gentile in the Kingdom, the mystery of Christ "which was never made known to any human being in past ages . . . that through the gospel preaching the Gentiles are to win the same inheritance, to be made part of the same body, to share the same divine promise in Christ Jesus" (Eph. iii, 5–6).

Thus all who belong to Christ are of the seed of Abraham, and the promises of the Kingdom are to us. But what sort of Kingdom? The Jews, as we have seen, seemed to expect an earthly Kingdom. The Prophets do not precisely and explicitly contradict them, but they give a mass of teaching which should have made the notion of a merely earthly Kingdom untenable and not even desirable. Thus Ezechiel (xxxvi, 24–26): "And I will pour upon you clean water and you shall be cleansed from all your filthiness: and I will cleanse you from all your idols.

And I will give you a new heart and put a new spirit within you: and I will take away the stony heart out of your flesh and will give you a heart of flesh. And I will put my spirit in the midst of you." And Zacharias (ix): "And he shall speak peace to the Gentiles and his power shall be from sea to sea, and from the rivers even to the ends of the earth . . . And the Lord their God will save them in that day, as the flock of his people: for holy stones shall be lifted up over his land. For what is the good thing of him, and what is his beautiful thing, but the corn of the elect and wine bringing forth virgins?"

Indeed it is plain enough, for us who read the Prophets now, that there was to be a spiritualization at every point: even at the point of priesthood and sacrifice where Israel had most scrupulously observed the Law. For the Jewish priests and the Jewish sacrifices were but figures of, and preparations for, something that was mysteriously to transcend them. The Messias was to be (Ps. cix) "a priest forever according to the order of Melchisedech"—a strange phrase, for Melchisedech, who had offered a sacrifice of bread and wine, was not a Jew. As for the priesthood, so for the sacrifices: "From the rising of the sun even to the going down, my name is great among the Gentiles: and in every place there is sacrifice and there is offered to my name a clean oblation. For my name is great among the Gentiles saith the Lord of hosts" (Mal. i, 11).

Everything in Israel was preparatory, looked forward to something which should complete it. The Law given by God to Moses was not a consummation. It was a preparation: a hard and heavy preparation: not maturity, but a superb training for maturity.

I

The Hidden Years

"And, in the fulness of time, God sent his son, made of a woman, that we might receive the adoption of sons."

(Galatians iv, 4–5)

NARRATIVE

Observe that the fullness of time, with all the mysterious spiritual resonances that the phrase has, actually *is* in time. It belongs to history. It has indeed been dated for us with some precision. Time came to its fullness during the reign of Augustus, who, having defeated Mark Antony and his ally, Cleopatra, ruled from 27 B.C. to A.D. 14 and out of the ancient Roman Republic and its conquests fashioned the Roman Empire, whose destiny was to be so closely linked with that of Christ's Kingdom on earth. We can come even closer (though not to His exact year, much less to a month and a day). Herod the Great, thirty years King of Judea, was close to the end of his life, and he died in 4 B.C. St. Luke tells us that Augustus decreed a census of the whole Empire: as a consequence Joseph, a carpenter, "a man of David's clan and family," went from Nazareth in Galilee to register in David's city of Bethlehem in Judea. With him was his wife, Mary, also of David's line, still a virgin and ever to be a virgin. And in Bethlehem she gave birth to Jesus, who was the Christ, the Anointed one, the expectation of the nations.

For this, the highest function to which any human person had ever been called, God had prepared Mary most exquisitely. Her own conception in the womb of Anne, her mother, had been in the ordinary way of nature. But in the doctrine of the Immaculate Conception, the Church teaches that from the

[3]

moment that she was conceived, sanctifying grace was by the power of the Blessed Trinity in her soul: thus, she was never stained by Adam's sin. Throughout her life she was, by the power of the same most Holy Trinity, preserved from all personal sin. In due course she was betrothed, to Joseph, a carpenter—whose glory in the eyes of God's church has grown steadily, for all that we have not one word of his recorded.

During the time of betrothal, God (as St. Luke tells in his first chapter) sent the angel Gabriel to Nazareth where Mary was. And Gabriel greeted her: "Hail, full of grace; the Lord is with thee; blessed art thou among women."

Then came his message: "Mary, do not be afraid; thou hast found favour in the sight of God. And behold thou shalt conceive in thy womb, and shalt bear a son, and shalt call him Jesus. He shall be great, and men will know him for the Son of the Most High; the Lord God will give him the throne of his father David, and he shall reign over the Kingdom of Jacob eternally; his Kingdom shall never have an end."

And Mary said to the Angel: "How can that be, since I have no knowledge of man?"

The Angel answered: "The Holy Spirit will come upon thee, and the power of the Most High will overshadow thee. Thus that holy thing which is to be born of thee shall be known for the son of God."

Thus she conceived. And to Joseph, profoundly troubled, an angel appeared in a dream and said: "Joseph, son of David, do not be afraid to take thy wife Mary to thyself, for it is by the power of the Holy Ghost that she has conceived this child; and she will bear a son, whom thou shalt call Jesus, for he is to save his people from their sins."

One other incident of that time is recorded. Mary visited a cousin Elizabeth, who lived in Judea and who was six months with child—the child who was to be John the Baptist. And Elizabeth greeted her: "Blessed art thou among women and blessed is the fruit of thy womb. . . . As soon as the voice of thy greeting sounded in my ears, the child in my womb leapt for joy."

And now in Bethlehem Jesus is born; in a stable, because there was no room in the inn, no room at any rate that would give any sort of privacy for childbirth. To the new-born child came shepherds, for an angel had appeared to them with the message, "In the city of David a Saviour has been born for you, the Lord Christ himself," and a multitude of the heavenly army had cried, "Glory to God in the highest, and on earth peace to men of good-will."

On the eighth day Jesus was circumcised. And on the fortieth, His parents brought Him to the Temple "to present him before the Lord there." Two people—Anna, an aged woman, and Simeon to whom God had revealed that he should not die "until he had seen that Christ whom the Lord had anointed"— recognized the Child for what He was. Holding the Child, Simeon said: "Ruler of all, now dost thou let thy servant go in peace, according to thy word; for my eyes have seen that saving power of thine whom thou hast prepared in the sight of all the nations: this is the light which shall give revelation to the Gentiles, this is the glory of thy people Israel." Then to Mary herself he said, "This child is destined to bring about the rise and fall of many in Israel; to be a sign which men will refuse to acknowledge, and so the thoughts of many hearts shall be made manifest; and thy own soul a sword shall pierce."

We do not know at what point the Magi—who were philosopher-priests from Persia—arrived in Jerusalem asking: "Where is he that has been born the King of the Jews? We have seen his star in the East and we have come to worship him." Learned Jews told of the prophecy that Christ would be born in Bethlehem and there they went, bringing the Child gifts of gold, frankincense and myrrh. King Herod, close to death and set upon establishing a dynasty of his own blood, had questioned the Magi closely and commanded them to return to him with news of what they might find. When they did not, he decided in a characteristic gesture to slay every male child under two in and around Bethlehem. But Joseph, warned by an angel, fl with Mary and the Child to Egypt. How long the family lived there we have nothing to tell us. But on Herod's death they returned—not to Bethlehem, for Archelaus, now ruling in Judea, was as bloody a tyrant as his father; but to Nazareth.

Of the next thirty years—till the time when Jesus came to be baptized by John—we have but one episode. When He was twelve, Mary and Joseph took Him to Jerusalem for the paschal feast. They were a day's journey on their way home, when they discovered that He was not with them. On the third day of anguished searching they found Him in the Temple, listening to the teachers and asking them questions and amazing all who heard with the quickness of His mind and the answers He gave. And His mother said to Him: "My Son, why hast thou treated us so? Think, what anguish thy father and I have endured, searching for thee."

But He asked them, "What reason had you to search for me? Could you not tell that I must needs be in the place which belongs to my Father?"

He went back with them to Nazareth "and lived there in subjection to them." Then come twenty years or so of which we have not one word beyond St. Luke's terse phrase: "Jesus advanced in wisdom with the years, and in favour both with God and men."

Needless to say this skeleton summary is no substitute for the reading of the first two chapters of St. Matthew's Gospel (which we may take to be Saint Joseph's account) and the first two chapters of St. Luke's (which we may take to be Our Lady's).

NAZARETH

A STRANGER of the West coming into the Holy Land does well to enter by the North, and to approach either by the Damascus road or the coast.

That is the way much the most of those who have found out this singular small piece of the world, with its enormous fortunes, have travelled. So came in the merchants from beyond the desert from the beginning of time, the caravans of Asia, the bales from India and Persia. They made either up the Euphrates to where it passes near habitable land, where Aleppo now is, and so down south along the edge of the mountains till they reached Damascus; or else straight across the waste from rare well to well until they struck Damascus directly from the east, and the first habitation of men for many days.

The Crusaders came down by the coast between Lebanon and the sea. But from the south was no general approach to Palestine, save by conquerors, and therefore he who would enter by the common door had best use the north.

Coming thus, the gate of the country is Nazareth. But one who is considering the unique significance of Palestine, the episode of these few years—half a young lifetime—which count indefinitely more than all that went before them—Nazareth is the true beginning of his journey for a reason more profound than geography and history: Nazareth is the Home.

Bethlehem is the actual birthplace, but Bethlehem is part

of the Tragedy. In situation as in the character of its events it counts with the Holy Places of the Passion. It is adjacent to Jerusalem and therefore to Calvary and the Tomb. It is associated with Herod's massacre and with the Flight of the Holy Family. The Birth stands hard by the Death and Sacrifice, a symbol of what most men find, that they end where they began.

But Nazareth was that place in which all the years in which a man is made were passed, from the first memories, through boyhood to maturity. Nazareth is the habitation, and the mother's house. To those of a full religion, Nazareth is especially filled with the silence of Our Lady and her presence.

It is in tune with all this: a happy, shining little town, climbing upwards, in a fold of high but gentle hills, the centre of those Galilean highlands which look so pure and cool from the half desert below and beyond Jordan. For as the Damascus road plunges rapidly down out of the steppe into the narrow, overheated trench of the river above the lake, the green heights of Galilee above and beyond are a small separate country deserving a name of its own: something much better than the arid wastes that follow in barren waves of stone southward into Judea: something more human and more blessed than the stifling gorge to the west, where the Jordan runs deeper and deeper, with an increasing fever of heat, to the abomination of the Dead Sea: something more private than the rich flat of Esdraelon, the broad sea plain to the west.

These Galilean hills have been called a watch tower, as indeed the separate height of Tabor, of the Transfiguration, on the south of them is, for it commands the whole land; and from it the Mediterranean, a long day's march away below, seems close at hand. They might be called also a citadel, but a citadel of peace, and Nazareth is their heart.

How much fresher it is than the other little towns of that worn land, and, as it were, younger! I would add: "How more

Christian!" The convents and monasteries have taken possession of it as they have not any other town—and the soul of it is
the shrine of the Annunciation. There is in that Sacred Place no
continuous antiquity as there is elsewhere. The church is of the
last few generations, and in a style neither recent enough to be
taken for granted nor old enough to be venerable.

The great church which Constantine built has long ago
suffered the attack of our repeated enemies and fallen to ruin,
only the stumps of its columns, some few, remain: here and
there fragments of its mosaic floor. The existing church is built
upon a fraction of the old site and on a different axis. But the
air of authenticity remains. It is the very spot. And if anyone
ridicule such a sense of certitude and call it an illusion or a
phantasy, let him take the matter more prosaically and ask
himself what, after all, would be probable, and whether the
vulgar scepticism of the nineteenth century was not much more
irrational and whether those who still follow it are not suffering
from a belated superstition?

I repeat—what, after all, would be probable? Eliminate all
that the sceptic does not admit to be true. Grant him, for the
sake of this argument, that the early Church was a pack of
enthusiasts suffering from the wildest illusions; even so, would
its members not retain a fixed knowledge of what were, to them,
the most important places in all the world and of all time? A
man may be laughed at for affirming that Kenilworth Castle is
haunted, but there is no doubt that Kenilworth Castle is there.
That is not an illusion and he must know it before he thinks
it haunted.

It is historically certain that the Christian community had a
continuous existence in Palestine for the better part of a lifetime after the Crucifixion and Resurrection of Our Lord. When
the final Roman attack on Judea came, there had been all those
years in which to familiarize its members with the places asso-

ciated with Our Lord's life. Is it conceivable that the home of
His childhood and the house which His Mother best remembered would have been forgotten?

It was a time of constant coming and going, especially in that
particular land. Nazareth was on the caravan road from Damascus to the sea and on the main road which ran northward from
Jerusalem. The time was a time of high civilisation and of
detailed record. Is it conceivable that the men of the first century, enemies as well as friends, would have neglected and forgotten the Home whence this New Thing—so detested by the
official Jewish world and the mass of the Jewish people, so
cherished as the salvation of the world by those who were to
found the Church—proceeded?

It is not conceivable to a man with any knowledge of how
men's minds work or with a competent use of his reason that
the site of Our Lady's Annunciation would be forgotten; and if
it seemed conceivable to the nineteenth century sceptic it was
because he had lost his commonsense. He prided himself on his
rationalism, yet all he so firmly believed was a mere mass of
affirmation flying in the face of human experience and of the
most obvious rules of history.

No, those who have lost the Faith may deny the Annunciation, for mysteries are not demonstrable, but that part of earth
which witnessed the Annunciation is certain enough, more certain than most of the sites that are pointed out as matters of
course in Profane History. A man may worship there in security;
he is in the very place.

I said at the beginning of this that Nazareth was, for various
reasons, the right entry into the Holy Land: the main gate.
There is a last reason which should be remembered and it is
perhaps the best.

Nazareth is Joy. We begin the Rosary with the commemoration of joy—we only go on later to the suffering. It is the process
of human life, for the beginnings of it are happy and its tragedy

THE BRIDE OF LIFE

WHEN OUR LADY went to visit her cousin in the "hilly country," everything seemed to be vibrant with joy; there was little John the Baptist, who very nearly danced into life; there was Elizabeth, dumbfounded with delight; and Our Lady herself broke out into a song of sheer joy:

". . . my spirit hath rejoiced in God my Saviour

"Because he hath regarded the humility of his handmaid; for behold from henceforth all generations shall call me blessed.

"Because he that is mighty hath done great things to me; and holy is his name.

"And his mercy is from generation unto generations . . ."

This indeed was the Bride of the Spirit speaking.

In giving her humanity to God, Mary gave *all* humanity to Him, to be used for His own will.

In wedding her littleness to the Spirit of Love, she wed *all* lowliness to the Spirit of Love.

In surrendering to the Spirit and becoming the Bride of Life, she wed God to the human race and made the whole world pregnant with the life of Christ.

"I am come," Christ said, "that they may have life, and may have it more abundantly."

Mary knew in what the joy of the world was to consist, what

is made by the passing of time. So in the greatest of hu
which was also divine, Joy came first and the Agony at
before the Glory, which last does not belong to this v
will find human joy at Nazareth, the blessed seclusioı
hood and the as yet unwounded years.

Nazareth was also the scene of the first tribulatioɪ
first opposition; but the note of the place and its meaɪ
the Holy Childhood, and the earlier maturity wheɪ
should come was still unknown to the world. Now i
man finds this about Nazareth: that such a note e
this day.

it would be that would make everyone call her blessed, for it would simply be her own joy.

Everyone who wished it could be wed to the Spirit: not only solitaries living in lonely cells but everyone in the world; not only young girls and boys or children who had been somehow spared from sin, but sinners too; not only the young but also the old: because the Spirit makes everything new. The life filling her own being, the life leaping in little John the Baptist, the life breaking out into her jubilant song, the life springing on the hills around her—all that would be given to everyone who asked for it.

She had given mankind the key. Indeed, she had unlocked and opened the door of every heart. Now men had only to leave it open.

ADVENT

Sing it early in the morning watch, sing it softly, softly into the world's dark ear.

Sing it on your knees, sing it as though under veils, sing it as women sing when they are with child:

For He who is strong has become tender, the Infinite has become small, His power now is kindness, the Exalted has put on humility.

He finds room in the chamber of a maiden: His throne will be on her lap—a cradle song will be enough praise for Him.

See, the days will not dawn for piety, and the nights are dark with awe.

I will kindle lights, O my soul, I will kindle joy to all the ends of your humanity:

Hail to her who carried the Lord!

EMBER WEDNESDAY IN ADVENT

꙰ THIS IS the golden Mass, O Holy Mary—
Drop down dew, ye heavens from above—
when lighted candles crowd the sanctuary.
O fields, bring forth the blossom of God's love.
This is the golden Mass, O longed-for Maiden.
Their swords to ploughshares and their mighty spears
to sickles turn. You come with gladness laden,
yet who will stanch the ocean of your tears?
This is the golden Mass, O Mighty Mother.
Open the portals, princes, open wide.
Through this sealed gate, He enters and none other
who openeth and will not be denied.
Short is the time of grace: O gracious One,
now in our souls, conceive and bear your Son.

MOTHER AND CHILD

The old masters are not afraid to paint the little new-born Lord Jesus quite realistically. The sweet, downy child's head is large in relation to the body, the limbs are painfully thin. He has one finger in His mouth, and lies sucking it while He thoughtfully rubs one rosy-heeled little foot against the other. The tiny infant lies on the bare, cold, earthy floor; at the best He is given only a handful of straw or a little white cloth spread out under Him.

One feels tempted to follow the example of the shepherds in the old mystery-plays and give the young mother good advice about child management. But the upright and slender young Virgin Mary kneels, deeply sunk in meditation and prayer. She looks at her little son whom she has borne in her womb and to whom she has given a body from her body, and in Him she sees her God and Saviour, the Creator who has chosen this world as His throne—the night sky above, with its myriad of stars, being but a corner of His mantle which He has cast around His mother and Himself.

St. Joseph, faithful and upright, stands on guard; and near him are the angels, trusty advisers to the carpenter. They have arrayed themselves in visible shapes, and made themselves very beautiful for the feast. We may imagine them in richly folded white linen tunics, like ministers at a festal mass, wearing garlands of flowers.

It is only their Master and their King who can come to such a festival without being decked out. The heavens are His and the earth. He has laid the foundations of this ball of earth and all that is upon it, and now He is coming to us as the lowest of all to serve us; for so it was foreordained in God's counsels from all eternity—God's secret counsels, at which we, in our smallness and weakness, so often take offence.

"Let not your heart be troubled," says Jesus to His disciples. "Fear not" is one of the last things He bids them. He says it also when He comes to earth, and He says it more emphatically than with words. Who can be afraid of a tiny baby? The half-crazy Idumean ruler in the castle up in Jerusalem—but he has been for so long a prisoner in his own wild kingdom of dreams that he has lost the taste for the sweet and simple everyday things of life. And the wild riders of the sky are afraid. But to men of goodwill, the King of Peace has come as a new-born babe in a crib, and He has chosen to come to us so weak and naked in order that we may each one do something for Him.

Is not this the last and most mysterious reason for the joy of Christmas—that the world has been turned upside down; that the Almighty has laid aside His insignia of office and receives our gifts, if we want to give them to Him. The mystery of the Atonement is introduced with a Christmas play, the real meaning of which is far beyond our poor comprehension; but for almost two thousand years the world has echoed every Christmas with the noise and the merriment of the children who come to visit the stable, and humanity has played itself warm and full of laughter around the Son of God who has become a little child for its sake.

Through the poetry and dreams of the Middle Ages one vision persists: Anti-Christ when he comes will suddenly appear as a full-grown man. He cannot make himself so small and humble as to become the son of a woman, for has he not brooded for aeons over his great plan of revolt and world destruction?

He cannot, therefore, possibly find time to play in a village street with other children in a land which is only a small offshoot of a world-power. It is only the Almighty who has created and upheld the universe who can afford to lie and rest among the shavings that lie on the floor of St. Joseph's workshop and hold Mary's hand when she goes to the well outside the town walls to fetch Him water.

The devil pops up at any time disguised in some human form or other. The most important point is, however, that the whole thing is a disguise. The tempter, the spy, worms himself in everywhere, in possible and impossible shapes. It is quite thinkable that he himself, for reasons that we do not know, has rather a predilection for appearing as the man with small crooked horns on his forehead, and goat-legged; but he can always easily dress himself up as a beautiful woman or venerable monk, or a poodle-dog or a staring pig or a headless cock. As long as the disguise is suitable. . . .

It is God who comes to us from eternity, faithful and loving, and binds Himself to us in chains of flesh and blood so as to fight with the human race for the human race, true God and true man among men. His heart, in which dwells all the fullness of the Godhead, has throbbed below Mary's heart. His mouth, from which St. John saw issuing the sword of judgment, has sucked at Mary's breast.

The maiden has lifted up her adored son, has wrapped Him in swaddling clothes, and holds Him in her arms. The Child Jesus leans His head upon His mother's breast, and His serious infant eyes look down upon us all over Mary's supporting hand. Then He snuggles up to her closer still and lifts His little right hand—now it is raised in blessing over the shepherds who come in. She must sit down with the Child so that the visitors can look at Him properly. The old chieftain from the East creeps forward on his knees towards the two and holds out a golden censer—perhaps the Child Jesus might find delight in playing with it;—listen how nicely the chain rattles! The Child's hand waves in the air for a moment and it kicks contentedly, then His hand sinks like a little token of love down upon the old man's head.

Humanity had made for itself pictures of goddesses with their children, the offspring of gods, in their arms. It had worshipped them—goddesses of Egypt, Babylon, China. Not one of them had the power to give an expression of peace to the child's body and limbs. They are wild and munificent, cruel and capricious, like the human nature they are meant to represent.

Then steps forward a child of the race—a woman. A young virgin full of grace who meekly answers the angel who brings her tidings from Him who has created both the maid and the angel. "Lo, I am the handmaid of the Lord; be it done unto me according to Thy word." And the Word became flesh and dwelt among us. Mary holds out to us her Child, the Child who is true God and true man, and He has come to save us, because each immortal soul is worth more than all the transient glory of the earth and the stars. And Mary's son tells us that all we do or do not do for one of the smallest of His little ones, that we do or do not do for Him.

The old pictures of goddesses decay, forsaken and forgotten. The memory of the orgies and bloody rites and dirges of their followers come down to us in confused myths and in adventure stories for the children who run, playing and smiling, around the Mother of compassion as she walks forward with Jesus in her arms.

Where she is driven out, the ghost of Herod steps in, and the people are bemused by the Idumean's dreams of dominion and glory, feasting in newly built palaces and deeds of violence in dark cellars, and in their hearts awaken Herod's hatred of his own offspring and his fear of children. And the old visions come up again, of goddesses of the fruitfulness of earth, the breaking of the buds and the fall of the leaf.

Each one presses her own child to her breast, ready to fight for it against the others. The children of Leto draw the bow again and there is no mercy for the sons and daughters of Niobe.

So let us follow the children who sing at the top of their voices:

> Adeste, fideles,
> Laeti triumphantes
> Venite, venite in Bethlehem

And when we give each other our Christmas presents in His name, let us remember that He has given us the sun and the moon and the stars, all the earth with its forests and mountains and oceans and all that lives and moves upon them. He gives us all green things and everything that blossoms and bears fruit —and all that we quarrel about and all that we have misused. And to save us from our own foolishness and from all our sins He came down to earth and gave Himself.

> *Venite adoremus Dominum.*

THE BURNING BABE

As I in hoary winter's night stood shivering in the snow,
Surprised I was with sudden heat which made my heart to glow;
And lifting up a fearful eye to view what fire was near,
A pretty Babe all burning bright did in the air appear;
Who, scorchèd with excessive heat, such floods of tears did shed,
As though his floods should quench his flames which with his
   tears were fed.
"Alas!" quoth he, "but newly born in fiery heats I fry,
Yet none approach to warm their hearts or feel my fire but I.
My faultless breast the furnace is, the fuel wounding thorns;
Love is the fire, and sighs the smoke, the ashes shame and scorns;
The fuel justice layeth on, and mercy blows the coals;
The metal in this furnace wrought are men's defilèd souls:
For which, as now on fire I am to work them to their good,
So will I melt into a bath to wash them in my blood."
With this he vanished out of sight and swiftly shrunk away,
And straight I callèd unto mind that it was Christmas day.

HEROD, THE MAGI AND THE STAR

The story of the Magi and of Herod massacring the Innocents at Bethlehem is sometimes set aside as a mixture of Bluebeard with a fairy story, which no grown-up person would take
seriously. Even those who would allow that the Gospels are in
the main historical still draw the line at such obvious legends
as the Magi and their Star. The killing of all the baby boys is a
tale gruesome enough to make children's flesh creep; and the
beautiful star resting over the crib and the mysterious Magi
bringing romantic gifts of gold, frankincense and myrrh, is just
the thing for youthful minds susceptible to the wizardry of the
East and marvels in the sky. But sober-minded people are too
rudely awake to the world of fact still to believe in fairyland.

Quite so. But facts can be stranger than fiction, and some
things, says the proverb, are too strange not to be true. Who was
the Herod who is said to have killed the babies at Bethlehem?
He was an old man of seventy-three when Our Lord was born.
We know his history well, he was one of the best-known figures
of his time. He was the Great Upstart in royalty of his days, the
Great Parvenu in the Court of Kings. His grandfather was the
son of a slave, so the tale went, and, though Herod reigned over
the Jews, he was no son of David, he was not even a son of
Aaron, or a descendant of the priest-kings who had ruled since
the Maccabees; he was not even a Jew, but a convert to Judaism,
who came from Edom, the national foe of Israel. He was foisted

on the Jews by the hated Romans; he was always surrounded
by a mercenary army, and reigned by the terror he inspired. But
let us give the man his due, he was Herod The Great in a
sense. He reigned undisputed master over a large country for
nearly forty years. Prosperity and peace, culture and magnificent
cities, marked the land of Palestine in his days. He made the
Temple at Jerusalem one of the wonders of the world for
grandeur and beauty, and he had built pagan temples, too, elsewhere when it suited him. Tranquility reigned where he had
power, for it was the irresistible power of the bloody despot. He
was great in a sense, but it was a monstrous greatness, England's
King Henry VIII was but a pale reflection of Herod the Great.

Herod began his reign by a series of condemnations and exe-
cutions of prominent noblemen amongst the Jews; with iron
hand he kept down insurrection. He had married Mariamne,
the granddaughter of Hyrcanus, the last of the Ashmonaeans,
priest-kings of Judea. Her brother, a lad of seventeen years, first
was made High Priest by Herod, and then assassinated by his
orders when in his bath. Five years later he had her old father
assassinated, and then he put Mariamne herself to death; two
years later he had her mother assassinated; three years later two
young distant relatives of hers, and a brother-in-law who had
shielded the lads; whilst about twenty years later he put both
the sons of Mariamne to death. Herod was married no less than
ten times, and his married life was a troubled one. Only five
days before his own death he had the eldest son of his first
wife executed, the son whom not long before he had proclaimed
heir to the throne.

As the massacre of the children at Bethlehem must have taken
place at most a few months before, this gave rise to the anecdote
preserved for us by a pagan writer, Macrobius (c. A.D. 410).
When Augustus, the Roman Emperor of the time, heard that
amongst the boys under two, whom Herod King of the Jews
had put to death in Syria, Herod's own son was killed, he said:

"It is better to be Herod's swine than Herod's son," for Herod affected strict observance of the Jewish food laws, and therefore, not eating pork, he would not slay swine. However, the anecdote, as told by this writer, fails to take into account that the son whom Herod killed a few days before his own death was a man of middle age. The acts of bloodshed perpetrated within Herod's own family were accomplished by others amongst his subjects—terrible by reason of their numbers. Josephus, who was born but thirty years after Herod's death at Jerusalem, tells how he had ordered the nobles, whom he called to him in his last moments, to be executed immediately after his decease, so that at least his death might be accompanied by universal mourning. Herod in his last days, so we read, did not spare "those who seemed most dear to him," but "slew all those of his own family who, looking forward to a change in the royal line, sided with the Pharisees in refusing to take the oath to the Roman Emperor."

The massacre at Bethlehem is a Bluebeard story, you say. But does anyone, who knows Herod's life, dare to say that the assassination of say twenty-five children—for there cannot possibly have been more baby boys under two in the small village of Bethlehem and its environs—would have caused qualms of conscience in the crazy old tyrant? If a set of distinguished foreigners came to Jerusalem and spoke about some royal prince whose birth they had read in the stars, and if the groaning people, who were yearning for the old king's death, and who rose in bloody revolution the moment almost that the breath was out of his body—if these people made this the subject of eager though subdued gossip, what else could Herod think but that this was some new scheme to tear the sceptre from his hands before he was dead? Herod struck blindly right and left; he had at least three of his own sons assassinated within four years of the first Christmas, and he threatened to have all the nobles of Jerusalem murdered at his death. Now this supposed Messias-Child, said to be

miraculously pointed out at Bethlehem, was but another attempt
"to change the royal line." What else could have suggested itself
to his maddened brain but the common procedure of assassination? A score of babies more to the bloody list of his crimes,
what did it matter? He had now set his mind on making his son
Archelaus succeed him, but, no doubt, half foresaw what would
happen. Within a few months the misrule and cruelty of Archelaus, who started his rule by a ruthless massacre of Jews, had
driven the Jews to ask protection from the Romans, who deposed
him, made Judea a Roman Province, and ended the dynastic
ambitions of Herod the Great. He felt, he almost knew, this was
coming; what wonder that he drowned his fears in blood?

But Jerusalem was a cultured city, you say, and Judea a
highly civilised country. No doubt it was—as civilised as Petro-
grad under Lenin and Trotsky. And who were the Magi?
Wizards of a fairy tale? Magicians with their famous wands?
Thus it might appear to someone who knows nothing of contemporary history. They were members of the priestly caste of
the Persian Empire, as well known in their own country of that
day as Anglican clergymen are known in the British Empire
of this day, and by no means unknown and unrespected in the
rival Empire of Rome. They could look back on centuries of
magnificent history, when they and the Persian Kings guided the
destinies of their vast countries. They were almost immeasurably superior to the crude idolatrous priesthood of Egypt, Greece,
Asia, or Rome, for they adored the One Good God, the Lord and
Maker of the world. It is true they had not reached the pure and
absolute monotheism of the Jews, for they believed this Good
God had still to struggle with an almost equal God of darkness,
but their religion was the highest that the human mind ever
achieved unaided by revelation. Their visit to Jerusalem and
reception by King Herod are no more improbable than the visit
of the Bishop of London to Paris and his reception by the Presi-
dent. When King Tiridates of Armenia went to Rome to be

crowned some seventy years later he was surrounded by Magi, who created an immense impression on the Roman people; and Nero the Emperor held a banquet in honour of the Magi and endeavoured to learn their secret lore. A few years before, Seneca, in a letter to Lucilius, refers to the Magi at Athens who offered a sacrifice to the spirit of Plato, the great philosopher.

A visit of the Magi to Herod, then, is not improbable: it is the reason of their visit that we cannot understand. What more wildly improbable than that they should be drawn by a star to come and adore a new-born babe at Jerusalem? Not so improbable, if you knew what people thought and dreamt of in those days. But probable or improbable, it is a fact, and an ounce of fact is worth more than ever so great a weight of theory. It is a fact that in those years there was a widespread expectation of the coming of a Saviour. The Jews, of course, were waiting for their Messias year by year: the unrest and frenzy of their expectations led to the war of their final destruction in A.D. 70. Somehow, this looking for someone to come had spread far beyond Palestine. Tacitus speaks of it, Suetonius speaks of it, people from the East, so it was said, would be masters of the world. People looked for "Salvation." Horace, in his sixteenth Epode, written about 30 B.C., utters a cry of despair that the Roman world is lost, people had better migrate to the mysterious islands of the Western Ocean, where a Golden Age would be reopened them. But Virgil answers these despondent verses in his fourth Eclogue in words referring to a New-born Child in whom all the hopes of the world are centered. The words are so strangely reminiscent of those referring to the Messias in the Prophet Isaias that many scholars hold that the Prince of Latin Poets had read the Prince of Hebrew Prophets. It is a fact that, through the Sibylline Oracles, Hebrew prophecies and Hebrew hopes were widely known outside Palestine. The Hebrew Scriptures had been translated more than two hundred years before into the Greek language understood throughout the East.

And could not the Magi know of the Jewish Prophecy in the Book of Numbers: "A Star shall arise out of Jacob?" Jews in vast numbers had lived in Persia for at least five hundred years. They were almost as numerous in the lands along the Euphrates and the Tigris as they were in Palestine. The Magi, who gathered their lore from the Sacred Books of the Chaldeans, as well as their own, were likely to be students of the Sacred Books of the Jews. Is not the Mazdean religion, with its beautiful doctrine of the Light-King, akin to some sublime passages in the Jewish Psalms? The Magi were the astronomers and, let us concede it, also the astrologers of their day. Astronomy was born on the Babylonian plains.

These Magi lived in a country in which a Jewish population had settled for over five hundred years—where, in fact, there were probably more Jews than in Palestine itself, where every town of importance had its "East End," as we have now in London. When Cyrus, King of Persia, allowed the Jews to return to their own country after his conquest of Babylon in 528 B.C., a goodly number indeed returned to Zion, and repopulated their devastated fatherland; but more, I should think, remained. They thought of Zionism as an ideal but not a practical consideration. They developed in the land of their exile a great literary activity, and their Babylonian Talmud was as famous as the Talmud of Jerusalem. If these Mazdean priests had nothing in their ancient books about a King to come among the Jews—a point which has not yet been definitely ascertained —they may well have joined some expectation of their own with the more precise expectation of Israel, which was waiting for the rising of the Star out of Jacob. The convert world of Judaism was much more widespread than historians at first believed, and these Mazdeans may well have been worshippers of the Most

High God, "Hypsistarians" as the Greeks called them, without
being full converts to the Jewish faith.

But the Star? Would not the whole astral system have been
disturbed if a star travelled across the sky to guide the steps of
the travellers from Persia to Palestine? Well, the Maker of the
starry skies has them sufficiently under control, I fancy, to allow
for a special star travelling across the boundless space above. But
does the Scripture text say that the Star travelled visibly across
the sky? If it does, that is the end of the matter; for God nothing
is difficult or impossible. But does it? Had we not better read "the
fairy story" over carefully before we smile at it? The Magi came
to Jerusalem saying: "We have seen His Star in the East, and
we have come to adore Him." Not a word about a star travelling
visibly across the sky before them. Still, they call it *His* star!
Quite so, some luminous body in the sky which they knew was
the harbinger of the coming of the King of the Jews. How they
knew it, the Gospel does not say. Through Sacred Book or
Sacred Oracle, through direct or indirect revelation, they knew;
let that suffice.

As a matter of fact, the text of St. Matthew does not force us
to admit of a star indicating by its movement the road to Bethlehem. The Magi did not need the Star to guide them. They
had just heard that the Messias was to be born in Bethlehem,
and the road to Bethlehem was a main road which everyone
knew. Having observed this remarkable constellation in their
own country, and learning that this new Star, as it appeared to
them, was a token of the new-born Jewish Messias, they went
on their pilgrimage. Whether they saw the Star while travelling
from Persia to Palestine all the time is neither said nor implied;
rather the contrary, for some time at least before they arrived
the Star was not visible to them. Otherwise, surely, when before
Herod and the priests, they would have pointed to the Star over-
head, and not have said: "We have seen His Star in the East,"

nor would St. Matthew have laid such stress on their joy at
seeing the Star again after leaving Herod.

When at Bethlehem they were indeed at a loss where to turn
to find the birthplace of the new-born King. They might have
asked the inhabitants as they had asked at Jerusalem, but that
they clearly did not do. Had they done so, there would have
been no need for their secret departure to hide the fact of their
having found the Babe from Herod. The Bethlehemites would
surely have given the information which would have saved their
own children. There, no doubt, God used the Star to indicate
the place where they found the Child and His Mother. How,
we do not know precisely. St. Matthew says: "Behold the Star,
which they had seen in the East, had preceded them (or, preceded them) until, going (or, in its course) it stood over where
the Child was." Perhaps the Star in its course, for stars rise and
set and travel across the sky as the sun does, reached the skyline
over the rocks in which the cave was hewn, or, in some other
wonderful way, indicated to the happy beholders the place
where the Word was made Flesh and dwelt amongst us.

He, who called all stars out of the deep and called them by
their names, and calling them, created them out of nothing; He,
who needed but to say: "Let there be light, and there was light,"
wished that the heavens should proclaim the glory of God on
the birthday on earth of His Only-begotten Son, who in His
Godhead had been born before the world was made.

ANNO DOMINI

You will have occasion for some time to come to write, more than once, the figures 1939.* Whenever you inscribe this mystic number breathe to yourself some word in memory of the man to whom you are indebted for that date. His name was Dionysius and he was an abbot in Rome during that strange time when the history of England disappears and runs underground like the river Mole: the darkness between Germanus and Augustine. For he flourished (as the phrase goes) about 1400 years ago in the earlier part of the sixth century, and it seems that the one date about him on which we can be certain is that he was dead by 540.

Now it was his computation of the date of the Nativity—or rather the Incarnation—which became gradually accepted throughout Christendom . . . very gradually. You cannot say that it had become common everywhere until well into the Crusades, nearly 600 years after his death, and I have read somewhere that his fixing of the era by which we now everywhere reckon the years was not taken over fully in Spain until the fourteenth century. You will find what I suppose to be the decisive phrase in Migne, that half of Migne which prints the Latin Fathers, and in the sixty-seventh volume thereof Dionysius writes: "We did not wish to mix up our memorials with impious and persecuting men" (he means, with the Roman emperors of the earlier pagan times), "but rather did we choose

* Need one say that this essay was written at the end of 1938?

to note the sequence of years from the Incarnation of Our Lord
Jesus Christ." And that date he put just after the middle of the
eighth century from the traditional founding of Rome, A.U.C.
753–754.

He was almost certainly wrong, as are most pioneers and
founders. How wrong we do not know. There are all sorts of
guesses based on all sorts of slight fragmentary evidence. For
instance, we have the death of Herod in 4 B.C.; but those who
understand these things (which I do not pretend to do) will
have it that his "year one" may have been anything from four
years too late, as is more probable, to seven years too early. But
it took root and you will not shift it now, neither you nor
millions with you: not all the Revolutionaries, nor all the over-
learned. I suppose it is about as firm a thing as the past has left
us, is the computation of the years A.D. and B.C.

This Dionysius was called, or nicknamed, "The Little," "The
Short," "Exiguus," and it is as Dionysius Exiguus that he is
remembered, to distinguish him among the other Dionysiuses,
from the Areopagite and the martyred apostle of Paris onwards.
The little we know about him is mostly from a few phrases
written by a fellow student of his, a younger friend who counted
much more than he, Cassiodorus. Cassiodorus is the larger figure,
partly because he was richer, partly because he did much in the
politics of his time. In part also because what he has to say about
the motley Imperial garrison of barbarian soldiers then in Italy
and their chief has helped a certain modern school to crack up
the Germans at the expense of the rest of us: a favourite game
of the nineteenth century. This friend, Cassiodorus, with three
generations of great wealth behind him, full of music, writing
much, wrote thus about Dionysius—

"There was also in my time among many great men Dionysius
the Monk, a Scythian by race, but altogether Roman: most
learned in Latin and Greek. He lived his life god-fearing like
a high master. There was in him a great carriage but with it
great simplicity, doctrine and humility. I would like to say more

about him but I must get on with my work." Whereupon Cassiodorus goes on to say more about him, after having promised not to do so, which is what one might expect of a public man dealing with public affairs. The rest that he has to say about his friend ends up very prettily—even finely: "He has left this evil time of ours and has been received into peace, and we must believe that his conversation is now in the household of God."

But Cassiodorus could not guess how vast a fabric would extend from the labours of this one man. He did not know that all these centuries after, the whole world of our white civilisation would be taking his date for our Era as a matter of course; nor did Dionysius himself know it. Had he known it, it might have spoilt his humility, though it is even said that he called himself, or was called, "The Little" by way of humble modesty. I prefer to believe that he was so-called because he was not tall. Thus he falls into the company of those many fixed names (or great men if you prefer to call them so), who had the advantage of few inches and therefore much energy; strong hearts with less work to do than have the hearts of taller men. He may be greeted by Napoleon and Wellington and Charles I of England and Canute and any number of others who perhaps when they were boys were ashamed of their stature but found, later on, that the defect was an advantage.

I have said that his system grew slowly in public esteem. I read that it was first adopted at all widely in England under the influence of Bede, the Venerable Bede, about two centuries after that system had been lodged, or at any rate crystallised. From England it spread southward, and Gaul was taking it up in a beginning sort of way within a lifetime, but the Papal Chancery did not use it for another 200 years.

No one ever made it official and no one can properly tell you how it developed roots so firm and so penetrating. But I say it again, it is established now more decidedly than any other act of all our long story.

NOËL

I

On a winter's night long time ago
  (*The bells ring loud and the bells ring low*),
When high howled wind, and down fell snow
  (Carillon, Carilla).
Saint Joseph he and Nostre Dame,
Riding on an ass, full weary came
From Nazareth into Bethlehem.
  And the small child Jesus smile on you.

II

And Bethlehem they stood before
  (*The bells ring less and the bells ring more*),
The landlord bade them begone from his door
  (Carillon, Carilla).
"Poor folk" (says he), "must lie where they may,
For the Duke of Jewry comes this way,
With all his train on a Christmas day."
  And the small child Jesus smile on you.

III

Poor folk that may my carol hear
  (*The bells ring single and the bells ring clear*),

See! God's one child had hardest cheer!
  (Carillon, Carilla).
Men grown hard on a Christmas morn;
The dumb beast by and a babe forlorn.
It was very, very cold when our Lord was born.
  And the small child Jesus smile on you.

THE GOD IN THE CAVE

❧ Traditions in art and literature and popular fable have quite sufficiently attested, as has been said, this particular paradox of the divine being in the cradle. Perhaps they have not so clearly emphasised the significance of the divine being in the cave. Curiously enough, indeed, tradition has not very clearly emphasised the cave. It is a familiar fact that the Bethlehem scene has been represented in every possible setting of time and country, of landscape and architecture; and it is a wholly happy and admirable fact that men have conceived it as quite different according to their different individual traditions and tastes. But while all have realised that it was a stable, not so many have realised that it was a cave. Some critics have even been so silly as to suppose that there was some contradiction between the stable and the cave; in which case they cannot know much about caves or stables in Palestine. As they see differences that are not there it is needless to add that they do not see differences that are there. When a well-known critic says, for instance, that Christ being born in a rocky cavern is like Mithras having sprung alive out of a rock, it sounds like a parody upon comparative religion. There is such a thing as the point of a story, even if it is a story in the sense of a lie. And the notion of a hero appearing, like Pallas from the brain of Zeus, mature and without a mother, is obviously the very opposite of the idea of a god being born like an ordinary baby and entirely dependent on a mother. Whichever ideal we might prefer, we should surely see that they are contrary ideals. It is as stupid to connect them because they both contain a substance called stone as to identify the punishment of the Deluge with the baptism in the Jordan because they both contain a substance called water. Whether as a myth or a mystery, Christ was obviously conceived as born in a hole in the rocks primarily because it marked the position of one outcast and homeless. . . .

It would be vain to attempt to say anything adequate, or anything new, about the change which this conception of a deity born like an outcast or even an outlaw had upon the whole conception of law and its duties to the poor and outcast. It is profoundly true to say that after that moment there could be no slaves. There could be and were people bearing that legal title, until the Church was strong enough to weed them out, but there could be no more of the pagan repose in the mere advantage to the state of keeping it a servile state. Individuals became important, in a sense in which no instruments can be important. A man could not be a means to an end, at any rate to any other man's end. All this popular and fraternal element in the story has been rightly attached by tradition to the episode of the Shepherds; the hinds who found themselves talking face to face with the princes of heaven. But there is another aspect of the popular element as represented by the shepherds which has not perhaps been so fully developed; and which is more directly relevant here.

Men of the people, like the shepherds, men of the popular tradition, had everywhere been the makers of the mythologies. It was they who had felt most directly, with least check or chill from philosophy or the corrupt cults of civilisation, the need we have already considered; the images that were adventures of the imagination; the mythology that was a sort of search; the tempting and tantalising hints of something half-human in

nature; the dumb significance of seasons and special places.
They had best understood that the soul of a landscape is a
story, and the soul of a story is a personality. But rationalism had
already begun to rot away these really irrational though imaginative treasures of the peasant; even as a systematic slavery had
eaten the peasant out of house and home. Upon all such peas-
antries everywhere there was descending a dusk and twilight
of disappointment, in the hour when these few men discovered
what they sought. Everywhere else Arcadia was fading from
the forest. Pan was dead and the shepherds were scattered like
sheep. And though no man knew it, the hour was near which
was to end and to fulfil all things; and, though no man heard
it, there was one far-off cry in an unknown tongue upon the
heaving wilderness of the mountains. The shepherds had found
their Shepherd.

And the thing they found was of a kind with the things they
sought. The populace had been wrong in many things; but they
had not been wrong in believing that holy things could have a
habitation and that divinity need not disdain the limits of time
and space. And the barbarian who conceived the crudest fancy
about the sun being stolen and hidden in a box, or the wildest
myth about the god being rescued and his enemy deceived with
a stone, was nearer to the secret of the cave and knew more
about the crisis of the world, than all those in the circle of cities
round the Mediterranean who had become content with cold
abstractions or cosmopolitan generalisations; than all those who
were spinning thinner and thinner threads of thought out of
the transcendentalism of Plato or the orientalism of Pythagoras.
The place that the shepherds found was not an academy or an
abstract republic; it was not a place of myths allegorised or dis-
sected or explained or explained away. It was a place of dreams
come true. Since that hour no mythologies have been made in
the world. Mythology is a search. . . .

The philosophers had also heard. It is still a strange story,

though an old one, how they came out of orient lands, crowned
with the majesty of kings and clothed with something of the
mystery of magicians. That truth that is tradition has wisely
remembered them almost as unknown quantities, as mysterious
as their mysterious and melodious names; Melchior, Caspar,
Balthazar. But there came with them all that world of wisdom
that had watched the stars in Chaldea and the sun in Persia;
and we shall not be wrong if we see in them the same curiosity
that moves all the sages. They would stand for the same human
ideal if their names had really been Confucius or Pythagoras
or Plato. They were those who sought not tales but the truth of
things; and since their thirst for truth was itself a thirst for God,
they also have had their reward. But even in order to understand
that reward, we must understand that for philosophy as much
as mythology, that reward was the completion of the incomplete.

Such learned men would doubtless have come, as these
learned men did come, to find themselves confirmed in much
that was true in their own traditions and right in their own
reasoning. Confucius would have found a new foundation for
the family in the very reversal of the Holy Family; Buddha
would have looked upon a new renunciation, of stars rather
than jewels and divinity than royalty. These learned men would
still have the right to say, or rather a new right to say, that there
was truth in their old teaching. But after all these learned men
would have come to learn. They would have come to complete
their conceptions with something they had not yet conceived;
even to balance their imperfect universe with something they
might once have contradicted. Buddha would have come from
his impersonal paradise to worship a person. Confucius would
have come from his temples of ancestor-worship to worship a
child. . . .

The Magi, who stand for mysticism and philosophy, are truly
conceived as seeking something new and even as finding something unexpected. That sense of crisis which still tingles in the

Christmas story and even in every Christmas celebration, accen-
tuates the idea of a search and a discovery. For the other mystical figures in the miracle play, for the angel and the mother,
the shepherds and the soldiers of Herod, there may be aspects
both simpler and more supernatural, more elemental or more
emotional. But the Wise Men must be seeking wisdom; and
for them there must be a light also in the intellect. And this is
the light; that the Catholic creed is catholic and that nothing
else is catholic. The philosophy of the Church is universal. The
philosophy of the philosophers was not universal. Had Plato
and Pythagoras and Aristotle stood for an instant in the light
that came out of that little cave, they would have known that
their own light was not universal. It is far from certain, indeed, that they did not know it already. Philosophy also, like
mythology, had very much the air of a search. It is the realisation of this truth that gives its traditional majesty and mystery
to the figures of the Three Kings; the discovery that religion is
broader than philosophy and that this is the broadest of religions,
contained within this narrow space. . . .

We might well be content to say that mythology had come
with the shepherds and philosophy with the philosophers; and
that it only remained for them to combine in the recognisation
of religion. But there was a third element that must not be
ignored and one which that religion for ever refuses to ignore,
in any revel or reconciliation. There was present in the primary
scenes of the drama that Enemy that had rotted the legends with
lust and frozen the theories into atheism, but which answered
the direct challenge with something of that more direct method
which we have seen in the conscious cult of the demons. In the
description of that demon-worship, of the devouring detestation
of innocence shown in the works of its witchcraft and the most
inhuman of its human sacrifice, I have said less of its indirect
and secret penetration of the saner paganism; the soaking of
mythological imagination with sex; the rise of imperial pride

into insanity. But both the indirect and the direct influence make themselves felt in the drama of Bethlehem. A ruler under the Roman suzerainty, probably equipped and surrounded with the Roman ornament and order though himself of eastern blood, seems in that hour to have felt stirring within him the spirit of strange things. We all know the story of how Herod, alarmed at some rumour of a mysterious rival, remembered the wild gesture of the capricious despots of Asia and ordered a massacre of suspects of the new generation of the populace. Everyone knows the story; but not everyone has perhaps noted its place in the story of the strange religions of men. Not everybody has seen the significance even of its very contrast with the Corinthian columns and Roman pavement of that conquered and superficially civilised world. Only, as the purpose in this dark spirit began to show and shine in the eyes of the Idumean, a seer might perhaps have seen something like a great grey ghost that looked over his shoulder; have seen behind him filling the dome of night and hovering for the last time over history, that vast and fearful fact that was Moloch of the Carthaginians; awaiting his last tribute from a ruler of the races of Shem. The demons in that first festival of Christmas, feasted also in their own fashion.

CHRISTMAS CAROL FOR THE DOG

THIS IS a carol for the dog
that long ago in Bethlehem
saw shepherds running towards the town
and followed them.

He trotted stiffly at their heels;
he sniffed the lambs that they were bringing;
he heard the herald angels sing,
yet did not know what they were singing.

With tail erect and tilted ears
he trotted through the stable door.
He saw the shepherds kneeling low
upon the floor.

He found St. Joseph watching by
Our Lady with her newborn Boy,
and being only dog, he wagged
his tail for joy.

There stationed by the Baby's crib
he kept good guard through the long night,
with ears thrown back and muzzle high
and both eyes bright.

When the three tall kings came at last
he barked a warning to each one,
then took his stand beside the Child,
his duty done.

Down into Egypt went the dog
when Herod slew the innocents.
He was not wise. He did not know
why, whither, nor whence,

but only, being dog, he knew
to follow where the Family led
to Egypt or to Nazareth.
And no one said

a word about the sharp-nosed dog
who stuck close to the Family then.
And yet, there must have been a dog.
This is a song for him. Amen.

THE PRESENTATION IN THE TEMPLE
14th Century French School

THE PRESENTATION IN THE TEMPLE

The prophets had foretold that this Temple—so much less beautiful than the first—was to be more glorious than it, because the Lord—*Dominator Dominus*—the Messias—was to come to it.

And now the Lord had come to His own Temple as a little, helpless child to be offered and redeemed by His parents. He was the Lawmaker, and the evangelists tell us that He accomplished all things according to the law of the Lord. Later He was to say: "I came not to destroy but to fulfill." He, the Lawgiver, fulfilled His own law by obeying it. No wonder the early Christians had such an ardent love for obedience. No wonder this virtue is one of the Counsels of Perfection.

Two things were involved in this prescription of the Mosaic Law, an account of which may be found in the books of Exodus, Numbers, and Leviticus.

When Pharaoh refused to let the Jews go forth from their Egyptian bondage, God struck with death all the first-born of the Egyptians. The Jews were ordered to kill a lamb and sprinkle its blood on their doorposts: their first-born would be spared. The lamb was a type of Our Lord Himself, the Lamb of God who was to die for man. Henceforth God declared His especial primacy over the first-born of Israel. The first male animal, the first son, belonged to God and was to be bought back by a price which was devoted to the maintenance of the priesthood and the Temple worship. Our Lord was taken to the Temple firstly to fulfill this law.

But, too, the Mystery is known as the Purification because Our Lady also was submitting to a Law. A Jewish woman, she submitted to this Jewish rite of Purification from the legal stain incurred by childbirth: she, the one spotless human being, accepted here the human burden of guilt: the utterly pure was purified. With the feast of the Purification Our Lady is already sharing her Son's burden of the sins of the world.

Often in the Gospels we are reminded of the greatness of the Temple—the centre of revealed religion, the supreme theatre of worship of the One True God and of sacrifice to Him. The priests in the order of their courses offering incense, passing through the wide courts, with all the splendor that a people could bring to the holiest place in the world. The apostles were later to say, marvelling, "See what stones and buildings are here." And Our Lord called it His Father's House. Every town and village might have its synagogue, but there was only one Temple.

What did this scene look like? A provincial family from a little village had come up to Jerusalem. The law prescribed that their offering must be received; the mother must be purified. They were not even rich enough to bring the lamb that was the normal sacrifice together with a dove or a young pigeon. They could only bring the offering of the poor—two doves: one for a holocaust, the other a sin-offering. Probably there was a line of waiting parents and babies. We can imagine one priest saying to another: "Have you got time to see to them? I'm too busy today."

It must all have looked rather a shabby side-scene amid the splendors of the Temple courts.

And Simeon and Anna. They were no part of the official priestly caste. They were probably like those old men and women of today who, as we sometimes say, "seem to live in the church"—saying their rosaries or sitting gazing at the Tabernacle. ("How do you pray?" the Curé d'Ars asked one of these. "What do you say?" And he answered, "I look at Him and He looks at me.")

For years Simeon had haunted the Temple, "looking for the expectation of Israel"; for years Anna had been serving God with fastings and prayers day and night. And these two recognized the reality so deeply hidden in this scene. Simeon's hymn will be sung forever in the Church's liturgy. He recognized Our Lord as the Messias, the glory of His people, Israel, but also as a "light for the revelation of the Gentiles." The opening of the door of God's revelation to all the world became visible to him as he gazed into the human face of God.

Did he know beforehand by his study of the prophecies how strange their fulfilment would seem to human sight? Or did it come upon him in a flash when he saw the mother carrying in her baby?

What did the Presentation mean for Our Lady? No word of hers is recorded, but only the words addressed to her by Simeon. This Joyful Mystery is also one of her Seven Sorrows—"Thine own soul a sword shall pierce." The flight into Egypt was soon to follow—the anguish of fear that must have haunted every step and could not even have died away when they were back at Nazareth. These were among the words she pondered in her heart.

St. Luke speaks only of the return to Nazareth, but we know from St. Matthew of the Flight into Egypt, which must have come between the Presentation and the return to Nazareth. Tradition says the Holy Family spent some two years in Egypt.

The Church has specially chosen words of Simeon for the celebration of the Feast of the Purification. Called Candlemas, it is kept with the burning of a multitude of candles, and

through the spaces of the church on a dark February morning
the shining candles are companioned by the constant repetition
of the antiphon *Lumen ad revelationem gentium.*

This mystery seems throughout to epitomize the contrast in
the life of Jesus between appearance and reality. Its very simplicity baffles the imagination. Dwelling on the feast, with its
strange name of the Purification, and on words spoken later by
Our Lord, Chesterton wrote:

THE PARADOX

These wells that shine and seem as shallow as pools,
These tales that, being too plain for the fool's eyes,
Incredibly clear are clearly incredible—
Truths by their depth deceiving more than lies.

When did the ninety and nine just men perceive
A far faint mockery in their title's sense
In the strange safety of their flocks and herds
And all the impenitence of innocence?

The sons of reason sin not and throw stones,
Nor guess where burn behind the battered door,
In the shining irony of Candlemas,
A hundred flames to purify the pure.

OUR LADY OF EGYPT

As you enter the Red Sea from the north you have Arabia to your left and, to your right, Egypt. Two thousand years before Christ's birth, Abraham detached himself from Mesopotamian civilisation, whose origins were as far behind him as he is behind us; he found his way into the land destined to become Palestine, and after a brief sojourn there entered another immemorially ancient civilisation and saw Pyramids of which, again, one was built as long before himself as he was before our Era. He returned to the north-east; but his descendants under stress of famine went back to Egypt, and five hundred years after him were led back to Palestine by Moses; and after another five hundred years David captured the rock-citadel of Sion and became the ancestor of Our Lord, born yet another thousand years afterwards. We, nearly two thousand years distant from Christ's birth. Abraham, two thousand years before Christ: the Pyramids, built another two thousand years before Abraham by men of a civilisation already old—the Great Pyramid you can still climb and from whose top you can scan that vast perspective.

No wonder that as you pass down the Red Sea memories crowd upon you and almost suffocate you from this side and that. And among them is the memory that from Palestine into Egypt the Holy Family once went, and the perception that at a certain moment you must be crossing their track. . . .

Between these two worlds, Asian and African, already suc-
cumbing, it is true, to the Roman, but still, at least in the case
of Egypt, thrilling the souls of their conquerors—moved the
shadowy little group: Joseph, Mary, their Child. You would
have said, "The absolute insignificance!" Yet it is they who have
survived.

True, they survive always, in a sense, in flight. Hunted from
one land into another; their houses successively destroyed;
always a tiny trio attracting to itself microscopic minorities of
wholeheartedly loving servants and indeed companions; but
still surviving. To which of those Sargons and Nabuchodon-
osors, of those Rameses or Amenhoteps, do men now *speak?*
pray? To what Caesar of that nascent Roman Empire do they
now look for succour? To which of those ancient rulers, or,
indeed, of our own, are the titles now given: "God-Manifest"—
"God-Saviour"—"God Present and Powerful"? To not one. But
there are millions upon millions, all over the world, who so
invoke that little Child. In but a very short while His Mother
too, was understood, especially in that East and in that South.
A strange proof, maybe, of the vitality of our Faith and also
of the slowness of our human minds is the gradual waking up
of the Catholic conscience to what had been implied in immemorial traditions, so that, for example, only century after
century, even epoch after epoch, was all that is involved in the
doctrine of the Real Presence explicitly perceived; and a millen-
nium and a half had to go by before the uniqueness of St.
Joseph's vocation and providential status was appreciated. Now
the entire Holy Family is followed lovingly by us, as it proceeds
through our modern deserts and into pagan Egypts, destined,
maybe, so far as the deserts go, to blossom like the rose; and, so
far as the powerful empires are concerned, to decay from within,
and so to offer no resistance to any shock that may assail them
from without. A modern author has composed a strange little
tale. A couple of Londoners, not too edifying either of them,

challenged a magician who claimed to control Time. The one asked to be transferred some fifteen hundred years backwards— he encountered, I think, St. Augustine or a fellow-missionary offering the Roman Mass within our coasts. The other awoke forwards, in a ruined London; a few of its natives lived timidly in huts along the Thames firmly controlled by their black masters. This sleeper-awakened was removed in a government-launch, and, on landing further up the river, encountered a black Dominican, in a church of mud and reeds, offering Mass among the devout though somewhat bewildered white natives whom he had reconverted. The tale is more than an allegory. We must, as men who have contemplated history, and also can take stock of our contemporary world, be able to foresee with serenity the collapse not only of our own British Empire, but of the whole of European civilisation; and, as Christians, we no less serenely look forward to the Offering of the Everlasting Mass somehow and somewhere in the world, for ever. Modern scientific apparatus provides no beginning of a basis for expect-ing modern white civilisation to survive (indeed, one might suppose it already to be killing itself off as fast as it can), any more than the world which made the Pyramids and the staring Sphinx has survived or will revive. But throughout all that uncharted future, Jesus, Mary and Joseph will take their way; and throughout it, Mass will be offered, and men will enter into Communion with the sole Saviour of human souls.

And there is, we may say, even a human reason for being sure of this. When you perceive that the race has always been trying to reach something—it knew not what, but surmised there must be something to which men's instinct imperatively was driving them, and without which they knew themselves unsatisfied— and when they have obtained the *real thing*, this they do not let go of nor ever do they lose it, as we seem to be doing, unless they are actually dying out. We have, indeed, no promise that this or that part of the human race will *not* die out, whether or not it has been Christian. But here I want to say that by a universal instinct the human race has always fumbled after God, and Salvation, and a Redeemer, and Sacrifice and Communion, and a Mother such as Mary is to us. And that beyond what the Christian Faith offers in this matter no one can go. Imagination, inventiveness, cannot give us more than the facts which reason and Christian history combine to provide us with.

Those who begin at the wrong end and picture to themselves the human race as evolving, none knows how, from something sub-human which got there none knows how, nor does anyone know why it should have started evolving, nor have moved in any particular direction—well, those who start without knowledge of origin or goal, or reason for development or law of development, have been accustomed to saying that humanity throws off, for its own consolation, illusions suited to its successive stages of evolution. Accustomed therefore to attribute to things the value only of their lowest form and to say for example that religion must have evolved out of something sub-religious and demonstrably false (like magic), and is therefore *in reality* worth no more than that, they have been in the habit of saying that Mary, the Virgin Mother of God, is but a somewhat more civilised version of innumerable pagan virgin-mothers, all of them divine; and in particular that the worship of Isis in Egypt (though also that of the Great Mother in Asia Minor and especially at Ephesus) gave both impetus and colouring to the cult of Mary.

To get rid of the clumsier part of this suggestion, let us recall that none of those pagan goddesses or heroines were virgin. They were married to some god; or, if unmarried, by no means necessarily, if ever, virgin: even if their children had a god for father, the method of their conception may indeed have been abnormal and usually grotesque or repulsive, but was always materialistic. Further, these goddesses were not really taken for historical figures; least of all were Egyptian Isis or the Asiatic

Great Mother ever thought of as having historically existed.
They were embedded in nature-myths, and so certain is this
that an older generation of speculative scholars used to try to
turn the Christian story, too, into a nature-myth like the rest.
I think that these vulgarities are now given up. Finally, despite
the attempt made by the more refined pagan philosophers to
turn those myths into ethical allegories, and to volatilise the
various goddesses until they all melted into one figure who
should stand for Nature, the Force of Life, and the like, they
remained thoroughly infected with immorality; and by far the
loveliest pages upon Isis come in a very obscene book. They
used also to say that the Hebrews "cleaned up" the ancient
Semitic legends about creation and so forth: well, if the
Hebrews, and they alone but always, purified the material supplied to them, that already would be sufficiently surprising: so
too, would it have been astounding if Christianity, and it alone,
could lay hold of a human instinct which had always and everywhere issued into the fantastic and the filthy, and rinsed it clean
of the obscenity and shown how it found its accurate place in
theology—in, that is, an intellectual system so complete that
in all its parts it hangs perfectly together, and yet is so alive
that it is all the while developing. There is very much that could
be said about the out-of-date idea that our cult for Mary somehow grew out of, or borrowed from, pagan cults that preceded
or surrounded the date of the writing of the gospels. We could
insist that Judaism never developed a virgin-mother-goddess
myth, and that the passages in the gospels dealing with Our
Lady are Palestinian in spirit through and through—St. Luke's
"gospel of the Infancy" exceptionally so. It clashed, therefore,
with normal Jewish tradition and expectation. And again, that
the early Christian generations were almost fanatical in their
horror of pagan worship. But this not being a lecture, we leave
all that to one side and conclude by recalling what we are justified in holding, given our knowledge that the human race was

created by God, has a God-given destiny, and is guided providentially thereto.

Well, God has "made men of one blood over all the earth, that haply, groping after him, they might find him" (Acts xvii, 26). We are bound, therefore, to expect that all men will display, though in different ways, what are fundamentally the same desires and needs. And indeed, men are much more like one another than they are unlike; and the simpler and less spoilt they are the better you see that that is so.

Now if there is any order in the world (and there is and must be, seeing that the All-Wise created it), man cannot be endowed with needs and desires that are contrary to his nature and lead him nowhere. It is then to be expected that all men will, in the rough, aim at what is good for them, and at what is meant for them. But it is not to be expected that they will aim with accuracy and success at precisely the right objective. Thus it is natural to the human reason to see a cause for every effect, and a startlingly special cause for a startling effect. So it is very easy for men to deduce, almost automatically, a special cause for a thunder-storm, and even to strike out the notion of a thunder-god. But if an inland man, complete with thunder-god, makes acquaintance with the sea, especially when stormy, he very easily can arrive at the notion of a storm-at-sea-god—and quite possibly suppose him to be the brother of the thunder-god. The starting-point was right, but the deduction wrong, though easily explicable. We need not give more examples of this.

Now "life" itself was demonstrably a mystery that fascinated the ancient world. It was naturally seen in terms of motherhood—not only of human motherhood, but of the motherhood of plants and animals, and, indeed, of Nature as a whole. Men were perfectly right in this generalisation: nothing *is* more amazing than the reproduction of life, or rather, than life itself. I do not think that I need point out, however, into what shocking aberrations the perception of this supremely mysterious fact, and the cults consequent upon it, could stray and did stray. Parallel with this was a floating admiration for and value set upon purity and even virginity. Seeing that purity is a very difficult virtue to retain, it is easily understood that these beliefs, values, and cults developed or maintained themselves far less easily than what was concerned with motherhood and new life. All the same, when men further became conscious of decay and death, and linked the idea of sin with these, they felt, too, the need of a rescuer—a divine rescuer, who should revive the world, revitalise it, and provide health and strength perhaps just for the following year with its harvests and vintages, perhaps for always; and as for men, even in the next world. The life-giving hero needed a mother, and a mother who should be in a special way his and no one else's. You see here, stimulated by purely human instinct, the elements of a belief in a virgin-mother of a rescuing life-giving god.

Foolish (to our eyes), sometimes cruel, even obscene as were the rites which often if not usually surrounded these desires and beliefs, we feel far from mere disgust or contempt for them, given that we Christians know that God was guiding the human race towards precisely *that*—the Virgin Mother of God our Saviour.

This is why, in that Red Sea between Egypt and Arabia with its distant hinterland of the Mesopotamian sands where so much still lies buried, I have never hesitated to let my mind dwell on that Egyptian moon-goddess Isis, whose husband Osiris was slain by the serpent of Evil, for whom she sought with tears, and who in the "Hidden World" became Judge of every soul for ever; and on the saving god, their son: nor, looking towards Assyria and Babylon, on that other goddess Ishtar who wept over the slain grain-god Tammuz, slain, but restored to life each spring: nor on those many other forms of hers around whose dedicated places the Israelites—always harking back to the idolatries whence they have been drawn—built groves. Again and again the groves were cut down by indignant prophets and loyal monotheist kings; again and again they were replanted and grew green despite the blood that was shed among them. Peering through that ghastly foliage I keep catching sight of the goddess' face, scowling, leering, summoning, maybe blank and irresponsive—but always, to me, a hint, albeit a caricature of something that was needed and that at long last was given.

No one, nowadays, I take it, builds groves to goddesses: Isis and Ishtar are relegated to museums: but if this means that man's primary reaction to the mystery of life and of the universe has ceased to be *worship,* I am sorry. I am not at all sure that I would not prefer even a distorted worship to none. A grotesque or even hideous sacrifice, to the total loss of the instinct for offering sacrifice; or the most explicable wrong-headedness which produced an Ishtar or an Isis, to that paralysis of the spiritual optic nerve which prevents men seeing the essential differences between Mary and all those ancient figures, or even, to that troll-like slit-in-the-eye which has enabled students to see Our Lady as but another "projection" of man's illusory desires.

We on our side are happily able to take the comprehensive view, and to register, and appreciate, alike the radical identity of God-created human aspiration, and the essential transcendence of the unique divine response thereunto. The real thing has at last, in the persons of Jesus and Mary, been given to men: men have got the substance instead of the ghosts: the waking truth in place of the nightmares. Nowhere, no-when, is this so manifest as between Egypt and Arabia, when the traveller's track cuts across the footprints of the Holy Family. The whole world is full of their partial images—to be transcended, because partial: not to be scorned, because images. The Church has always condemned idolatry *and* iconoclasm—it is for us Catholics, to lay hold upon what is complete; what is Reality Alive!

MANCHILD

To THINK God learned to walk,
in Nazareth.
Later there'd be hard
walking to do,
with heavier falls.

And talking: in Nazareth
God played Adam's game—
naming things,
bringing out words:
and saw His own begetting
imaged, in the word's spring
from the intent regard.

A grave infant world
studied for Calvary,
studied for Genesareth,
prepared to say thrice;
Simon Peter, lovest thou me?

Mary was never asked
if she loved God.

A CARPENTER'S SON

He was a carpenter's son, from Nazareth.

I wish to begin with the utmost simplicity, and by saying that this was true. True in the sense that our Lord was truly man—and, legally, the son of Joseph.

When a Jewish girl was solemnly betrothed to a Jew she became legally under his protection and passed out of her father's control, even if she did not leave her father's house. When Our Lady was betrothed to St. Joseph by law she was responsible to him, and he for her. I will ask you, though, only for one moment, to consider the appalling hour during which St. Joseph perceived that she would be the mother of a child who was not his own. Strictly speaking, it was his duty to hand her over to the law, and it was the duty of the terrible Jewish authorities to cause her to be stoned. Such was the agonising preface to the history of our Lord, agonising, need I say, not only to St. Joseph but to the immaculate Virgin Mother of God. But the incredible purity of Mary had diffused its fragrance around itself: Joseph was, the Gospel says, a "just" man—he knew by instinct that, whatever had happened, there could be no imaginable taint in her whom by now he appreciated sufficiently to know *that* at least; and he was making arrangements to send her quietly away, so that no one should hear about what had happened. Then it was that God Himself let the mind of this simple working man know that he need have no fear; he kept Mary with him and he assumed full paternity, in the eyes of the world, of the child that was born; and legally, and in every way that human society could perceive and accept, he ranked himself as father of her child, and never did Jesus, during His childhood, adolescence or afterwards, do anything which could humiliate or disconcert St. Joseph. I beg of you to delve into this episode so little spoken of, and to venerate the persons who went through so really dreadful an experience. But it is not of the legal and social parenthood or humanity of Christ that I wish now to speak. Jesus Christ could not in any sense have been called son of Joseph, had He not been truly man. It would have been an illegitimate fiction, a wanton delusion, so to call Him, had He been anything short of it. But to be a man involves at least your being partly body. A body is not a thing you "have," but a thing you are. We are not body plus soul, soul in spite of body, soul inside a body, but *persons, body-souls.* Our Lord grew. He "increased in stature," say the evangelists.

He was a baby—Christmas does not allow us to forget that; if you had met Him then, you would not have been able to do towards Him more than you can towards any lovable little baby that looks at you with its blue whites to its eyes and catches hold of your thumb with its incredibly strong minuscule fingers ending in pink nails so tiny as to be almost laughable. You cannot say anything to such a baby; you can do nothing but love it; but it always knows if you do. He was a little boy, and you know how very little boys will trust you—take you for granted —never begin to dream that you are going to be unkind to them— instinctively sheer away from you if you begin taking airs or putting on affectations towards them—are very hurt if you do not accept their views of things exactly in the way that they accept them. Little boys can be made very lonely if you act the aloof grown-up, but far more lonely if you pretend you are a child, which they know very well you are not. Jesus was next a growing lad, and only for one moment is the curtain lifted upon those years—during an episode of three days, when, upon the occasion of a pilgrimage to Jerusalem, He stayed behind and was lost to Mary and to Joseph. They found Him, and thereafter, His history relates, He stayed at Nazareth, being "subject unto them." He learned and gradually performed His work as smith and carpenter in a town which, though small, was a very active one. Nazareth lay near two roads, up and down which trade flowed continuously and also the Roman soldiery, and also the caravans taking people to and from the summer-court of Herod Antipas at Sepphoris. When our Lord was about ten, He, and all the folk of Nazareth, watched that town on its hill four miles away going up in smoke when the Romans, because of an abortive insurrection, burnt it; those Romans crucified two thousand men of the neighbourhood as an object lesson—Mary could not go to her well, nor Jesus to the social meeting-place of any oriental town, the Gate, without seeing—or trying not to see—poor human corpses rotting upon crosses. He knew—perhaps she dreamed—what was to happen after twenty years, not away in Galilee, but in Jerusalem, the holy city, the dear city, which yet should crucify its Lord.

A CHILD MY CHOICE

LET FOLLY praise that fancy loves, I praise and love that
    Child
Whose heart no thought, Whose tongue no word, Whose hand
    no deed defiled.
I praise Him most, I love Him best, all praise and love is His;
While Him I love, in Him I live, and cannot live amiss.
Love's sweetest mark, laud's highest theme, man's most desired
    light,
To love Him life, to leave Him death, to live in Him delight.
He mine by gift, I his by debt, thus each to other due,
First friend He was, best friend He is, all times will try Him
    true.
Though young, yet wise, though small, yet strong; though man,
    yet God He is;
As wise He knows, as strong He can, as God He loves to bliss.
His knowledge rules, His strength defends, His love doth cher-
    ish all;
His birth our joy, His life our light, His death our end of thrall.
Alas! He weeps, He sighs, He pants, yet do His angels sing;
Out of His tears, His sighs and throbs, doth bud a joyful spring.
Almighty Babe, Whose tender arms can force all foes to fly,
Correct my faults, protect my life, direct me when I die!

THE WORD MADE FLESH

I

The Word

IN THE BEGINNING *was the Word, and the Word was with God, and the Word was God. . . . And the Word* was made flesh, *and dwelt among us, (and we saw his glory, the glory as of the only-begotten of the Father), full of grace and truth* (John i, 1, 14).

The doctrine of the Trinity (that within the divine Nature are three distinct Persons) is the inner, the innermost, life of God, His profoundest secret. He did not have to reveal it to us. We could have been saved without knowing that ultimate truth. In the strictest sense it is His business, not ours. He revealed it to us because He loves men and so wants not only to be served by them but truly known by them. It is the surest mark of love to want to be known. The revelation of the Trinity was in one sense a more certain proof even than Calvary that God loves men. To accept it politely and think no more of it is an insensitiveness beyond comprehension in men who quite certainly love God.

God knows and loves, for these are the proper operations of Spirit. Because He is infinite, His knowledge and love are infinite. It is in the further consideration of God living within His own nature a life of infinite knowledge and infinite love that we shall come to some further knowledge of the three Persons and of their relations one to another.

We begin with the relation of the Second Person to the First. For this relation, Scripture provides us with two names: the Second Person is the *Son,* and He is the *Word.* It must be understood that these two words refer to one and the same vital process in the Godhead. But the second takes us deeper. Let us concentrate upon it.

In the Old Testament (Ecclus. xxiv, 5) we have a hint of a word—"I came out of the mouth of the Most High"—a word which is also a son—"the firstborn before all creatures." But the explicit reference to the Son of God as the Word we get from St. John, and so, we may believe, from Our Lady, since Christ Our Lord on the Cross entrusted her to St. John that he might be her son and she his mother. To open his Gospel he writes: "In the beginning was the Word, and the Word was with God, and the Word was God . . . And the Word was made flesh and dwelt among us. And we saw his glory, the glory as of the only-begotten of the Father." Thus He who became man and dwelt among us, that Jesus of whom St. John was to write his Gospel, was the only-begotten of the Father—with that phrase we are back at the concept of the Son; and He who lived among men as Jesus of Nazareth, Who was the Son of God, was the Word of God: and the Word was God.

It is clear that if God has a word it will not be a vocal word, a thing of air, shaped by lungs and throat and tongue and teeth. God is not like that. God is a pure spirit and His word must be a word in the mind, *verbum mentale,* in other words a thought or idea. We must follow very closely to see what is the meaning of

> the thought or idea in the mind of God,
> which was in the beginning with God,
> which was the only-begotten Son of God,
> which became Flesh and dwelt among us.

God's revelation tells us that God, knowing Himself with infinite knowledge, thinking of Himself with infinite power, generates an idea of Himself. With that piece of information the closed circle is suddenly opened, the barrier is down and the whole vast inner life of God invites us.

An idea is, so far as we can make it so, the mental double or image of the object we are contemplating; it expresses as much of that object as we can manage to get into it. Because of the limitation of our powers, the idea we form is never the perfect double or image, never totally expresses the object, in plain words, is never totally adequate. But if God does, as we know from Himself that He does, generate an idea of Himself, this idea must be totally adequate, in no way less than the Being of which it is the Idea, lacking nothing that that Being has. The Idea must contain all the perfection of the Being of which it is the Idea. There can be nothing in the Thinker that is not in His Thought of Himself, otherwise the Thinker would be thinking of Himself inadequately, which is impossible for the Infinite. Thus the Idea, the Word that God generates, is Infinite, Eternal, Living, a Person, equal in all things to Him Who generates It—Someone as He is, conscious of Himself as He is, God as He is.

This is the second Person, the Word, the Son. So it is that St. Paul can speak of the Son as "the image of the invisible God." We sometimes speak of a son as the image of his father —even the living image. This Son is. It is of the essence of a son, any son, that he should be like his father; it is of the essence of an idea, any idea, that it should be like what the thinker is thinking of. The Infinite Father generates an Infinite Son, resembling Him infinitely; the Infinite Thinker, thinking of Himself, generates an Infinite Idea, resembling Him infinitely.

Thinking on the word Word, we can now take a further step.

For though the thought is not the thinker, the thought is in the nature of the thinker; it is not a separate nature, as the nature of a son in all our human experience is a separate nature from his father's. Thought is within the very nature of the thinker. Thus we have God within His own Nature generating an Idea which because it *is* an Idea is wholly in that one same Nature, and because it is an adequate idea contains that Nature wholly. The Son has nothing that He has not received from the Father; but the Father has nothing that He has not given to the Son. The One has the Divine Nature as unreceived; the other as received: but each has It in Its totality, and there is no shadow of inequality between them.

The Second Person, as we have just seen, proceeds from the First by way of knowledge. The other primary operation of spirit is love, and it is by way of love that the Third Person proceeds. To a point the two "processions" are parallel. The First Person knows Himself; His act of knowing Himself produces an Idea, a Word; and this Idea, this Word, the perfect Image of Himself, is the Second Person. The First Person and the Second combine in an act of love, love of one another, love of the glory of the Godhead which is their own; and just as the act of knowing produces an Idea within the Divine Nature, the act of loving produces a state of Lovingness within the Divine Nature. Into this Lovingness, Father and Son pour all that They have and all that They are, with no diminution, nothing held back. Thus this Lovingness within the Godhead is utterly equal to the Father and the Son, for They have poured Their all into it. There is nothing They have which Their Lovingness does not have. Thus Their Lovingness too is Infinite, Eternal, Living, Someone, a Person, God. Observe that here again we are still within the Divine Nature. For love is wholly within the nature of the lover. But this love wholly contains the Divine Nature, because God puts the whole of Himself into love.

Was Made Flesh

God the Son took to Himself a human nature, not merely wearing it as a disguise or taking it up as an instrument He might use, but making it His own as my nature is my own, making it His own so utterly that we can express the new relation only by saying that He, God the Son, became man. He did not take a human nature simply to be able to do the things that a man does, to act the part of a man, to pass for a man. Let us say it again, He became man. To the question, "What are you?" He could answer with no mitigation or reservation, "I am man." That would not have been the whole answer, for it would not have reached His divine nature. But it would have been wholly true. The relation between His nature as man and His person was as direct, as intimate, as the relation between my nature and my person. He could say: "I am man" as completely as I can say: "I am man." Indeed He could say it with better title, for He was more of a man than I. His human nature was not diminished by sin as mine is.

Notice again that it was a *real* human nature and a *complete* human nature. Take the reality first. The human nature of Christ was not simply a human body animated by a human soul, thus possessing all that the definition of a man requires, suddenly appearing among us. He actually belongs to us. His soul was a direct and individual creation of the Blessed Trinity, just like your soul and my soul; but by His body He was conceived of a human mother, just as you and I.

Of a human mother, notice, but not of a human father. In the sense in which other human beings have a mother and father, He had a mother only. The bodies of other human beings result from the action of an element supplied by their father upon an element supplied by their mother. In the case of Our Lord the effect upon the female element normally produced by the male element was produced simply by a creative act of the will of God. Thus He is a member of Adam's race on His mother's side; He is a Jew on His mother's side; but not upon His father's side, for in the order of human generation He had no father. He was descended from Adam as we all are, but not as much as we all are. None of us derived our souls from Adam, but we all derived our bodies from Adam; whereas He derived His body from Adam only as to part. It follows that we are all related to Him—through her, and only through her: we are all His maternal relations, His mother's people.

His was a real human nature: and it was a complete human nature, lacking nothing whatever that human nature requires for completeness. We read in Hebrews (iv, 15): "He was like us in all things but without sin"—sin not being required to complete human nature, but always operating to diminish it. To grasp the completeness of Our Lord's manhood, we have only to consider the elements of which manhood is composed, body and soul. His body was a real body, though conceived by miracle: He was born as an infant and grew through boyhood to manhood; in His body He knew hunger and thirst; when His body was scourged, it bled; when it had a weight to bear too heavy for it, it fell; when it was damaged beyond a certain point, it underwent that separation from the soul which is death.

Just as He had a human body, He had a human soul to animate it, a soul which like other human souls was a created spirit. He could cry in the Garden of Gethsemane, "My soul is sorrowful even unto death." Again, His soul had the faculties of intellect and will, human intellect and human will. He who by His divine intellect had all wisdom could in His human intellect "grow in wisdom" (Luke ii, 52). In the Garden He could say to God, "Not My Will but Thine be done," thereby indicating that though His human will was totally united to the Divine Will, there was question of two wills and not one.

The co-existence in Christ of a human intellect with the

divine intellect may at first seem more difficult to conceive than the co-existence of two wills. A human intellect proceeds toward knowledge discursively as the philosophers say, step by step as ordinary men say. The external world makes its impact upon the bodily senses; and from the evidence of the external world which thus gets through, the soul forms its concepts, and compares its concepts to form judgments; and as its experience increases, its knowledge grows. But all this in a necessarily limited way. It does seem difficult to conceive that the one identical Person who by His divine nature knew all things could also proceed to acquire by the operation of His human intellect scattered sparkles of the infinite light of knowledge in which He already lived. It is, I say, hard to conceive, yet not inconceivable. The human nature and the divine nature belong to one person, but they are not one nature. The one person could operate, really and truly, in both natures. If Our Lord wanted to lift a load, He could have lifted it either by the effortless fiat of the divine will or by the hard effort of the human muscles. Our Lord's human nature was a reality, His human senses and His human intellect were reality. His human senses could not do other than receive the impact of the external world; His human intellect could not do other than act upon their evidence to form concepts and judgments. The Godhead did not swallow up the manhood.

While we are upon this question of Our Lord's human intellect, there are two other things to be said about it. It has been the steady teaching of theologians that Our Lord's human intellect had both infused knowledge and the Beatific Vision. What it must have been like for the one human mind to move along so many roads at once we cannot well picture. But there is no contradiction in the idea of the mind moving by one road to a goal it has already reached by another. The point to be grasped is that neither infused knowledge nor beatific knowledge is beyond the power of human nature to receive from God.

Many men have had infused knowledge—though not continu-ously—and all the saved will have beatific knowledge.

Our Lord, then, as man had a real body with a real soul, with a real intellect and a real will. His emotions were real too: He loved St. John; He wept over Jerusalem and over dead Lazarus; He stormed at the Pharisees.

But if Our Lord had a real human nature with a real natural life, then He needed the supernatural life too, to accomplish those things which are beyond the power of nature. By merely human natural power, He could not see God direct any more than we could; but His human nature was capable of receiving sanctifying grace, just as ours is. The work of grace in the soul is appropriated to the Third Person of the Blessed Trinity. The Second Person as God possessed all things; but as man He needed the indwelling of the Holy Spirit both for that elevation and sanctification which every human nature needs, and for the special guidance and illumination His human nature needed for the unique work which as Son of God He was to do in it and through it. Our Lord then had sanctifying grace in His soul. He did not have faith or hope because, possessing the beatific vision, He did not need them; but He had charity in the fullest measure possible to a creature: for, at the risk of wearying, we must constantly remind ourselves that His human nature was a creature: like ours.

II

The Public Ministry

"What I was born for, what I came into the world
for, is to bear witness of the truth."
(John xviii, 37)

NARRATIVE

I

IN THE FIFTEENTH year of the reign of Tiberius Caesar, says St. Luke—the year 27 A.D.—John the Baptist began such a whirlwind preaching campaign as Israel had never known. He was that John, son of Mary's cousin Elizabeth, whose birth was announced by the Angel Gabriel five or six months before Christ's, who was to be filled with the Holy Ghost from his mother's womb, who was to go before the Lord, as St. Luke tells us; who was not the Light but was to give testimony of the Light, as St. John tells us. He exhorted all Israel to penance and baptized multitudes; but, when men thought he might be the Christ, he insisted that the Christ was to come and was to baptize them with a baptism mightier than his. To John came Jesus, then about thirty, demanding to be baptized: and after His baptism the Holy Ghost descended as a dove upon Him, and a voice came from Heaven: "Thou art my beloved Son, in whom I am well pleased."

Immediately upon His baptism, Jesus was led by the Holy Ghost into the desert, where He spent forty days in prayer and fasting; was tempted by Satan and vanquished him; began to gather disciples; and at a wedding in Cana, a few miles from Nazareth, performed His first public miracle and so ended His hidden life—at the request of His mother He changed water into wine.

From Galilee where all this happened, Jesus went to Jerusalem and there did the one thing that would mean that everyone in Palestine to the smallest child would hear of Him—He drove the money-changers from the Temple. Still in Judea, He had the conversation with the Pharisee Nicodemus in which He told of the baptism He would institute—"unless a man be born again of water and the Holy Ghost, he shall not enter into the Kingdom of Heaven," as well as of the death He would die—"As Moses lifted up the serpent in the desert, so must the Son of Man be lifted up."

II

With the arrest of John the Baptist by Herod Antipas—who ultimately slew him—Jesus left Judea to open His own ministry in Galilee, lingering a little in Samaria on the way. In Galilee He healed a ruler's son, preached in His own town of Nazareth but established His abode in Capharnaum, by the Lake of Tiberias (the other name for the Sea of Galilee), probably in the house of Simon, a fisherman, whose name He changed to Peter, Rock. His ministry proper had begun. He preached, of penance and the coming of the Kingdom, and worked miracle upon miracle—including the miraculous haul of fish which was followed by the definitive call of Peter, James and John to join themselves to Him.

By now the opposition was beginning to take shape. At Capharnaum He healed a paralytic but first forgave his sins, which led to an accusation of blasphemy. He called to Him a tax-gatherer (who was to be the apostle Matthew) and in his house sat at table with Matthew's disreputable friends—which led to an accusation of moral laxity, and unfavorable comparison with the rigidly ascetical life of John the Baptist and his followers. Then there were problems about the Sabbath—His followers plucked ears of corn on that day, and He Himself healed a man with a withered hand. He answered their complaints unanswerably. And He claimed to be Lord of the Sabbath. Thus early, Pharisees and Herodians, so ill-assorted allies, began to plan for His destruction.

Then comes one of the decisive things—the Sermon on the Mount. It was preceded by a whole night "passed in the prayer of God," after which He made the definite choice of twelve to be His apostles. Then the crowds thronged, not only from Galilee where He was, but from Judea, from Jerusalem itself, and from Tyre and Sidon on the Mediterranean coast. He healed the sick—"distressed with pain and sickness of every sort, the possessed, the lunatics, the palsied." Then He went up into a mountain, and the most famous of all sermons began. First, the Beatitudes—Blessed are the poor in spirit, the meek, those who mourn, who hunger and thirst after righteousness, the merciful, the peacemakers, all who are persecuted for God's sake. Then a great body of moral and ascetical teaching, exalting love but giving stern warning of Hell for the un-loving. Much of His moral teaching is a restatement and interiorization of the law of Moses. He had come not to destroy the law but to fulfill it: but the formula He used—"Moses said to you. . . . But I say to you"—claimed a superiority to the Law that stunned his hearers more even than His claims to be Lord of the Sabbath.

Back in Capharnaum He healed the servant of a Roman officer, whose phrase "Lord I am not worthy that thou shouldst enter under my roof" is enshrined in our Eucharistic liturgy. At Naim he raised a widow's dead son to life. The discussions and dissensions about Him went on. His fame grew but the doubts grew too. John the Baptist in prison sent disciples to Him to reassure themselves; the Pharisees were furious that He allowed a harlot to anoint His feet; some of His relations thought He was mad. But the travelling and the teaching went on all over Galilee. We have come to the time of the first great group of parables—of the Sower, the Seed growing secretly, the Cockle, the Mustard Seed, the Leaven, the Treasure hid in a field and the Pearl of great price, the Net, and the Householder—in which the nature of His Kingdom begins to emerge, a spiritual Kingdom, not that earthly one of the Jewish hope.

Capharnaum is on the west of the Lake of Galilee. After six or seven months there, He brought His teaching and healing to the eastern shore—there most notably He allowed unclean spirits driven from a man to enter a herd of swine. Back in Galilee comes what must surely be one of the agonizing moments of His life—He preached in His own town of Nazareth. His own people rejected Him and tried to kill Him: not altogether surprisingly, since He had talked of times when God had favoured Gentiles rather than Jews.

Once more He crossed the lake and went to a desert place near Bethsaida. A crowd of five thousand followed Him: there was the, by now almost routine, teaching and healing: and towards the end of a day in which none had eaten, Jesus fed the crowd by a miraculous multiplication of five loaves and two fishes. Out of this miracle, He drew the teaching given in the synagogue at Capharnaum, and set out by St. John in his sixth chapter, of Himself as the Bread of Life—"Unless you eat the flesh of the Son of Man and drink his blood you can not have life in you. The man who eats my flesh and drinks my blood enjoys eternal life, and I will raise him up at the last day. My flesh is real food, my blood is real drink. He who eats my flesh and drinks my blood lives in me and I in him." It was too much even for many of His disciples, who simply left Him; but the Twelve remained with Him.

The best part of a year had passed since Jesus had taken up His abode in Capharnaum. Now He went to Jerusalem for Pentecost, infuriated the Jews further by healing a paralyzed man on the Sabbath, accusing them of unfaithfulness to Moses

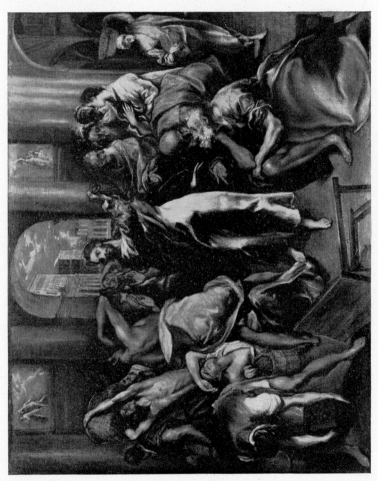

THE PURGING OF THE TEMPLE
El Greco

and making a frightening claim for Himself—"all men should honour the Son as they honour the Father." But He did not stay in Judea, for they sought to kill Him and He had much yet to do. So He taught again in Galilee, where scribes and Pharisees followed Him from Jerusalem to question Him, but could hardly have enjoyed the experience; went to the sea-coast cities of Tyre and Sidon and back to Galilee, once again fed a crowd, four thousand this time, by a miraculous multiplication of food.

St. Peter and the other apostles were with Him in these goings and comings and had already been entrusted with a teaching and healing mission of their own. Their faith had been tested hard by the teaching that they must eat His flesh and drink His blood, but with one exception they were still wholly His, yet with no clearness in their own minds whether or not He might be the Messias, whether or not He might be human or more than human or divine. They were sure of one thing only: that He had the words of eternal life: and they had one strong hope, that when He founded the Kingdom He talked of so much, they would hold high rank in it.

To us, reading in the light of all that has happened, their slowness of comprehension seems beyond comprehension. Now at least Jesus made a more determined effort to clarify their minds—about Himself, themselves and His Kingdom.

At Caesarea Philippi, in the north of Galilee, He drew from Peter the confession that He was the Christ, the Son of the living God—which is at least an assertion that Jesus is the Messias, and (given all they had heard Our Lord say of His equality with the Father) surely an assertion of His divinity. Jesus met Peter's confession with the announcement that He would build His Church upon Peter, who must have found the next series of events a little dazing. He has just heard that he is to be the head of Christ's Kingdom on earth—think what that meant to a Jew with the thousand-year expectation of the Kingdom, raised to a new power by a year or more of constant companionship with a Messias beyond any Old Testament dream. Within a few minutes, he hears Christ warn the apostles of His own coming suffering and death and hears himself called Satan—the tempter—by Christ for urging Him not to undergo so much agony and infamy. The week that followed could hardly have been long enough to lift the pain and fear and humiliation from Peter's mind: but at the end of it Christ raised him once more to the heights—spiritually, of course, but physically too. For He took Peter and James and John into a high mountain—Tabor probably—and there was transfigured before them, the glory that was ever His being allowed for that brief while to shine through and be seen of men. With the Transfiguration Jesus' ministry in Galilee is really at an end. On their way back to Capharnaum, He once more tells of the suffering and death that must come to Him, adding the grim detail that He is to be betrayed, and the explicit statement that on the third day He will rise again. There is now a great mass of teaching, directed it would seem at the apostles, forming them for the work they must do: culminating in the injunction that we must forgive not seven times but till seventy times seven.

III

From now, Jesus is in Judea, where His death is planned and certain. In Jerusalem the scribes and Pharisees ply Him with questions, and His answers leave no place for compromise. When they bring Him the woman taken in adultery, He challenges any man who is sinless to throw the first stone. He speaks more and more clearly of His own divinity. He heals a man born blind and the Pharisees hold a full-scale investigation. He tells a lawyer, set upon knowing whether all the 248 commands and 365 prohibitions of the Law were of the same rank, that there is a first and a second among them, that the two great commands are to love God wholly and love our neighbour as ourself. In the parable of the Good Samaritan He rejects Jewish exclusiveness wholly. But His own main interest, perhaps, is in the formation of His followers. He gives to Martha and Mary at Bethany the great lesson that contemplation is the higher and holier state; and upon a disciple's request that He teach them how to pray, He gives us the Lord's Prayer.

The Pharisees continued importunate: suggested that He cast out devils by diabolic power. He answered their hostility with a great storm of denunciation, and they were set more implacably than ever in their determination to destroy Him. When, in response to their irritated question "How long dost thou hold our souls in suspense: if thou be the Christ tell us plainly," He answered, "I and the Father are one," they took up stones to stone Him. But He would not let them slay Him yet. He crossed over Jordan and there for a while remained. To this period belong another great mass of parables—of the Banquet, the Great Supper, the Lost Sheep and the Lost Coin—which seem clearly enough to say that the Jews have forfeited their priority: then the parables of the Prodigal Son, and of Dives and Lazarus which underline the same truth unmistakably: as do the parables of the Pharisee and the Publican and the Labourers in the Vineyard which came soon after. One cannot be certain of the order of events just here. There is the healing of the ten lepers (with only the Samaritan returning to give thanks) and a magnificent body of teaching on the Second Coming and the Last Judgment, on the providence of God, on riches and poverty, on marriage and virginity, on the necessity of becoming as little children.

The determination of His enemies to destroy Him was given its last edge of sharpness by a miracle He worked at Bethany— He raised the four-day-dead Lazarus, brother of Martha and Mary, to life. A miracle of that magnitude, and only a mile or two from Jerusalem itself, was too much: "If we let him alone, all will believe in him and the Romans will come and take away our place and nation." Jesus retired for a little while to Ephrem, some fifteen miles away. It was noted that He did not come up to Jerusalem before the Pasch: and orders were given that anyone who knew where He was should give information: He must be left no more at liberty.

It could only be a matter of days now, as He knew. He gave His apostles the most detailed foretelling of His betrayal and scourging and death, but also of His resurrection.

THE SITUATION IN PALESTINE

⊰ St. Luke tells us that John the Baptist began his preaching in "the fifteenth year of the reign of Tiberius Caesar, Pontius Pilate being governor of Judaea, and Herod being tetrarch of Galilee, and Philip his brother tetrach of Ituraea and the country of Trachonitis, and Lysanius tetrarch of Abilina: under the high priests Annas and Caiaphas . . ." (Luke iii, 1–2). This medley of names, titles and duties warns us from the start that we have to deal with a complex state of affairs. The fact is that the political unity re-established in Palestine by Herod the Idumaean at the cost of an atrocious war of three years' duration (40–37 B.C.) had been again broken down. This half-Jew, crafty and cruel, who was to complete his reign with the massacre of the Innocents, did at least enforce order and obtained, even if he did not merit it, the name of "the Great." He reigned from 37 to 4 B.C.

In his time the Temple was magnificently rebuilt, peace was maintained, the pride of the sacerdotal families was humbled, and the marked hellenism of the prince, together with his constant devotion to the more powerful of the Romans, was limited by a sure instinct for the critical point beyond which Jewish endurance would give place to despair and revolt. The dark intrigues of the palace and the unforgivable murders which blackened the last years of the reign did not prevent Augustus from ratifying the chief features of the Idumaean's will. This divided his land between his three surviving sons—he had put to death his three elder sons. By this will, Archelaus received Judaea; Herod Antipas (who beheaded John the Baptist and appears in the story of the Passion) was given Galilee and Peraea; while Ituraea and the north-eastern districts went to Philip.

By the year 30 only the last two retained their dominions. In Judaea (properly so-called) Archelaus made himself so unpopular that his subjects forwarded to Rome a petition against him. Augustus received it in A.D. 6 and in consequence placed the province directly under a Roman magistrate, who was a mere procurator (we should call him a Lieutenant-Governor) of the Pro-consul of Syria, and resided on the coast at Caesarea, whence communication with Rome was none too easy. His habitual absence from Jerusalem, to which he went every year with a strong escort at the time of the Feast of the Passover, together with the care taken by the Romans to leave to subject peoples a portion or a shadow of autonomy, meant that the high council of the nation, the Sanhedrin, which had been almost abolished during Herod's reign, regained a certain amount of independence. Composed of seventy-one members, "princes of the priests" (chiefs of the principal families of sacerdotal caste), "scribes" (doctors expert in the interpretation of the Law), and "elders" (senators) the Sanhedrin was presided over at great functions by the high priest. In the time of Jesus, this tribunal was in actual fact the sole Jewish authority in matters political and religious. . . .

We see in the Judaea of those days, less perhaps than elsewhere, but in the same way, rich and poor, "the great ones of the flesh" and the small, persons of quality and the populace. As always happens, the first class are the better known to us: it is they who, in very great measure, make history, and it is always they who write it. And it is chiefly with them that we are con-

cerned in this chapter. But if we were to forget the others we
should run the danger of not understanding the Gospels, and it
is the Gospels which offer us the most vivid pictures of these.
Leisured artisans, and fishermen who could be more easily detached from their boats than labourers could be uprooted from
their soil, the apostles of Jesus almost all belonged to that little
world of true Israelites, without guile and without artifice,
formed on the model made familiar to us by the Wisdom literature and the Psalms.

The Master praised them in the person of Nathaniel (John
i, 47) and, which is much more, he called them to him. Jewish
scholars who strive to explain and to diminish the contrast
between the Gospel and the Pharisaic ideal, locate the difference in the fact that, far from repulsing these men as incapable
of sharing in the Kingdom of God, Jesus opened the door wide
to them. He went lower than that, even to sinners and publicans,
but chiefly he talked familiarly and in friendly fashion with
the ignorant, the rude, and "this accursed multitude which
knoweth not the law" (John vii, 49).

Above these masses of the people we find, ruling them or at
least distinct from them, at this period in Judaea, "the rich and
prudent" whose importance was assured to them by their birth,
fortune and knowledge of the Law.

The *Herodians* are three times mentioned in the Gospels
(Mark iii, 6; xii, 13; Matt., xxii, 16). Without constituting a
particular sect, analogous to those which will be described
below, these politicians, who were resigned to the Roman rule,
and were devoted to or rallied to the power of the Idumaean
princes, were recruited from the families which the state of
affairs existing under the Herods had not too much offended
or injured. They saw in this government a more or less tolerable middle term half-way between total subjection to the
Empire and an independence which they no longer believed to
be possible. The words spoken at the meeting of the Sanhedrin

about the miracles and increasing popularity of Jesus express very fairly the timid wisdom of the Herodians and the proximity of Rome which made them desire, and almost love, the scarcely national dynasty of the Herods.

At the other extremity of the political rainbow, a turbulent, fanatical group, the *Zealots*, were jealous observers of the Law, and, as such, were Pharisees and no more. What enabled Josephus to distinguish them from the main body of the Pharisees was the fact that, being before all else nationalists, the Zealots were the declared enemies of all foreign domination. Already formed in Gospel times, this turbulent minority increased as a consequence of the troubles which followed the ephemeral reign of Herod Agrippa I, who died in 44. It fomented and fanned the successive revolts which led to the capture and sack of Jerusalem in 70.

The *Essenes*, who are known only through occasional (though detailed and friendly) passages in Philo, Josephus and Pliny the Elder, have greatly aroused the curiosity of scholars and have driven not a few amateur historians to delirium. They formed cenobitical groups, freely recruited, and their chief centres were situated around the Dead Sea. According to Josephus they numbered as many as four thousand. Their origin is unknown: but traces of them are found possibly towards the middle, and certainly towards the end of the first century B.C. After undergoing a postulancy of one year, they were initiated and given a knife, a belt and a white robe. They kept themselves, worked with their hands, as a general rule preserved celibacy, did not keep slaves and did not engage in commerce.

As all goods were held in common, meals were taken together, with a grave and religious solemnity. Their scrupulous, concerted, almost ritualistic care of personal cleanliness, and their abstention from blood sacrifices, might make us think that the Essenes were very different from other Israelites.

In reality, they were (although following their own particular course) true Jews, faithful to the fundamental beliefs of Judaism, strict observers of the Law, and especially of the Sabbatarian precepts, great readers of the Holy Books, who sent their offerings regularly to the Temple at Jerusalem. If Schürer goes too far in calling them "decided Pharisees" (for their faith seems rather to have turned towards the immortality of the soul than to the resurrection of the body), if certain characteristics seem to betray foreign origin and discipline (possibly Greek or Pythagorean, more probably Iranian), the Essenes remain for all essentials within the religious body of Israel. In any case, nothing could differ more from primitive Christianity, which could at the most see in them an example, when for some time it put into practice at Jerusalem the common holding of property. In other respects, that is to say in almost all its characteristics (its rigid legalism, its scrupulous attention to corporal and saving purifications, its moral rigorism extending normally to prohibition of marriage, and its aloofness from all that was sinful, common or profane), the Order was absolutely contrary to the spirit and the habits of Jesus. It could be more justly asked whether certain of the Master's criticisms were not aimed at the refinements and exclusiveness of the Essenes . . .

Let us come to the great parties, which were opponents and rivals on many points, but which a common interest could partially draw together and unite against Jesus: the *Sadducees* and the *Pharisees*. The distant origin of these sects has been sought for in their conflicting tendencies, the one rigidly Jewish, the other more open to foreign influences, which divided the Jewish leaders throughout the period which followed the return from exile in the middle of the sixth century.

At first the severe tendency, closed to all compromise, which was favoured by the leaders of the migration, Esdras and Nehemias, and by the fact that the greater number of the social leaders of the people had remained in Mesopotamia, undoubtedly reigned supreme. It is the period of the *Soferim,* i.e., the commentators on the book *par excellence,* the *Sefer-ha-torah* (book of the Law). Promulgated again among this group of devout Jews, the Law became truly the *form* of this people, in the Aristotelian sense of the word, the intimate regulator of its life, its specific principle of order and of hierarchy. In it was sought every rule for public and private organisation, every solution for the extremely complex cases which were raised by the return to Judaea of the caravans from Persia, coming as they were amongst a scattered population of pagan or semi-pagan occupiers. From this necessity there sprang the important occupation of the scribe, the commentator on the sole rule of God. Sprung generally from modest origins, often laymen, though not always (Esdras himself was of the sacerdotal caste), the scribes favoured with all their power whatever tended to separate Israel from the people amongst whom they lived, with the object of restoring an autonomous state. Mixed marriages, therefore, intercourse with pagans or the semi-Jews of Samaria, and anything approaching idolatry, were zealously denounced.

On the other hand, some of the most important of the priests who had returned from exile, pastors and leaders of the people in this theocracy in which the two powers were confounded, remained in contact with the Persian authorities, and even went so far as to unite themselves in marriage with influential families not of pure Jewish race. Such was the case, for example, of the high priest Eliasib: he was united to the family of Tobias the Ammonite, and one of his grandsons, the son of Joiadah (and therefore the son and grandson of high priests) married a daughter of Sanaballat the Horonite. And Tobias and Sanaballat, sworn enemies of Nehemias, opposed with all their might the rebuilding of the walls of Jerusalem undertaken by the latter.

We can see in these two tendencies, the one aristocratic and liberal, represented by the high sacerdotal caste, and the other more humble and rigidly closed to all foreign influence, an anticipation of the future.

Yet the origin of the parties of the Sadducees and Pharisees does not go back so far; it must be sought in the obscure period which separates the end of the era of the scribes and the death of Simon the Just from the brutal attempt of Antiochus Epiphanes to hellenise the country (roughly 270–175 B.C.).

Then was completely shattered the unity of the sacerdotal and learned oligarchy, the legendary "Great Synagogue" of later Jewish tradition, which maintained on the whole for two centuries, despite varying fortunes, a certain general understanding amongst those faithful to the Law. Whatever form that assembly may have had (and we must not be too quick to see in it the features of the future Sanhedrin), it united the double authority of the great priestly families and the doctors (priests or laymen) who gave the people from day to day the interpretation of the Law. The members of the first group, who were the more rigid the more liberty they took for themselves, and were satisfied with a literalism which cut short all casuistical discussion, stood theoretically, if not practically, for the written Law without gloss. The others strove to give to the sacred texts a flexibility which would enable them to be adapted to a change of circumstances; this they sought to do by the double means of a subtle exegesis of the letter of the law, and a traditional interpretation, a kind of oral law, which later took form in the Mishna. It was probably on that point that the separation took place.

From whichever side the initiative came, the somewhat ill-sounding name of the Separated (peruchim, Pharisees) was applied to those who abandoned the high authorities of the Temple. Thus it was indicated that they formed a body apart and were seceders. They themselves did not call themselves by this name, but preferred that of haberim (colleagues, companions, fellow-workers). But the other name prevailed, and it is as Pharisees that all ancient tradition knew them. In contradistinction to them, and before political circumstances led them

to reintroduce certain Pharisees into the supreme council of the
nation, the representatives of the priestly caste were called or
called themselves the sons of Sadoc (Sadducees), in allusion no
doubt to a prince of the priests of the time of David and Solomon, Sadoc, whose real or fictitious descendents were regarded
as the sacerdotal family *par excellence.*

Each party was wedded to its own opinions, while the mass of
the people, naturally closer to the Pharisees, oscillated between
currents which sometimes came near to intermingling, only
speedily to resume their separate and often antagonistic courses.
The Sadducees were ambitious, and consequently opportunist,
very tolerant in the matter of alliances, understandings, and
compromises with pagans and half-Jews, hard towards the poorer
people; they were unscrupulous in increasing their personal
fortunes from the enormous contributions of money and other
offerings which flowed into the Temple from all parts of the
Holy Land and from the Dispersion, but they professed an un-
swerving conservatism in matters of the Law. They reduced
the whole of Revelation, at least all that was of absolute authority, to the five books of Moses, rejecting or disputing, as
illegitimate or imaginary, more recently developed beliefs on
the resurrection of the body, the world of spirits, and the
Messianic Kingdom. The Law alone, and in its strict letter, was
of weight with them. It was less as priests (many of the priests
were Pharisees) than as aristocrats and leaders of a dominant
faction, as interpreters of Revelation and of the Law, that this
minority, full of haughtiness towards the lowly, and bending
only to the great, stood in opposition to the Pharisees. These
men, well-born and endowed with worldly goods, looked with
jealousy on the progress of a caste formed outside themselves,
and criticised their adversaries as innovators and rebels. They
deplored the growing prestige brought to the Pharisees by their
zeal, their knowledge, and their rigorism. They found these
casuists an obstacle and an embarrassment.

But we should not imagine that the whole Sadducean party was of the type stigmatised by the Talmud:

"House of Boethus? Woe is me!
Woe is me by reason of their bludgeons.
House of Annas? Woe is me!
Woe is me by reason of their viperish hissings.
House of Cantharos? Woe is me!
Woe is me by reason of their calumnies.
House of Ismael, sons of Phabi? Woe is me!
Woe is me by reason of their clenched hands.
They are high priests, their sons are treasurers, their sons-in-law are inspectors of the Temple, and their footmen belabour the people with clubs."

We must not judge the whole party by the radically exclusive members, and the insolently secular attitude of the families which monopolised the office of high priest. Scholars are inclined to see in the *Ecclesiasticus* of Jesus the son of Sirach a book that is representative of the primitive Sadducees; from this we should have to conclude that the sect had a theology of its own, though very conservative in nature, and that it treated the prophets with honour, if it did not put them on a level with the five books of the Law. . . .

As opposed to the Essenes, dreamers absorbed in moral and ritual matters, and the Sadducees, aristocrats by race and politicians by instinct, the "Companions" (*haberim*), the "Devout" (*chasidim*)—who soon came to be called the Pharisees and have remained such for us—formed a party which was before all things religious and national, a kind of Holy League, the Jewish party pure and simple. Their whole aim was in the first place to purge the people of God who had returned to the Promised Land, from foreign infiltrations and influence, and then to preserve them from the aggressive, cunning and sometimes (as in the time of the Seleucidae) violent propaganda of surrounding paganism. In this defence of the Jewish spirit and customs, the essential wall or, to use a metaphor dear to the rabbis, the protecting hedge of Jahweh's vine, was the Law of Moses. Recruited from all classes of society, including the most humble, without distinction of priests and laity, and counting among their number the majority of the intellectuals, scribes and doctors, the Pharisees were thus before all the men of the Law: its interpreters, its avengers, and at need its martyrs. St. Paul, when he wishes to express his passionate attachment to the Law, is content to say: "An Hebrew of the Hebrews. *According to the law, a Pharisee*" (Phil. iii, 5). In saying that, he says all.

In their absolute trust in the Torah, some inclined to make it independent, to some extent, even of God. The little collection called *The Sentences of the Fathers,* which represents Pharisaism in its most authentic aspect, and gives us the best of it for the period reaching from the first century B.C. to the end of the second century A.D., practically identifies the scribe with the saint: knowledge of the Law sanctifies after the manner of a sacrament. Rabbi Meir (about 135) said: "Everyone who gives himself to the study of the Torah for its own sake is worthy of every good. What is more, the whole world and its fulness is not worth more than he."

In these thoroughly religious pages God is scarcely named. The Law takes up all the space, because, for a Pharisee, it virtually signifies the whole of divine truth, so far as it is accessible to the human mind. And they had for it the respect that is due to God: the most innocent distraction during the study of the Torah is culpable, as being one which interrupts a prayer.

Rabbi Jacob (who died in 175) said: "If a man walks about while studying [the Torah] and interrupts his study to say 'How beautiful is that tree,' or 'How beautiful is that wild spot,' Scripture holds such words to be a sin which makes his soul guilty."

In this way the Pharisee drew from the Law the rules for the whole conduct of his life, private and public. This last fact, which endowed the scribe with the very power of the State, was bound to lead to conflicts with the political powers. And in fact neither the Hasmonaean princes from the time of John Hyrcanus, excluding the personal reign of the old Queen Alexandra (78–69 B.C.), nor the Idumaeans accepted this tutelage. But whether favoured or suspected, sometimes even persecuted, the *Separated* never ceased to be feared by reason of their power with the people. This power, which Josephus states, with obvious exaggeration, to have been practically unlimited, was certainly great and often preponderant. It was based in great part on the manner in which the Pharisees had decentralised and in a certain sense laicised and democratised the religion of Israel. The Temple remained its centre; the hegemony of the great priestly families, and especially of the high priest, continued to be exercised; but even there, in the Temple, the Pharisees had their influence, and had caused daily prayers to be established, and instituted a sort of delegation of pious laity representing the people of Israel at the daily sacrifice. Outside the Temple, by means of the synagogue and worship in the home, they had severed the line which bound the whole religion of the people to the Temple. The rabbi and the father of the family tended more and more to supplant the Levite and the priest. Finally, in matters casuistical and the application of the Law to daily life by means of subtle exegeses and traditional interpretation, a sort of unwritten Law commenting upon the written one—in these matters the Pharisees were supreme, and for an Israelite desirous of devoutly fulfilling his duties, indispensable. Women especially (as Josephus noted) looked upon them as their oracle.

Less dependent than the chosen priesthood on political vicissitudes, less entangled than the Zealots in militant xenophobia, the bulk of the Pharisees represented, from the time of the Machabees to the fall of Jerusalem, the kernel of Israel, the heart of Judaism by their ardour in observing, imposing and explaining the Law, by their minute knowledge, which though literal and rigid was yet real, by the hold which their puritanism gave them over the people, and by the religious feeling which made them favour the more purified and spiritual doctrines.

So, too, it was through the *Separated* that the Jewish people survived the appalling catastrophes of the first and second centuries. The barriers established, or re-erected, around the race; the traditions jealously maintained within these closed groups; the supple resistance which gave way only in order to obtain; the political opportunism which bowed to every *de facto* government to snatch from each of them toleration and the maximum of possible concessions; the enormous mass of sayings, prescriptions, decisions, and recollections which crystallised into the two Talmuds: all these are the work of the Pharisees. And it is sufficient to read the Gospels to see the preponderant part played by them in the opposition encountered by Christ.

This very opposition makes impartiality more difficult for the Christian historian towards the principal enemies of Jesus. But he himself has plainly taught us that truth alone delivers. And while proving that they became by their blind obstinacy and the malice of their leaders the enemies of the Kingdom of God, we willingly acknowledge that the Pharisees played a useful and sometimes a glorious part during the century and a half which preceded our era. Those who spied upon Jesus were the descendants, buried in the formalism of the Law, and sometimes poisoned by sterile pride, of the great men who had freed Israel from the yoke of the Gentiles at the price of their blood. All that was best in the literature which preceded the advent of Christ bore as a rule the imprint of the beliefs, the hopes, and the passions which were theirs. And even in the time of the Saviour, an impressive minority did not sin against the light. In this matter the *Acts of the Apostles* are very helpful in completing the testimony borne by the Gospels. They show us in the youthful Church a great number of recruits from the party of the Pharisees; beginning with St. Paul, they were not the most unimportant.

In conclusion we must note that, while stigmatizing their merciless literalism, their complacent casuistry and their pride, Jesus aimed much more at the vices of conduct, the abuse of holy things, the canonization of human tradition, the ill-inspired zeal of the *Separated*, than at their doctrinal position. On the characteristic questions of the resurrection of the body, the existence and the action of spiritual forces, the Master was in agreement with them. Nor did he disdain to employ (though moderately) their exegetical methods. He acknowledged their relative authority in the domain of the interpretation of the Law: "The Scribes and Pharisees have sitten on the chair of Moses. All things therefore whatsoever they say to you, observe and do: but according to their works do ye not" (Matt. xxiii, 2–3).

CAPHARNAUM AND THE LAKE

⟡ HE MAKES but a false picture of those supreme three years during which the Godhead created the Catholic Church, if he imagine them to have been passed amid a pastoral and simple people of the more debased oriental sort, such as we find for the most part in that desolate countryside today.

The scene of the Gospels and, in particular this lake of Tiberias, which was the nucleus of all that went before the Passion, the stage on which or from which doctrine and revelation were proclaimed, was, in Our Lord's day, a scene of greatness, wealth and splendour; of high civilisation and of man by his creative power adding all that he could add to nature.

Where there were so many rich there were many, many more of the poor; but the world in which Our Lord and His Apostles moved, the surroundings of all that story—of the teaching from the boat, of the Transfiguration, of the Sermon on the Mount, of the casting out of devils and of that turning point, the confession of St. Peter—was a world which, to the eye and to the ear and to all the senses of those who passed through its thronged porticoes, was a high and exalted world, comparable to, but far more dignified than, the wealthy centres of today in our teeming western Europe.

Its civilisation was Greek. That civilisation was superimposed upon an older population, mainly Jewish in faith (though largely also Pagan), Semitic in tongue but in dress presumably and in general habit much what the rest of the Mediterranean people were. The dress was *not* what the Arab dress is today: *not* the modern Oriental garments in which it is still fashionable to represent Our Lord and His Apostles.

Stand on the high land to the north and east of the little shore plain of Genesareth, and look down those few miles of water, eight miles across at their broadest stretch. You see the lake narrowing down to the southward, the high hills closing round about it, forbidding to the left and to the right; at the extreme end of your view the lump of land on which lay Gadara, and the opening of that oppressive trench, deep dug below the level of the Mediterranean, the Jordan valley. Here and there you see a few new houses springing up, much more rarely the ruins, often but a stone or two, of something older; empty wastes of reed on the flat shores and some way off on the western bank, the only agglomeration which seems worthy of a name, rather a large ramshackle village than a city, still called in its degra- dation Tiberias, and still overhung by the dark rock on which was planted its citadel. For the rest, nothing. You are fortunate if you so much as see one sail on that flat, shining oval of water.

But in those old days it was a pageant. All round the shores of that inland water was a succession of fine towns, in an almost uninterrupted ring, passing one into the other as do those pleasure-places which we built today along the shores of the Channel, but how much more glorious!

Capharnaum was a great place, there to your right, where even now for three-quarters of a mile or more, its unhappy stones lie scattered upon the Galilean grass. Bethsaida, to your left upon the flat, where the upper Jordan pushes its delta into the north of the lake, had all the loveliness of Greece stamped upon it; and beyond again the string of white columns and walls in place after place along the eastern shore; in between and above them the groves of chestnut trees, on the heights the outlying Greek towns of the Decapolis.

On the extreme limit of your view, where the lake ceased, Tarichaeae, where the pickling of fish from the lake supported an industry which sent its delicacies all over the Roman world. Hidden between that point and the other great and noble town of Tiberias were the baths which the wealthy sought not only from all that country, but from far away, for their healing. Men counted nine towns at least, apart from intervening suburbs and villages, along that short ring of coastal land.

There in Capharnaum stood up the grandeur of the Great Synagogue, with its high Corinthian columns and the carving of the Manna in between.

It was in this building, majestic with the outward order of Greece, consecrated within by the traditions and teaching of those who had maintained for centuries the worship of the Most High God, that Our Lord first proclaimed the Eucharist.

There, in the Great Synagogue of Capharnaum, to its crowded hall, were these strange words first said: "I am the living bread which came down from heaven. If any man eat of this bread he shall live for ever: and the bread that I will give is my flesh for the life of the world . . ."

Those strange words were said, and they were bewildering. In the buzz of talk arising on this could be discerned such a protest as this: "How can this man give us his flesh to eat?" But the silence that followed was broken by the reiterated words: "Except you eat the flesh of the Son of Man and drink his blood you shall not have life in you."

If you turned, standing on that rising ground above the lake by Chorozain, and looked northward, you saw the snows of Hermon rising high into heaven nearly 10,000 feet above the lake, barely thirty miles away, and dominating all that land. On the flanks of that great mountain at its feet some twenty odd miles from where you stood, was the little paradise (as it then was) of Caesarea Philippi. There the living waters gushed out of the limestone with a wealth of greenery about them; the marble columns of a temple shone upon the cliff above, and the Greeks, delighting in so much beauty, dedicated the groves to Pan and to the Nymphs. Thence ran the great Roman road to Damascus.

It was here, in Caesarea Philippi, that loveliest corner of what was still then everywhere a lovely land, that the famous question was asked and answered: "Whom do you say that I am?" . . . "Thou art Christ, the Son of the living God." And here it was that openly and by a solemn published word the indestructible title of the Catholic Church was proclaimed: "I will build my church and the gates of hell shall not prevail against it."

The site is symbolical. It is an origin in every way, is that very height of the Jordan valley. There stretch southward, past the lesser mere, then past the sea of Galilee, then down the long trench to the Dead Sea, and the mass of bare stony heights which are Judea, all the scenes of this Story. Thence runs for its hundred and thirty miles the countryside on which all the future of the world from that day onwards has turned.

And thence it was that Our Lord turning His face southwards towards all that land, began His Journey to that appointed end, to Jerusalem, to the Passion, and death upon the Cross.

Such was the setting of the story; such the Kingdom of this World, as it moved past the Apostles in their goings back and forth with their Master; everywhere the might of a great culture and the splendour of its sculptured stones and the wealth of its commerce and the crowds of its superabundant people.

Stand on that same height and look around you today. There is nothing. Magdala, the City of Pleasure, drawn luxuriously along the shore, has utterly departed; a hut or two and a bush. Great Capharnaum is the scattered stones hidden in growth on which men dispute whether it was really there or no; Chorozain is a doubtful name, a wretched hamlet; a traditional low cliff may be, or is, the mark of what was once Gerasa. And Tiberias, itself once a high city with three miles of walls, might be any one of the squalid overgrown villages which the wreck of civilisation has left like flotsam behind it.

So utterly has the blight and devastation of the half-barbaric conqueror reduced this land that even the names of what was once so great have become obscure.

No story is more famous than that of the Gadarene swine—yet only now are men, quite recently, fairly assured (but not yet quite assured) that the spelling is erroneous; that the true place of the miracle was not Gadara at all—how could it have been six miles from the lake shore and cut off from it by the deep valley of the Yarmuk?—but rather Gerasa.

Men dispute on Bethsaida: stood it here or there? Caesarea Philippi is not; the excellent title which Greek fancy gave it— the Place of Pan, Paneas—is preserved in Arabic corruption —"Banias," a fortress in ruins also; but of all the beauty and wealth that stood there, nothing.

The Decapolis to the east, the Greek cities, are (all save Damascus), a desolation; and the refrain perpetually recurring is the same everywhere—ruins . . . ruins . . . ruins.

THE LAKE

When Our Lord left Nazareth and began His public predication, He went down first to the Sea of Galilee close at hand. There it was He began to choose the Apostles; there it was that the great Story openly began.

On this account the Sea of Galilee (which is also called the Lake of Tiberias) has become the most famous sheet of water in the world.

Nazareth itself stands in the folds of rolling highlands which reach the height of from two to three thousand feet above the sea, the highlands of Galilee. These hills are the distinctive feature of the country, standing separate as they do from the stony hills of Judea to the south; and from them down to the lake shore (a matter as the crow flies of fifteen miles but by the new road of seventeen) is a drop of over 2,000 feet, over grassy country with here and there a village, such as Cana of Galilee, within an easy walk of Nazareth, where Our Lord worked his first miracle.

The road goes on, still falling, past the broad sward of Hattin, where was fought one of the most important battles in history, the battle in which the Christians lost the Holy Land, seven hundred and fifty years ago. It continues, the valley of the Upper Jordan opening before it, and the deep hollow in which the Lake lies, its waters at last apparent before you and the dark steep hills beyond, which correspond upon the east of the Jordan trench to what the hills of Galilee are upon the west.

So at last, at the end of half a day downwards, you come to the shore at the place which gave the Sea of Galilee its Greek and Roman name: the town of Tiberias.

I know many others have spoken with enthusiasm of the beauty they found in this deep cup, buried between the opposing hills. It was not beauty which affected me when I saw it; the landscape is stern, and I will maintain of this great site as of all else southward, down to Bethlehem itself, of all else in this land save Nazareth, that it carried more air of tragedy than any other.

Mighty things were done, the greatest of spiritual victories and the triumph of the Resurrection at the end—but I can only believe that the Passion has chiefly imprinted itself upon all that land wherein Our Lord taught, gave the signs from Heaven, and suffered, at last, the Agony.

Though here, on this placid oval mirror of the Lake, placid save for those very sudden storms which rise and are gone sometimes in an hour, such storms as you always find in the enclosed waters of mountain lands, there is no name or spot recalling the mighty tragedy, yet that tragedy broods over it.

It was first the knowledge and personal experience, it was later, when that generation had died, the Faith, of Christian men, that the tragedy was succeeded by glory. And doubtless, to a full vision, all this land, from happy Nazareth in the north to Bethlehem, three days' journey away to the south, is lit, as by a sudden sunrise, with the Resurrection. It should be so. But to me as I first looked on that landscape it was not so, and I think would not be so were I to return there a hundred times. Rather the solemnity as of a profound horror, the sombre silence of the hill-sides that hang so awfully about it, were filled with a precognition of what was to come.

Here all the first wonders were wrought; here first from Magdala, a little northward along the shore, came the woman whose association with the Story will be spoken of till the end of the world. Here were the multitudes who heard the Voice, here, further to the north again, stood Capharnaum, which should be filled with memories of revelation, of the beginning of doctrine, of the appearance of the Kingdom of God, and with nothing else.

But we know, and not we alone, that all this was to fail very quickly in the eyes of the world. It was to last three years, it was to end in a local climax at Jerusalem; it was not to be of very great immediate fame; and the close was to be intolerable pain of body and the worst suffering of the expectant mind—jeers and tortures and a dreadful death. The land has not escaped the stamp of that Deicide.

I note also that as the world progressed in its gradual apostasy, as doctrine faded from its intelligence, and as the meaning of all that was here done was lost to it, so did what is called "the modern mind" begin to sentimentalise over the landscape of Judea, and particularly over these waters of the Lake: insisting upon, exaggerating beauty, when it should rather have had before it the awful business which transformed the world.

And let me say this too—although I know I am here far from repeating what others have said whose eyes have fallen upon the sacred soil—there seems to me to be in a sense upon all the places of the Predication, the public life of Our Lord, and not only in Jerusalem, the living echo stamped upon it of the Lamentation which Jesus made over the walls of the city, fore-seeing their destruction.

For Tiberias also, and all the places round about, bears that mood of desolation and ruin which fell upon the Holy Land when the lesser thing conquered the greater, and the men of the desert, with their new degraded heresy, swept over and destroyed the splendours inherited by Christendom from the old Pagan world, whence our civilisation came.

Tiberias was stately and splendid, with the Grecian column everywhere and the marble statuary and colonnades which you may still see overthrown, lying in ruins, of city after city from Palmyra in the desert to Petra in the far south. All that loveliness, all that dignity, has gone; and the squalor has replaced it which follows everywhere at last the sweep of the Moham-medan conquest.

Magdala has been wiped out; a few stones and a house or two of no presence, a tree or two, and the reeds along the lake are all that remain. On the slope above stand the new villas of wealthy immigrant Jews. Capharnaum is not even a name. The Greek proportion and beauty, the Roman soldiery and order, the full life and wealth of that countryside, with its capital called after and, as it were, dedicated to the glory of the Empire and its head—all these have gone. And that feeling which oppresses every man who goes eastward of the Adriatic comes upon one almost fiercely here on these desolating shores.

Yet in the midst of all this, appearing visionary above the physical emptiness of what was once so active and so filled, moves the profound pageantry of the opening Gospel. Here were the words first said (in Aramaic, it is believed, to the poorer people, but surely in Greek to many) which were the prelude. Their strength gives substance to the deserted places, and peoples the shore and the slopes above.

If you look eastward over the water you see within you the stilling of the storm, and also the figure passing swiftly over the water to the astonished fishermen upon the boat. That boat, which was the poor possession of Cephas, called also Peter, is a vessel which can never founder, which shall not be cast upon a beach in age and broken up, as other vessels are.

The Sea of Galilee is today bereft of life and filled with its presence. It is empty to the eye and silent to the ear, but a multitude fills it, and the splendour of palaces and temples, many cities, wealth, the noise of soldiers, and in that setting the unique and novel gem, on that field the sowing of the seed; on that platform the foundation of the Church.

MINISTRY IN GALILEE

⋙ GOD CAME TO TEACH men truth and to free them from sin; so He came to the places where truth was threatened and sin flourished. He elbowed His way into the crowded market-place, walked the dusty roads, thundered against the violation of the Temple at the very height of a feast. He did not sit back content with His perfection and graciously stooping to forgive any sinners who might come to Him. He went out on the highways and byways seeking the sinners, pursuing them like the Hound of Heaven He was, eagerly, anxiously, relentlessly.

He came that through Him we might have easy access to God. We needed His help, for it is not an easy thing to go to God, particularly when we are weighed down with sin; even though we know there is no place else to go, we still have our human pride and our human fear. The enemies of Christ unwittingly made clear to the sinners of all future ages what confidence and courage His familiar life with men had poured into the human hearts of His time by accusing Him of surrounding Himself with sinners and publicans. Sinners ever since have laughed with joy to learn that the men who had the most reason for terror were precisely the ones who came to the feet of the Son of God.

Of course they came to Christ; He had made Himself one with men. He did not embrace the rigid fasting and penance of John the Baptist, for He did not wish to tower above men, striking terror into their hearts; rather He came down among men that they might more easily walk into His divine heart. He gave a perfect example in the absolutely necessary things, and among these rigid abstinence from food and drink is not included. Abstinence is not an end in itself but a means by which men might attain to control and continence; the sinless Christ had no need of this means, so He lived as other men, eating and drinking.

All through His life, Christ felt the privations and tasted the joys of poverty. On His own testimony, He was hungry, thirsty, and without a place whereon to lay His head. Nor was this a condemnation of riches. It was no secret in Christ's time that riches can be an occasion of pride and offer opportunities for sins that are not open to the poor man; but then neither were the men of that time ignorant of the fact that poverty can be no less an occasion of sin, indeed, an occasion of all those sins a man will commit to seize the riches upon which his heart is set. It is neither riches nor poverty that count; but the poverty of spirit which is a casting aside of the trinkets of the world in the realization of how little they contribute to the perfection of man's life.

Men do not need riches for human living; they simply cannot get along without fellowship and law. It is small wonder that Christ insisted so strongly on these two. He came to perfect the imperfect law, yet His observance of that imperfect one was most exact; He came to liberate men from the burdens of the Old Law, but first He carried the burden Himself. None of His contemporaries could accuse Him of sin. He was no lawbreaker; for He would not have us miss the fact that the fruits of sin are degradation, subjection, and tyranny, not the liberty and perfection He came to give us. Even His indignant declaration that the Son of man was Lord of the Sabbath was not a rejection of law but a condemnation of misinterpretation and vicious perversion of law. Clearly the law of the Sabbath was not meant to forbid divine works; it did not prohibit the works necessary for life, even for corporal life; above all, it did not prohibit what pertains to divine praise and worship.

Now and then, the commands of the law seem unbearably heavy. If our human nature does not point this out to us, there is an angelic nature always ready to whisper it to us; for our fight for perfection is not only against our own nature, but against the princes, the powers, the dominations of the angelic host who lost their own battle long ago. The abstract assurance of divine help against these vastly superior forces is a grand comfort; in the actual heat of the battle, it is a more solidly comforting thing to our human hearts to have before our eyes the concrete story of divinity's own strategies against satanic cunning.

The temptation of Christ was just another of the devil's bad mistakes. He had to guess; and he guessed wrong. Not even an angelic intelligence could pierce through to the divinity of Christ, for that is something to be believed, not seen; the devil could see the sinless life of Christ and suspect the mystery, then remember the infant helplessness of Christ and doubt that God could make Himself so lowly. He could not believe, for belief flows only from a good will. Up to the last minutes of Christ's life, then, the devil was on tenterhooks about this strange Man; was He really God, or was He merely man?

It was fortunate for us that he made the mistake of trying to find the answer to that question. At least, his mistake protects us from foolish pride or smug security in our own sanctity. For sanctity is no guarantee against temptation; it is an invitation to it. The devil hates saints, they approach so closely to God; and, with the stupid stubbornness that has marked all of his career, he continues to batter his head against the divinely protected wall again and again. Really, sanctity and good works constitute a kind of diabolic desert where there is neither shade nor rest for the evil one. Indeed, sanctity is a desert place in another sense, for the corridors of sanctity are seldom crowded and man always faces his greatest dangers alone; so it was that Christ underwent His temptation when He was alone in a desert place. It was His invariable custom to face first the hardest of the things He demanded from us.

He went at that difficult task in a fashion that leaves no doubt in our minds as to the method we must pursue. There is no better preparation for future temptations than present fasting and penance. We know very well that there is no time in our lives when we can depend upon quiet security, rest on our arms idly waiting for the next fight to come up; surely we cannot take any chances on the grounds that we have worn down our strength with laborious good works. It was to a tired and hungry Christ, tired and hungry from fasting and penance, that the devil came. Whatever the cause of the fatigue, it is just at that time, with our body protesting a bit, that the devil is most likely to make his attack; he was never one to overlook so powerful an ally as our sense appetite.

His diabolic strategy in the temptation of Our Lord is worth noting well. Since temptation must always come from the outside as far as our soul is concerned, it must be by way of a suggestion. Being what we are, suggestion has no chance for infiltration except along a path already made smooth for the journeys of our heart. The devil does not shock a saint into alertness by suggesting great crimes; he starts off with little, almost inoffensive things to which even the heart of a saint would make only a mild protest. So it was with the temptation of Adam; so also with the temptation of Christ. These two heads of the race could not be grossly attacked; they were to be subtly fooled. To our first parents, the devil made an intellectual appeal, a suggestion to that element of curiosity in all of us, asking: "Why did God forbid this particular fruit?" With that wedge securely in, he became bolder, appealing to pride and vainglory with a promise that their eyes would be opened; it was only when definite progress seemed to have been made that the full horror of the temptation was made plain in his invitation to the extreme pride of rebellion—they should become like gods.

When the devil approached Christ, he used practically the same strategy—there is, after all, very little room for originality in the line of sin and temptation; he was perhaps a little more subtle with Christ, paying Him the same dubious compliment a bandit pays his victim in approaching him with extreme caution. He tempted Christ first with what even the most spiritual of men desire, the food necessary to sustain the body: "If thou be the Son of God, command that these stones be made bread." From there, he went on to that to which even spiritual men are too often victim, ostentation and vainglory: "If thou be the Son of God, cast thyself down . . ." (from the temple). With inevitable grossness, he advanced a temptation that appealed not to spiritual but to carnal men, the appeal of the riches and the glory of the world, going even so far as contempt of God: "All these will I give thee, if falling down thou wilt adore me."

The first thrust was not successful. Wisdom in the tempter would seem to indicate a complete change of attack, a search for some even subtler approach. But the devil is not wise, which is one of the reasons why he is a devil; the planned attack had to go forward, in spite of the failure of the first necessary maneuver, stupidly becoming clumsier at every step. It is no sin to trust in God, quite the contrary; but to plunge off a great height in deliberate temptation of God, demanding a miraculous rescue, that is a different matter. To desire riches and the honors of the world is not necessarily wrong; but to be willing to abandon God and adore the devil to attain those ends, there is no excuse for that. Christ was quite patient with the first two temptations, for, after all, He had come to conquer the devil by justice not by overwhelming divine power; at the third temptation, He lost all patience. He did more than reject the temptation, He dismissed the devil with a brusqueness that must have been gall to so proud a spirit. This temptation was not to be tolerated for an instant; for it was a direct attack, not on the things of men, but on God Himself.

That outburst of divine indignation sent the devil slinking away, still mystified by the God-man. When he had gone the angels came and ministered to their Master. We shall read once more of an angel ministering to a tired Christ; then it will be on the edge of His passion, as here He was on the threshold of His public life. Each was a beginning; and it is at just these moments that comfort is needed, for beginnings, particularly beginnings of divine things, are hard. Since then, it is not an angel but the Master Himself who brings comfort to the hearts of men courageous enough to begin.

From the desert, Christ returned to the cities of men and set off on His career of bearer of divine truth to men. Much later, this part of His life would be summed up with a simplicity whose beauty forbids adornment: He had done all things well. He spoke with the appeal and persuasiveness of an orator reading the hearts of his audience as plainly as the page of an open book; He denounced evil with the thundering authority of a supreme legislator; He confirmed His doctrine by stunning miracles, even more by the calm, persistent, quiet sinlessness of His life. All this was but the vehicle of His message. The doctrine itself surpassed anything that teachers of men have ever conceived; and it answered the deepest demands of the hearts and minds of men.

Yet, looked at objectively, the actual proposal of this doctrine seems to have been miserably limited. It was strictly held within the narrow limits of Palestine and, even there, was restricted to Christ's own people, the Jews. Why did not Our Lord preach to all men? How could He expect the same results from the lesser teachers to whom He commissioned this world-wide preaching? The point is that the lesser teachers actually achieved greater results, thereby showing more plainly the power behind that teaching.

Christ's restriction of His preaching to the chosen people was part of that orderly procedure so perfectly proper to God's action. The promises of a redeemer and a messias had been made to the Jews, not to the Gentiles; the Jews, then, should receive the fulfillment of these promises. They were the chosen people, they had had generations of preparation; they should be given the first chance to welcome the Messias. . . .

He came to the Jews in fulfillment of divine promises, in the name of God's love of the race. His love was the strong love of God, a love great enough to be terribly severe. By their malice, the leaders of this chosen people were impeding the salvation of the whole race; they were rejecting the doctrine of Christ which alone held out hope of salvation; their vices were corrupting the life of the people. This was not the time for a lover of the people and a teacher of truth to tread gently lest he hurt the feelings of some who were considered great among men. Of course Christ cried out against them, sparing them nothing; yet there was the full vigor of divine love in that violence, a love that embraced the leaders perhaps even more strongly than the people who followed them. . . .

When in the last days of His life, Christ was called to account, He could say with complete truth "I have spoken nothing in secret." He had not come to hide divine truth but to manifest it; He was not a miserly Master huddling over His knowledge in dark corners, gloating over His exclusive possession of it, afraid to share it lest He lose His mastery. The things He had to say needed nothing of the garments of sly ambiguity which hide the ugliness of the obscene and allow it to slip furtively into the souls of men. Christ taught publicly: to crowds in the temple, on the sea shore, in desert places, on the high road. To the little group of apostles and disciples, He talked incessantly. He let slip no opportunity to publish His truth. Some things He spoke to the multitudes in parables, giving them the milk of children because they were not capable of the meat of men; clearly, it was better for them to have this than nothing at all. Even these parables were explained in detail to the apostles to whom it was given to know the secrets of the kingdom of God that they might instruct the children of men.

Many years after, closing his own attempt to put the teachings and deeds of Christ in the prison of written words, St. John admitted the hopelessness of it: "There are also many other things which Jesus did, which if they were written every one, the world itself, I think, would not be able to contain the books that should be written." The world could not contain the books, only heaven can; it is quite impossible to contain the sublimity of the teachings of divine wisdom within the narrow confines of words. Christ Himself wrote no words beyond those few He scrawled in the sand to scatter the accusers of the adulteress; how significant that it should have been sand in which He wrote! He did His real writing on the hearts of men and thus forever scotched the petty error that His doctrine was not more than is contained in the written Scriptures. . . .

While the written word did not befit the dignity of Christ, His miracles certainly did. There was nothing confining about them; rather, they threw open the vast spaces of infinity to the human mind. Indeed, their whole service is to lift the mind of a man above the limits of nature by bringing him into sharp contact with the Author of nature. A miracle is a wave of divine power that lifts men up to the crest and lets them see the distant shore if only for an instant. More concretely, they are worked either to confirm the truth or to show the presence of God in the man who does the works of God. On both counts, Christ fittingly worked miracles.

The miracles of Christ, like all true miracles, were worked by divine power, for miracles are such precisely because they outstrip the powers of nature. It is true that Christ reached out

and touched the leper to cleanse him, it was His human voice
that awoke Lazarus, Magdalen knew from His loving glance
long before He spoke that her sins were forgiven; but the hand,
the voice, the eye were merely instruments of divinity, channels
which carried the power of God. Christ, even as an Infant in the
manger, had both the divine power and the human instrumen-
tality of that power, for He was both God and Man. It is, however, an extravagance of unbridled imagination to picture the
childhood and adolescence of Christ as a gloriously triumphant
journey leaving an uninterrupted wake of miracles behind it. If
there was bread in the house at Nazareth, it was because it had
been earned by Joseph and his Son: if the clothes were clean, it
was because Mary had washed them.

There was no point in miracles until some truth was to be
confirmed; until it was time to manifest the divinity of Christ
to all men. The first miracle, then, is that recorded as such by
St. John, the changing of water into wine at the marriage feast
of Cana. It is comforting to remember that this first miracle was
worked at Our Mother's request, that it was for such a human
end as saving the host of Christ from embarrassment, that it was
a benediction of such a human thing as marriage. I have often
wondered what the bridegroom said to the master of the feast
in answer to his complaint about saving the better wine until
the last. Probably he just smiled and shrugged his shoulders,
hoping Christ would not give him away.

From this beginning to the very end, all the miracles of Christ
had the common purpose of confirming the truth of divinity,
of manifesting to men the presence of God among them. All
were, of course, works transcending natural powers; all were
done in Christ's own name. Again and again, He insisted that
it was in confirmation of His claim to divinity that He worked
miracles; if what He said were not true, then God Himself
would have collaborated in a gigantic lie.

Certainly, the scope of the miracles of Christ was a plainly

written documentation of His mastery over all the universe, that
is, of His divinity. Angelic beings bowed to His command in
every expulsion of the demons from their possessed victims;
the heavenly bodies offered their homage and submission when
they covered their face against the spectacle of the death of God.
Most constantly, however, His miracles revolved around His
fellow-men; of these, the outstanding ones are the healing
miracles, the miracles whose final goal was not the salvation of
the body but the soul. After all, He had come to save men, to
enlighten their minds, and relieve them of the burden of sin.
That no least doubt of His divinity might remain in the minds
of men of good will, all irrational creation gave Him unquestion-
ing obedience.

These were proud days in the lives of the apostles. The simple
fishermen of Galilee were living familiarly with the Lord of the
universe. Before their eyes, Nature tumbled over itself in its
eagerness to obey Him; the eyes of faith showed them the greater
miracles of grace within the souls of men; they shared His confidence, listened to His patient reiteration of divine truth, even
partook of something of His infinite power on that mission where
they were told to heal the sick, raise the dead, give freely of what
they had freely received.

They returned from that journey bubbling over with enthusiasm, swelled a little with consciousness of self, to be met with
the laconic word of the Master: "Let us go apart and rest a
while." That is, let us stop for a minute to think, to remember,
to pray; after all, you are the same men you were before, not
God. As the days of His life grew shorter, His warnings of His
passion and death grew more plain; to the apostles, they were
steadily unwelcome, even a little frightening, shaking that
confidence and sense of power that had so recently come to
them.

They had some reason for fright. He was starting them off
on a long journey over a road that was rough and steep. His

divine wisdom could easily understand that the comforting memories of three intimate years with Him would hardly be enough for them. In the kindness of His heart, He gave them concrete, ocular evidence of some of the joys that awaited them at the end of the journey. For an instant, there on Tabor, Christ unveiled to His beloved three the glory of His human soul shining through His human body.

Understand, this transfiguration was a revelation of human glory. It was essentially the same brilliance that is a permanent quality of the bodies of the saints after the resurrection, the brilliance that would have been constantly shining forth from the body of Christ had not a constant miracle been worked to prevent what would have overwhelmed men as it did the apostles on Tabor. This glimpse of glory completed the dim sketch of the glory of the human body after the resurrection. Other vague details had been drawn when Christ passed through the closed womb of the Virgin, when He walked upon the water, when He passed unharmed through the hands of the Jews who attempted to apprehend Him before His hour had come.

This apex of human glory was not only for the men who were to come after Christ, but for those faithful ones who had preceded Him. Fittingly, then, Moses and Elias were present at that preview of glory in the name of all who had gone before; Peter, James and John, in the name of all who were to come after. Those five witnesses were really a mighty company; the Law and the Prophets, the Head of the Church, the first of the apostolic martyrs, the most beloved of the disciples and greatest of the evangelists, the Sons of Thunder, and the Rock upon which Christ was to build His Church.

The transfiguration of Christ was really a revelation of the full significance of our position as adopted sons of God. By that adoption, we are made conformable to the natural Son of God, imperfectly now by grace with its glory for the soul, perfectly in heaven with its glory for the body and soul. We enter the life of grace by baptism, the life of heaven by the light of glory. As at the baptism of Christ, so here again at His transfiguration, there is the divine witness to His natural Sonship and a divine promise as to our adopted sonship. As at the baptism the Son was baptized and the Holy Ghost appeared hovering over Him in the form of a dove, while the Father's voice was heard approving; so here on Tabor, the Son was glorified, the Father testified, and the Holy Ghost hovered over the scene in a luminous cloud.

They came down from the mountain a little shaken to set about the business of suffering and dying. But now, what a different task it was, not only for them but for all men; for here was the goal that explained all the hardships and difficulties of the journey—the vision of glory within a man now, shining through His very body in heaven. Here was the secret of the glory of man: a human sharing in the divine life.

PHILIP SPEAKS

WHEN WE RETURNED and told Him all we had done,
I, for one, was emptied out like a husk
that has scattered its seed upon hard ground.

We had not had time even to eat;
always the open hand,
always the blind eyes,
always the deaf ears,
always the wound to be healed.

My thoughts were like wild birds
beating the bars of the cage
for empty skies.

Even now the smell of the people
clung to my hair and clothes.
A rotten sweetness of oil and musk
that smells like death, it hung in my hair.

Their voices went on and on in my head,
monotonous waves wearing my mind away.
(Rock is worn by the waves to sand.)
I wanted to shut my mind, that my thoughts might close
on my own peace; I wanted to close

the peace of my love in my heart,
like dew in a dark rose.

He told us to rest.

We went in a small ship,
the wind and water moving in her.
She lived in their sweetness of life, a bride.
Her sail, a white wing—unmoving—moved with the tide.
She lay to the wind, and we gave our hearts with a sigh
to the breath of the Spirit of love.

But when we came to the shore
the people were there;
they had found us out:
always the open hand,
always the blind eyes,
always the deaf ears,
always the wounds to be healed!
They were there,
swarming there, everywhere—
insects there in the sun
when someone has lifted a stone.
I knew they would drain Him
and wring Him out—wring Him out
to the last drop of the fountain-water of Life
I was sick of it all,
with a dry husk for a heart.

But He saw the flocks wanting shepherd and fold;
pity in Him rose in a clear spring
for the world's thirst, and love was a pastureland.

So it went on all day:
always the open hand,

always the dull mind,
always the slow heart,
always the nameless fears;
and self-pity, self-pity and tears;

until the sun went up in the blaze of the day's heat,
and with red wine burning through thin gold,
it was lowered slowly onto the altar-stone
of the darkening world, where the sheep were in fold.

We thought, "Now it is night; He will send them away;
the hour is late." We said, "This is a desert place.
Send them away, Lord, to buy food and be fed!"
But He: "You give them to eat!"

The grass in that place shone exceedingly green.
I remember, because when the brain is dust
the cool greenness of grass is absurdly sweet.

"There is a lad here," said Andrew,
"with two little fish and five loaves of bread.
But what are these, if this crowd must be fed?"
"Bid them sit down on the grass, and give them to eat," the Lord
        said.

The lad was one of the crowd; he went as he came.
As long as the world lasts, the world will remember him,
but no one will know his name!

They sat down on the grass.
My heart contracted, my mind was withered up;
but Christ poured out His tenderness,
like wine poured out into a lifted cup.

Always the open hands,
always the blind eyes,

always the mouth to be fed;
and I, for one, was emptied out like a husk
that has scattered its seed upon hard ground.
But He saw the flocks wanting shepherd and fold;
pity in Him rose in a clear spring
for the world's thirst, and love was a pastureland.

The Lord blessed the bread.
He put it into our hands
and it multiplied,
not in *His* hands but in *mine!*

Even now, remembering this,
my thoughts shut like a folding wing;
my mind is a blank sheet of light
in the mystery of the thing.

I gave and my hands were full, again and again;
pity in Him fell on my dry dust:
it was summer rain,
and the husk of my heart expanded and filled again
and was large with grain.

For me, the miracle was this:
that a clear stream of the Lord's love—
not mine—
flowed out of my soul,
a shining wave over my fellow men.

These things I have told you happened a long while since.
Our cherished Lord is dead; He was crucified.
Now, as then, we go about in the crowd, telling His love
and how He rose from the dead and, risen in us,
He lives in the least of men.
But I think nobody understands,

until I touch their wounds and they know
the healing of *His* hands.

On the night of the Pasch, before He died,
He blessed the bread and put it into my hands,
to increase and be multiplied to the end of time.

Now, if I turned my face from the market-place,
I should be haunted,
hearing the rustle of wheat in the darkness—
striving, pushing up to the light.
I should hear His words, falling like slow tears
in the upper-room,
when He prayed that we all be one,
even as they are one, the Father and Son:

falling like slow tears
over the sown fields;
and I should see the world
like a young field of wheat
growing up for the grain,
watered by Christ's tears.

Always the open hands,
always the blind eyes,
always the slow mind,
always the deaf ears,
and always Christ, Our Lord,
crowned with the flowering thorn
and ringed with spears.

I know—now that I never see
the print of His feet in the dust
where the Son of Man trod—
that in every man, forever,
I meet the Son of God.

PERFECT MAN

᠕ THE POWERFUL IMPRESSION which Jesus made at sight on ordinary people and especially on the sick and on sinners certainly owed something to his appearance, which drew all to him and held them, even if it was primarily due to his spiritual and religious power. His eyes with their burning, wakening, reproving looks must have been especially striking. Does not he himself say "the light of thy body is the eye. If thy eye be single, thy whole body shall be lightsome"? It is significant that Mark, when reporting some important saying of Our Lord, not seldom uses some such expression as "And looking round about on them he saith."

Coupled with this exterior comeliness we get the impression of health, power, energy and well-being in the appearance of Jesus. According to the unanimous witness of the Gospels Jesus must have been a thoroughly healthy man, inured to fatigue and with a great capacity for work. In this he is differentiated from other important founders of religions. Muhammed was a sickly man, tainted with an hereditary disease and with a shattered nervous system, when he unfolded the banner of the prophet. Buddha was mentally a broken-down and worn-out man when he died. We never hear of Jesus that he was visited by any sickness. All the sufferings which came to him were due to his calling, to the privations and sacrifices which his messianic mission laid on him. His body must have been hard-

ened in no common measure. A proof of this is seen in his
habit of beginning his work in the early morning. "Rising very
early, going out he went into a desert place and there he prayed"
(Mark i, 35); "When day was come, he called unto him his
disciples: and he chose twelve of them" (Luke vi, 13); his joy
in nature breathes the same fresh, healthy, unspent sensibility.
The hills and the lake were especially dear to him. After a tiring
day's work he loved to climb to some lonely height or late in
the evening get himself taken on to the shimmering water of
the Lake of Genesareth and stay out far into the night. We
know further that the whole of his public life was one of wandering, coming and going from Galilee to Samaria and Judaea
and even as far as to the district of Tyre and Sidon. And he
made these journeys with the simplest provision for the way,
as he would also have his disciples do. "Take nothing for your
journey, neither staff, nor scrip, nor bread, nor money, neither
have two coats" (Luke ix, 3). Hunger and thirst must therefore
often have accompanied him. His last journey from Jericho up
to Jerusalem is rightly pointed to as an astounding feat. Under
a burning sun, along roads in which there was no shade of any
kind, through a desolate rocky waste he had to mount some
3,500 feet in his six hours' climb. And the most astonishing
thing is that Jesus was not tired. On the very same evening
he took part in a feast which Lazarus and his sisters had made
ready for him. By far the greatest part of his public ministry
was spent not in the comfort of a home, but in the open, exposed to all the rigours of the climate.

He was born and died in remote places. Between the manger
of Bethlehem and the hill of Golgotha he spent a life more
homeless and poor than that of the birds in their nests and the
foxes in their holes. If he ever entered a house, it was one
belonging to acquaintances or friends. For himself he had not
where to lay his head. There can be no doubt that Jesus must
have spent the night in the open many hundreds of times and

that it was not least this that made the birds of the air and the lilies of the field so familiar to him. Only an absolutely sound body could have been equal to such demands on it. Moreover, this wandering life was filled to overflowing with labour and toil. Again and again Mark notes the fact that they had not time to eat (cf. Mark iii, 20; vi, 31). Till late in the evening the sick kept coming and going. And with the sick there came malevolent enemies, the Pharisees and Sadducees, and word wrestled with word, mind with mind, and racking disputes took place, leading to dangerous moments of tension and conflict. In addition there were the tiring explanations he had to make to his own disciples and the heavy burden which their want of understanding and their self-seeking laid upon him. Any sickly or even weak constitution must have given in or broken down under the strain. That Jesus never on any occasion gave in, not even in the most tense or dangerous situations, that, for instance, in the midst of a raging storm on the Lake of Genesareth he went on peacefully sleeping until his disciples woke him, and that suddenly roused from his deep sleep he immediately grasped the situation and dealt with it, all this is proof how far his nature was from being excitable and temperamental, what complete control he had over his senses, how sound he was in body.

Was there also a sound mind in this sound body? . . . The first to slander him by saying "he is become mad" were his own relations (Mark iii, 21). And his adversaries among the Pharisees only put the same thing in their own way when they assumed that an evil spirit was working in him (Matt. xii, 24).

The evangelists give us unequivocal information on this point. What struck them most in his human nature and what they were always underlining was the tremendous clarity of his thought, the sure consciousness he had of his aim, and the resultant inflexibility and finality of his will. If one wished to attempt the impossible and to sum up his mentality in one phrase, he would have to set down this resolute virility and fixity of purpose with which Jesus sees his Father's will as his appointed task, and carries it through to the very end, even to the pouring out of his own blood. His very turn of phrase, with its ever-recurring "I am come," "I am not come," gives expression to the stern determined Yea and Nay of his life and the inflexibility of his purpose. "I came not to send peace, but a sword"; "I am not come to call the just, but sinners"; "The Son of Man is come to seek and to save that which was lost"; "The Son of Man is not come to be ministered to, but to minister, and to give his life a ransom for many"; "Do not think I am come to destroy the law or the prophets. I am not come to destroy, but to fulfil"; "I am come to cast fire on the earth; and what will I but that it be kindled?" Jesus knows what he wills and he knew it from the beginning. In the scene in the temple at Jerusalem when he was but a twelve-year-old lad, he gave clear and plain expression to what his life's work was to be. "Did you not know that I must be about my Father's business?"

The temptations in the desert are, psychologically regarded, a victorious settlement with the satanic possibility of using his own messianic powers for his own self-glorification and selfish ends and not for the construction of the Kingdom of God. We can see here with the utmost clearness how plainly, at the very start of his ministry, Jesus sees the new way, and how resolutely he treads it, the way of self-surrender and of sacrifice for the heavenly Father's sake. In the days that followed it was not only his enemies who sought to divert him from it. On at least three occasions we can trace influences from within his own circle at work to force him to abandon the *via dolorosa* on which he had set out. At Capharnaum these are already vaguely in evidence in the secret opposition of his own kindred. They came to a head in Peter's determined protest at Caesarea Philippi: "Lord, be it far from thee, this shall not be unto thee." And they led once, when Jesus spoke of the eating of his flesh and the drinking of his blood (John vi,57), to a mass-defection of his own followers. "After this many of his disciples went back; and walked no more with him." But Jesus pursued his way, determined, if need be, to follow it alone and solitary. He has no reassuring words on this occasion for his disciples. He only puts to them the short, sharp question, "Will you also go away?" Here we have Jesus, the man of clear will, whose every action reveals the fixity of his purpose. In the whole of his public ministry not one single instant can be found when he had to reflect on an answer or when he hesitated in indecision or when he reversed a statement or an action. And he demands the same inflexible and steadfast purpose of his disciples. "No man, putting his hand to the plough, and turning back, is fit for the Kingdom of God"; "Which of you having a mind to build a tower, doth not first sit down and reckon the charges that are necessary?" or "What king minded to make war does not first made a muster of his troops?" It is his own method quite personal to himself that he here enjoins on his disciples.

Unconsidered action, vacillation, any coming to terms or compromising, these are not for him. His whole life and being are a Yea and Nay, nothing else. Jesus is always the complete man, always prepared, for he never speaks or acts except out of his whole clear consciousness and his own firm will. Hence he and he alone can venture the imperative "Let your speech be yea, yea: no, no: and that which is over and above these is evil" (Matt. v, 37). His whole nature and life are a unity, a completeness, a transparency, are fundamental clarity and truth. He bore so clearly the marks of the true, the upright, and the strong, that even his enemies could not escape this impression. "Master, we know that thou art a true speaker and carest not for any man." Here, in the unity and purity and transparency of his interior life, lies the psychological point whence started his life's struggle against the Pharisees, those "whited sepulchres," representative of the spurious, the finical, the purely

exterior and the narrow in religion and life. From this point his
way led directly to the Cross. It was, psychologically speaking,
his tragic fate that he throughout remained true to himself, to
that genuineness and loyalty to himself and his Father's will
which was his nature.

Jesus is in every respect an heroic, epic figure, heroism incarnate. And it was this heroic spirit, this unconditional staking
of their lives for the known truth, that he demanded also of his
disciples. The heroic is to him a matter of course. To the rich
young man who had observed all the commandments but one
thing was wanting, that he should sell all he had and follow
Jesus. The true disciple must be so valiant, so resolutely pur-
poseful, that he will not even take the time to bury his own
father. "Let the dead bury their dead." His concern must not
be for the dead but for the living. What makes a disciple a
disciple is that he "hate his father and mother and children and
brethren and sisters, yea and his own life also"; that is to say,
in the Aramaic figure of speech, that he set all these aside in
order to follow Jesus.

This concentration and focussing of the will on his goal, this
initiative and energy, make Jesus the born leader. He called
Simon and Andrew, "and immediately leaving their nets they
followed him." He called James and John "and leaving their
father Zebedee in the ship with his hired men, they followed
him." He cast out them that bought and sold in the temple and
none ventured to resist him. His is a masterful nature, a regal
disposition.

The disciples felt this. Hence their diffident awe of the
Master, their strong sense of the gulf separating them from him,
which kept them at a distance. Again and again the evangelists
note how they wondered among themselves at his words or
actions, how these struck terror into them (Mark ix, 5; vi, 51;
iv, 40; x, 24, 26), and how they did not dare speak to him
(Mark ix, 31). Mark describes the start of the last journey to

Jerusalem with the significant words: "And Jesus went before them, and they were astonished, and following were afraid." This same timidity and awe also affected the multitude. "And they were afraid," "and all men wondered." He was not like one of them, neither was he like one of their own leaders, the scribes and Pharisees. He was one having authority. So strong was the impression of towering ascendency in the figure of Jesus that the people sought the loftiest images and names to find words to express it. Is he John the Baptist? Is he Elias? Is he Jeremias, or one of the prophets? Jesus was fully conscious of the essential difference between himself and all other men. Hence he loved solitude. So soon as he had spent himself in preaching to and healing the multitude, he withdrew into himself and betook himself to some lonely spot or on to some silent hill. Again and again this is noted by the evangelist. "And having dismissed the multitude, he went into a mountain alone to pray." It was a solitude *in sinu patris,* that is to say, a solitude shared with the Father. But it was nevertheless a withdrawal from the multitude into himself, a silence of his concentrated forces, a silence whence as from some hidden well the living water gushed forth.

It was a psychological necessity that this tremendously concentrated and disciplined will, this pent-up spiritual power, should discharge itself in stern language and bold action when powers of evil arrayed themselves against him. On such occasions Jesus could wax wroth and show his displeasure like any prophet of the Old Testament, an Osee or a Jeremias, or like Moses when he threw the tables of the law to the ground. This must be recognized, if we would get to know Jesus. In Jesus there dwelt not only mighty powers held in restraint and a disciplined will, but the fire of a holy zeal. We need only test his words and actions for their emotional content to verify this. "Begone, Satan," was how he frightened away the devil who came to tempt him. "Go behind me, Satan, thou art a scandal unto me," was how he rebuked Peter when the latter wished to break down his will to pursue the road which led to the Cross. "I know you not, whence you are: depart from me, you that work iniquity," is what he will profess to those who have neglected to do good to his suffering brethren on earth. It is not quiet, peaceful reserve of spirit that we have here, but deep emotion and passion. Not a few of his parables breathe the same fiery spirit. In them the thunder rolls and the lightning flashes, as in the parable of the cockle: "The Son of Man shall send his angels, and they shall gather out of his kingdom all scandals and them that work iniquity. And shall cast them into the furnace of fire. There shall be weeping and gnashing of teeth." Similarly, too, in the parable of the fishermen's net: "The angels shall go out and shall separate the wicked from among the just. And shall cast them into the furnace of fire: there shall be weeping and gnashing of teeth." The same angry sentence is also pronounced in the parables of the ten virgins, the talents and the sheep and the goats. In the parable of the unmerciful servant the king "being angry delivered him to the torturers until he paid all the debt." Again, in the parable of the marriage of the king's son, the king "was angry, and sending his armies, he destroyed those murderers and burned their city." And when later on the king saw a man at the feast who had not on a wedding garment, he in unconcealed anger gave the order: "Bind his hands and feet, and cast him into the exterior darkness: there shall be weeping and gnashing of teeth." And in his similitude of the faithful and unfaithful stewards, the lord of the house returns unexpectedly and orders the latter to be "beaten with many stripes," and "appoints him his portion with the unbelievers."

There can be no doubt but that the temperament which gave birth to these parables was charged full with emotion. Of sentimentality there is not a trace. As for the polemics against the scribes and the Pharisees, against the ruling caste, against the teachers of Israel, and the judgments passed on them, they flame with indignation. "Woe to you scribes and Pharisees, hypocrites; because you devour the houses of widows, praying long prayers. For this you shall receive the greater judgment . . . You blind guides, who strain at a gnat and swallow a camel. . . . Woe to you scribes and Pharisees, hypocrites: because you make clean the outside of the cup and of the dish: but within you are full of rapine and uncleanness" (Matt. xxiii, 14, 24, 25). The same temperamental vehemence and heat breaks out in not a few of his actions, especially in the cleansing of the temple when "he cast out them that sold and bought in the temple, and overthrew the tables of the money-changers and the chairs of them that sold doves. And he suffered not that any man should carry a vessel through the temple" (Mark xi, 15 sq.). And it is also displayed in the malediction of the fig-tree on which there was not yet fruit, "for it was not the time for figs." In both these cases his wrath took a form likely to alienate those who regarded these events by themselves. The merchants in the court of the temple thought that they were acting fully within their rights; for they had, with the knowledge and consent of the Jewish authorities, leased their trading rights from Annas. Then again the fig-tree was quite blameless in not having any fruit in early spring. But it was distinctive of the prophetic, and particularly of the Messianic method, to announce by apparent paradoxes, and by unintelligible acts, the new unprecedented, revolutionary character of the Messianic message. The very paradox of his actions will necessarily call attention to the prophet and his revolutionary influence. Hence the evangelists have a special interest in the cleansing of the temple, and each of them gives an account of it (Matt. xxi, 12 sq.; Mark xi, 15 sqq.; Luke xix, 45 sqq.; John ii, 14 sq.); and in telling the curse put upon the fig-tree Mark is careful to add the words, "for it was not the time for figs" (xi, 13). It is in the unusual that the Messias is manifest to them. In the seemingly unfair and inconsiderate casting out of the merchants from the temple, they see the solemn proclamation of the newly arisen Messianic worship of God in spirit and in truth, of the new Messianic temple and of the destruction of the old, a proclamation destructive of all merely earthly ambitions. The apparently senseless curse put upon the fig-tree is, to their minds, precisely because of its harsh unintelligibility, a prophetical symbol of the approaching sinister curse on Israel, that fig-tree which the Lord had himself planted, and which had remained unfruitful in good seasons as well as bad. There is hardly another place in the Gospels where the Messianic background, against which the life of Jesus as related in them is enacted, is more evident. Whosoever does not see this background can only misunderstand Jesus.

Jesus was not one to tread delicately, he was no timid weakling when the need arose to bear witness to the truth. His was a fighter's nature. But here, too, in the midst of the fight, he always remains himself, he never forgets himself, never loses control. His anger is always an expression of supreme moral freedom, the act of one having full knowledge, of one who could say, "for this came I into the world, that I should give testimony to the truth." It is because he was so consistently true to his Father's will, because he was only "Yea and Nay" that he reacted with equal severity against anything that was ungodly or hateful to God, whether this found expression in perverse theological formularies or in the decree of a ruler. And the story of his life proves that in harmony with his uncompromising words he was ready to stake his own life for the truth and to die for it.

TRUE SON OF ABRAHAM

ﭻ Our Lord had the normal experiences to which human flesh is heir—hunger, thirst, fatigue, responsiveness to all that can challenge the senses. That He was hungry, we know. In days when earning had ceased, but publicity and, in consequence, alms had not been obtained and made normal, He and His companions were driven to plucking the ears of wheat as they passed by the field's edge, and rubbing them between their hands so as to get the grain. He was tired, and at Sychar sent His disciples ahead into the city to buy food while He Himself sat down "thus" under the shade beside the ancient well, and asked a local woman to give him something to drink. . . . True, in the eagerness of the apostolate which forthwith became possible, He asked no more for the cool water and could not bring Himself to want to eat what the disciples carried back; but the fact remained, true hunger and true thirst had been there first. He was so tired on that occasion when they crossed the lake, that He could not take His place at the oar, but went to sleep "with His head upon a cushion." I must confess to you that after that first crowded day at Capharnaum, when at last the thrilled crowds had left Him and then very early next day returned to make the most of Him once more, and found Him not, for He had "risen up, very early, while it was still dark, and gone out into a lonely place to pray"—all this touches me, yet perhaps not so suddenly or poignantly as the recollection that between whiles, our Lord, the Saviour of the world, had been lying asleep, on mat, beneath rug, head on bolster, fast asleep, in the little house of Peter. Is any one thing more human than to go to sleep?

But the days came when it was a danger to receive Him; when the little village would not, in fact, receive Him when He wished to enter it after the long dusty tramp, to find His meal; and even, when He would have to say, very gravely, though not bitterly, to one who professed a wish to follow Him, that the foxes had their holes and the flying birds their nests, but that as for Him, He had not where to lay His head. That was when, upon lime-stone rock and under tamarisk or juniper, our Lord found for the night such shelter as He could.

I am not going to pursue our Lord's human experiences beyond these bodily ones, into either those mental ones which are concerned with deep personal joys or sorrows; or into those emotional ones which are proper to the having, say, of friends. But you must let me just allude to one little explosion, as it were, of intense appreciation of beauty on His part which is so incidental that we seldom notice all that it implies. He is speaking of God's Providence, and how it prolongs itself into all parts of nature—animal nature—not one sparrow falls to the ground without God, who is its Father, knowing all about it and making it, somehow, *right;* and indeed, into inanimate nature. Owing to God and not to us, the flowers spring up and grow—it is not they who clothe themselves; they weave not neither do they spin . . . and then, suddenly, our Lord glances off, as it were, from this thought into a kind of ecstasy at their sheer beauty—indeed, He had the incentive: Palestine in spring is a mass of anemones, cyclamen, iris: blue, lilac, palest pink and crimson, yellow and cream and purple—but what an exclamation is, as it were, wrested from Him: "I tell you, not Solomon, in *all* his glory, was arrayed like *one* of these!" You might find in ancient literature some instances of the more or less convinced rehearsal of that classical cliché which declares that nature is more beautiful than art; but on the lips of a Jew, of one given indeed to admiring the force and even violence of nature, the richness of tilth and luxuriance of vine or forest, but perfectly imperceptive, you would think, of the more tender charm and of the delicacies of living things that were not human —this cry of ecstasy, I repeat, this sweeping elimination of Solomon, the very symbol of magnificence, is something completely new, something that entrances us with its humanity when we encounter it, and enough to make us gratefully rejoice in the *total* humanity of Him who was known as Joseph's son, and chose for His habitual title, "Son of Man."

He was also true son of Joseph, son of David, son of Abraham, because He *thought in the way proper to such a man*. We are all half consciously inclined to assume that the really right way of thinking is the one in which our fellow-countrymen think, and that other nationalities somehow deviate from it—inculpably, no doubt, and without being able to help it; but all the same, their thoughts are rather "queer" and the simpler sort of tourist undoubtedly feels that it is rather perverse of a Frenchman so much as to talk French, and as for Czech. . . . It remains that nations and races really have their *way* of thinking; and by that I do not mean that they entertain a perfectly different set of thoughts from ours, but that they think the same things in a different way, and clothe their ideas in correspondingly different words, and, above all, in a quite different costumery, so to say, supplied by an imagination immemorially furnished in a particular way. Now when Our Lord thought of Tyre and Sidon, when we might think of Brighton or Blackpool, Marseilles or Monte Carlo, Shanghai or Buenos Aires (or any two other towns which we find it more convenient to criticise than our own), He really did most naturally think of them. He was not playing a part, and, as it were, saying to Himself: "Tyre and Sidon are the sorts of places that these Palestinians require to have men-

tioned to them—I will introduce some local colour." When
Solomon, the Queen of Sheba, this or that prophet, was alluded
to by Him, it was not as though we, in Italy, might courteously
choose to mention Dante or d'Annunzio rather than Shakespeare or Rupert Brooke. When He argued as He did with the
Pharisees He adopted methods strange to us—not as an Englishman, laboriously or with that instinctive skill which makes the
really useful civil servant overseas, might adapt his mind and his
palaver to Swahili or Matabele; but He spoke like that because
such really were the processes of His human mind—Jewish
processes proper to that age, because he *was* a Jew, living exactly
then.

Moreover, He loved that land of His with all His heart. He
had, personally and so far as His actual life-time went, a very
circumscribed mission. "I am not sent but to the lost sheep of
the House of Israel." The pagan officer, whose boy He cured, the
pagan woman to whom He said (seemingly so roughly) that
it was not right to take the household bread and toss it to the
dogs—and who (dare I say?) defeated Him so exquisitely by
answering that anyway the little dogs beneath the table ate the
crumbs that happened to fall from it—extorted His half exultant,
half agonized admiration: "I have not yet found such faith—no,
not in Israel itself!" But primarily, and genuinely, His efforts personally went to save "at least in this its day"—in the last few
hours more for which that day was destined to last—His own
People. Jerusalem was the centre of the spiritual life of any Jew;
twice did our Lord cry His heart out when, from Mount Olivet,
He saw the walls that so soon were to be laid low. But even so,
Christ was, as we might say, a north-countryman; He came from
Galilee; and no one can fail to "sense" the sorrow, the bitter,
bitter grief, of His heart when for the last time He said goodbye
to those hills and to the lake and took His way towards Jerusalem, where they would kill Him.

NATIONALITY

BECAUSE He was a man
As well as He was God,
He loved His own goat-nibbled hills,
His crumbling Jewish sod.
He bowed to Roman rule
And dared none to rebel
But Oh the windflowers out of Naim
We know He loved them well!
He must have loved its tongue,
His Aramaic brogue,
As much as any Norman loves
The accents of La Hogue.
Discountried and diskinged
And watched from pole to pole,
A Jew at heart remains a Jew—
His nation is his soul.
Had he upon that day
Of headlong cloaks and boughs
Surrendered all mankind to race
And lifted David's brows,
They would not on His cross
Have writ as mocking news
That He the man from Nazareth
Was monarch of the Jews.

As heifers' to their young
Christ's bowels yearned to His sod.
He was the very Jew of Jews
And yet since He was God—
Oh you with frontiered hearts,
Conceive it if you can—
It was not life alone He gave,
But country up for man.

THE PATIENCE OF CHRIST

"Burning heat by day, and biting frost at nights, till my eyelids lost the power of sleep"—so Jacob describes his twenty long years of service under Laban. And the Son of Man had not where to lay his head; all day he taught the multitude; at evening he answered the questions propounded to him by his apostles; sometimes it was only by denying himself sleep altogether that he could find time for prayer. In all this, he would be a model for his priests; they were to be, all the time, at everybody's disposal, they were not to keep office hours. And whereas we are accustomed to remember how tired Our Lord must have been *physically* by the labours he undertook during the years of his active ministry, we are apt to forget how tired he must have been mentally. After all, his nerves, no less than his muscles, were ordinary human nerves, capable of exhaustion. Nothing is so fatiguing, I fancy, as the pressure of multitudinous other human lives on our own. How easily we priests recognize the types of people who surrounded our Lord with their comments and their questionings! The unfriendly critic who wants a reason for everything: "How is it that thy disciples do not fast, when John's disciples and the Pharisees fast?" The eager inquirer who, after all, never comes up to the scratch: "Lord, give me leave to go home and bury my father first." The person who cannot understand what a priest's job is and what it is not:

"Master, bid my brother give me a share of our inheritance." The pious female who pesters you with her compliments: "Blessed is the womb that bore thee . . ." and all the rest of them. Our Lord met them all, and always with a patient word. Day in, day out, they never left him alone.

E TENEBRIS

Come down, O Christ, and help me! reach Thy hand,
  For I am drowning in a stormier sea
  Than Simon on Thy Lake of Galilee:
The wine of life is spilled upon the sand.
My heart is as some famine-murdered land
  Whence all good things have perished utterly,
  And well I know my soul in Hell must lie
If I this night before God's throne should stand.

"He sleeps, perchance, or rideth to the chase,
  Like Baal, when his prophets howled that name
    From morn till noon on Carmel's smitten height."
    Nay, peace I shall behold before the night,
  The feet of brass, the robe more white than flame,
The wounded hands, the weary human face.

NEVER MAN SPAKE

The historical Figure had disappeared. The foot-prints on the shore of Galilee had vanished. The miracles, if any had been wrought, could no longer be investigated. But something yet remained. There were certain recorded utterances which could be examined here and now. If the supreme claim of the Christian philosophy as to the nature of its Founder were true there should be something more than remarkable in the nature of those utterances; something that would reveal itself to the cold and impartial tests whereby we estimate the values of isolated passages in great literature; something in the very quality of those utterances (apart from all other considerations) that came up to the level of the supreme claim. . . .

The mental process by which we recognize and appreciate the comparative values of isolated passages in great literature, or discover the author in his work, is not an analytical one. It differs from those of the textual critic and the theologian. But it is rational. There is a profound philosophy behind it; and its principles belong to the great history of aesthetics from Plato to Hegel. Whatever failings it may have in its adventures among contemporaries, it knows nothing of partisanship or prejudice among the masterpieces of the remote past. Its function there is a spiritual one, the recognition of spirit by spirit, through material forms, or the harmonies of language. It is in their

qualities that it knows them, and it asks for no other cor-
roboration. . . .

Doubts and controversies may arise over inferior examples,
where the artistic values are themselves obscured. But only
those who do not know the exquisite precisions and certainties
of the highest level of art would distrust their evidence in the
noblest cases; and in actual fact it is by their evidence alone
that the highest achievements of creative genius in art and
literature hold their immortal place in the history of mankind.
Höffding, dealing with the symbolic element in religious ideas,
had taught that the religious consciousness approximates to the
aesthetic point of view, and adopted the mental process of the
latter as an essential part of his philosophy of religion. Kant,
Hegel, Schiller, Wordsworth and many others, by many independent considerations, had already justified him. It was the
mental process with which I was most familiar; and I was
haunted by the feeling that it had something of the first importance to tell me about the utterances of the central Figure
in the history of religion; and especially, to begin with, that
quiet personal reassurance addressed to a mourner at a graveside: *I am the Resurrection and the Life.*

Through all the veils of translation, in Greek, Latin, or English, it seemed to convey values unlike any other that had fallen
from human lips. If we compared the loftiest utterances of
Socrates or Shakespeare with that sublimely simple statement
of its Author's *personal* mastery over the entire kingdom of
death, the distance between them was at once seen to be an
infinite distance. This infinite distance required an adequate
explanation from the literary critic no less than from the theologian. A difference beyond measure seemed, at first sight, to
postulate a Cause beyond measure.

Shakespeare, the accepted master of merely human speech,
might by a considerable expenditure of rhetoric impress us with
his power to write a poem that would "live."

CHRIST THE GOOD SHEPHERD

"So long as men can breathe, or eyes can see,
So long lives this, and this gives life to thee."

But his words are gnats dancing in the sun compared with the
stupendous implications of that quiet reassurance, addressed
to a woman mourning for the dead, and not only to her, but to
all those who have ever looked down speechlessly into a grave—
I am the Resurrection and the Life.

I am not here discussing the truth of that quiet reassurance,
all the more heart-shaking for its profound and infinite calm,
nor am I resuscitating the familiar and powerful, but not wholly
convincing argument, "either a madman or God." I am looking at the problem for the moment from the point of view of
pure literature, and the values whereby we estimate its greatness, those strange values of the eternal world which, in certain
inspired moments, seem to emerge from the almost miraculously
perfect arrangement of a few colours on a canvas, a few recorded
words from the lips of Socrates, a few lines on a printed page,
or a combination of three sounds in music, from which there
emerges "not a fourth sound, but a star."

"The Divine," said Hegel, "is the centre of all the representations of art." In the highest moments of art and literature, our
temporal world has always been seen *sub specie aeternitatis*. At
such moments the masters of human expression have felt within
themselves a spark of the divine flame, and acquired as Hart-
mann said, in his *Philosophy of the Unconscious*, the will
and power to think and feel as if God were in them. At such
times they seem to reveal fragments of the secret plan of the
universe. They overhear phrases of the universal harmony and
record them for men. But, however far these human masters may
have risen above themselves in that process or have felt themselves inspired by a power greater than their own, there is not
a measurable, but an utterly immeasurable distance between
their utterance, and those quiet, superhuman, *personal* reassur-

ances: *Let not your heart be troubled. Neither let it be afraid. Ye believe in God. Believe also in Me.* . . .

Come unto Me, all ye that are weary and heavy-laden, and ye shall find rest to your souls.

There is egotism enough in literature, God knows; but what merely human being has been able to round the whole infinite circle from the supreme proclamation of Self as God's equal to the utter humility of a Self prepared to wash the dust of the wayside from the feet of one who would sell him for thirty pieces of silver.

Hereafter ye shall see the Son of Man coming in the clouds of heaven.

Take my yoke upon you and learn of Me; for I am meek and lowly of heart.

Were there ever such evidences of lowliness offered to God or man before? Could such evidences be offered—had the words any meaning at all if they came from a merely human being? How was it possible for any finite mind to ascend and descend thus in a single breath between earth and heaven—to claim the full majesty of the Eternal at one moment, and brood like a dove in the heart of a child at the next?

Whether the awful claim be true or not, the words have a character of their own, which sets them apart from all other human words, and requires an adequate explanation. Glib suggestions that the man Christ Jesus never uttered them are not enough. For my present argument, it matters not who formed the sentences attributed to Him. As Rousseau said in his Émile: "Never could Jewish writers have found such a tone or such a teaching: in the Gospels are qualities of truth so great, so striking, so totally inimitable that an inventor would be more surprising than he who uttered them."

Four such inventors, all simple, all on the spiritual heights, and all liars, would be more astonishing still. For those who desired to accept the "idea" in detachment from concrete earthly "facts" and historical events (most of them "illusory"), the life of the "Galilean peasant," who had so profoundly affected the world as to rearrange its whole scheme of thought, and the very stones of its architecture, had the symbolical truth of a great poem, in which the most illusory "facts" were themselves curiously perfect parables, or symbolical embodiments of eternal truths. . . . If we cannot believe that five loads feed a multitude, we are yet forced to observe that the story is an exquisitely accurate parable of the strange process whereby the mind, heart and spirit of the civilized world have been sustained for nearly two thousand years by the bread of life in one man's word. The very tale is sacramental. The "facts" themselves are the five loaves, and after they are consumed there remain endless fragments of super-substantial Bread. Wherever we touch them they have this virtue. Whether it be the account of an episode, or the record of a word spoken, they had the authenticity and authority of a spiritual law, transcending Nature perhaps, and overruling natural laws, but not contradicting them. Here and now, our water was changed to wine. Here and now the blind were made to see. The "facts," as they were recorded, glowed with an inner light, illuminating the heights and depths of the intellectual and spiritual world. They answered a thousand philosophical riddles, not as the philosopher answers, in empty abstractions, but as the masterpieces of art answer, in their sacramental use of things we daily see and touch and handle.

But these "facts" were not set before us in a masterpiece of art. They were set before us by very simple narrators—whose very earnestness made them fragmentary; yet, when the masters of art have endeavoured to elaborate or glorify or round off those fragments, the simplest words of those humble fishermen have always dwarfed their proudest efforts. Two words of St. John make all the harmonies of Dante and Milton sound like a tinkling cymbal, and one glimpse of the seamless purple at the foot of the Cross brings all the magnificence of Tintoretto down into the dust.

The "facts" were not recorded in masterpieces of art. The symbolism is not planned. It is the natural and inevitable symbolism of facts that accord with and reveal a profound Reality. They were delivered separately by men who were earnestly striving to make a true record of events which they thought of immeasurable importance to their own souls and to the whole world. Whether their attempts be regarded as a failure or not, there is no parallel in the history of the world for so earnest an attempt on the part of four men to make their testimony as to the facts of any event whatsoever. Elaborate histories have been written by scholars. Beautiful legends have been rounded into shape by poets; but of any similar attempt to bear witness, merely for the sake of bearing witness, to a series of alleged facts, for which the testifiers and millions of their followers were ready to offer up their lives, there has been no shadow of a semblance. If those broken narratives, then, had that profound, symbolical, sacramental inner truth, to which the philosophy of Europe has paid its tribute through its deepest minds, there is something more to be accounted for than criticism has yet envisaged. An artless report of the alleged facts can hardly strike deeper than the masterpieces of spiritual and intellectual art, unless there be something more in the "facts" themselves than sceptics are usually prepared to admit.

It seemed possible that they shone with all those strange lights and reflections of the Divine because they themselves actually encompassed and enclosed a Light that our darkness could not comprehend.

The biographical "facts," however, might all be minimized or explained away. The alleged physical miracles all happened long ago and, in every case, even though Hegel decreed the

historical Figure to be "unique," they were on *a priori* grounds
ruled out by the modern mind.

But this other miracle of the spirit, this Pentecostal flame,
shining through all the veils of language and translation, in the
four-fold record of the things He said, was there for all to see.
The words themselves were a gleam of the divine self-revelation.
Even as He speaks the words, He prophesies their power; and
the quality of the prophecy can be investigated, here and now,
as when He uttered it. *Heaven and earth shall pass away, but
My words shall not pass away.*

The values of that utterance—subjected to the coldest standards of literary criticism—are not human. The voice of the
Eternal is in it, before whom even the suns and universes dissolve like a shadow, and all the ages of Time are but a moment.

Compare it with any other human utterance, and the immeasurable distance at once appears again, the infinite difference
which requires an infinite explanation. Consider, for instance,
the words in which that great statesman, Lincoln, expressed the
determination of the New World that "government of the
people, by the people and for the people shall not perish from
the earth." They embody an ideal, and a noble ideal; and yet,
compared with those other words, they sound like a tinkling
cymbal. They are of the earth, earthy. The political forum
echoes in them. It is at least imaginable that someone may have
applauded.

The words of Christ are of another order. They are not to
be measured by the duration of "the earth." They are of the
eternal world, and move us with the strangest apprehension of
the human spirit, the sense of *das Heilige.*

And yet—here is the most striking distinction between them.
The statesman's utterance appears to be entirely unegotistical.
It is concerned with earthly interests, it is true; but they are
the interests of "the people." The other utterance appears to

be so completely the annunciation of a Self that it dismisses the whole of the rest of the universe as nothing in comparison. In all the utterances of Christ, even in his reassurance of the mourner at the graveside, there is this personal annunciation—*I am the Resurrection and the Life.*

If any other human lips could ever have made a measurable fraction of such a claim it would have sounded like an insane boast. It is only because the claim is not fractional, but complete, that it has never occurred to any one to regard it as a "boast" or as incompatible with a divine humility. The utterance is its own evidence, as no other ever has been; for its kingdom, its infinitude, is within it. Any madman might say things equally impossible from the human point of view; but he could not simultaneously overwhelm us with that strange sense of the infinitely holy, or move the depths of innumerable hearts to adoration for two thousand years by the sheer majesty —and awful humility—of his words. We might also say that the supreme claim of the words would be utterly intolerable if they were not true. But the words have been cherished in the hearts of countless millions, to whom they conveyed the values of God. . . .

This was exactly what had been affirmed by the masterminds of Christendom for nearly twenty centuries, after the most elaborate and profound consideration of all the available facts, by the greatest intellectual and religious councils that the world had ever known. They thought they had an adequate explanation of that constant, profound and solemn mood of the central Figure of religious history, who quietly took His personal identity with the supreme Being for granted, and sometimes directly affirmed it, or with the utmost subtlety implied it, in words that bow the head and break the heart with their beauty. Our immediate conscience almost allowed us to say that, if the affirmation were untrue, it could not have been made in those words. There would have been a false note somewhere, a fault of character, a flaw in the tone; and there is none, even in the broken and stumbling human record. We may be more than sure, therefore, of the original glory of the Aramaic. It is a commonplace of criticism that translation dulls the finer lights and shades of all the masters of literature. Here and there, it is sometimes affirmed that by some rare chance a translator of genius has improved on an inferior original. But in this case there has been no question as to where the original greatness lay, and it shines through four records. It shines, moreover, not only through the Greek, the Latin, and the English, but through every language into which it has been translated, transfiguring even those that are in decadence, with something of its own sacramental splendour.

Taking all these instances together, even this poor literary test gives us a glimpse of the Personality that, across the ages and through all the obstacles of the material world and the dull vesture of our mortality, speaks instantly to what is real in our own personalities, and merely by saying what He says, proves that He has the sole right in the universe to say it. . . .

It was through neglect of these values, which could be perceived here and now, in the actual record, that Renan and so many others went astray. They tried to build up their own independent record, and plunged it in a thousand inconsistencies. Renan's *Vie de Jésus,* that "French novel" as it has justly been called, attempts to depict a beautiful character who is at the same time a despicable impostor; one who could lend himself to a trick at the tomb of Lazarus, and dream of love-affairs in the Garden of Gethsemane. The direct literary test of the values in the Gospels themselves annihilates Renan. Before the fire of one of those burning utterances the romantic creation of Renan shrivels like "a scribbled form, writ on a parchment." It was disregard of the purely "literary test" that so blinded him to the values of character and personality.

There were other definite results that this merely literary test seemed to offer, again and again, and their force was cumulative. No man whose ear had been attuned to great literature could doubt, for instance, that through all the veils of language and translation this proclamation of a unique Self persisted; and that the Voice which said "I am the Resurrection and the Life" was the same as that which said "Be of good cheer, *I* have overcome the world." It was the same voice that said "*I* am the vine, ye are the branches," and "Before Abraham was, *I AM.*" Was there ever an assertion like this of a *personal* domination over the relativity of Time?

Those who point to the fact that the assertion of the complete dominion over death occurs only in the fourth Gospel (the most divine of all) are still confronted by equally stupendous implications elsewhere, such as "All power is given unto Me in heaven and on earth"; and "Lo, I am with you all days, even unto the end of the world." If the actual expression in the fourth Gospel is more vitally beautiful, is there not a more vital explanation of this than the suggestion that its author was more of a theologian or philosopher than the writers of the other gospels? To me it seems that we overhear in those ineffable cadences and undertones a direct echo of the living voice which it was natural that the beloved disciple should have caught more perfectly, more profoundly, more exquisitely than another. Its pity had breathed upon him as his head lay upon the divine breast. It is the only adequate explanation of that infinitely tender preparation of his mind for the great farewell, murmuring, with a compassion impossible to man, the consolation that no other could give: "It is expedient for you that I go away. . . . I will not leave you comfortless. I will come to you."

Let it be regarded from yet another side. Suppose for the moment that the record is really true, and that this "historical Figure approaching us in Time" did indeed embody the "values of God." Nobody with an ear attuned to great literature can doubt for a single moment, in that case, that the words attributed to Him by the simple recorders were absolutely worthy even of Him. The words from the Cross, for instance, "Forgive them, for they know not what they do," in which the divine Sufferer manifests the divine compassion towards those who nailed Him there, are yet again a proclamation (implied and acted out this time, not asserted) of His own infinitude. But let it be taken with all those other instances, and especially with what is to me the unanswerable instance—*I am the Resurrection and the Life*—and we feel at once that those sentences are perfectly fitting for those divine lips. We should not feel that, in using them, He was falling short of His infinite majesty and holiness.

But it is exactly in the attempt to invent fitting utterance for the Divine—that the masters of merely human expression have always failed. It is one of the commonplaces of literature that even the august spirit of Milton, using the language at perhaps its noblest period, failed and failed miserably in the words that he puts into the mouth of the Son of God. It is a commonplace of criticism that the speeches of his Satan are among the most magnificent ever penned; that, in describing the unattainable light of Heaven he attains sublimity, but that, both in *Paradise Lost* and *Paradise Regained*, except where he directly borrows from the great original, he is utterly inadequate. Thousands can quote line after line of those burning words that he attributes to the fallen archangel. We all remember that courage:

> "Never to submit or yield,
> And what is else not to be overcome."

But who remembers two consecutive lines of the words that Milton puts into the mouth of the Son of God? There are few who remember a single phrase. The following lines are perhaps the best of them:

"I through the ample air in triumph high
Shall lead hell captive, maugre hell, and show
The powers of darkness bound. Thou, at the sight
Pleased, out of heaven shalt look down and smile
While, by thee raised, I ruin all my foes,
Death last, and with his carcase glut the grave."

They deal with the same subject as what I have called the supreme instance of the Divine utterance in the New Testament; and by a curious accident an exact ground for comparison is offered here. The noblest measure in the English language, the measure into which its finest utterances have fallen as though in accordance with a natural law, is the measure in which Milton wrote his epics, and Shakespeare wrote the greater part of his dramatic works. The greatest line of Shakespeare himself in that measure is perhaps the line in Hamlet,

"Absent thee from felicity awhile."

It is merely an accident, from the human point of view, though perhaps in the eternal aspect a breath of inspiration, that an obscure translator, in the age of Shakespeare, should have written, not only the greatest single line in Shakespeare's own measure, but a single line that in itself outweighs all the wonders of his combined works, and compresses more meaning into its ten syllables. It is a line that has been spoken as the final living truth over myriads of graves, and has burned through myriads of desolate minds with a new conviction of immortality. What criticism can fathom that profound calm or explain it?

"I am the Resurrection and the Life."

Art and literature are confronted here by a Presence that shrivels them into insignificance; and there is no answer to its instant question—"Whom say *ye* that I am?" but the answer of Peter, "Thou art the Christ, the son of the living God."

TEACHING UPON THE TRINITY

ONE RESULT of reading the Gospels is that we find what Our Lord shows us about God by being God. Another is that we find what Our Lord shows us about God by what He has to say of God. There is a lot to be said for making one's own list of the texts in which Christ Our Lord tells us of God, grasping them in their context and returning to them again and again. Most of them, naturally, treat of God in His dealings with and judgments of the human race. Save perhaps in the proportion of statements about God's love to statements about His justice, it would be hard to find among these anything that has not already been told us in the Old Testament. There is a new atmosphere, but if it is impossible not to feel the difference, it is almost impossible to lay a precise finger on it—if one happens to know the Old Testament at all well: everything makes us realize how vast a communication about Himself God had already given His chosen people.

In a handful of statements Our Lord covers the ground of the philosophers: God is a spirit (John iv, 24); He is perfect (Matt. v, 48); He dwells in secret (Matt. vi, 18); He is good and He only (Matt. xix, 17); to Him all things are possible (Matt. xix, 26); He has never ceased working, that is maintaining creatures in being (John v, 44); He is the one only God (Mark xii, 33).

It is a vast reassurance to the mind to have God as it were ratifying the words with which human language has tried to utter Him. It is true that no word of human speech, no concept of the human mind, is adequate; but word and concept are not therefore useless, for God has used them. We may have precious little notion of what they mean in an infinite nature, but the little *is* precious. They do not give all light, but light-giving they are. God uses them for that.

Our Lord uses them: God had already used them: for not here either do we find anything that is not in the Old Testament. But there is a third sort of statement, which does constitute a new element in God's revelation of Himself to men. As we read what Our Lord tells us of God, we are bound to become conscious of two elements constantly recurring, and recurring in combination—the element of oneness and the element of plurality.

II

I say that this was new. There are in the Old Testament stray hint and gleams of it, but they are no more than that. Thus in the first chapter of Genesis, God says (verse 26), "Let *us* make man to *our* image and likeness" and in the next verse we read, "And God made man to *his* image and likeness": the plural words "us" and "our" seem to suggest that there were several persons; the singular word "his" that they were somehow one. I do not mean that the human writer of Genesis knew how apt to the reality of God were the words that he wrote: but God Who inspired him knew it. Anyhow, it did not strike the Jews, even by Christ's day, as requiring any special comment. To us again there is something fascinating in the fact that the word for God, "Elohim," is plural: yet it takes a verb in the singular, and if an adjective goes with it, that is in the singular too. But again it did not strike the Jews, or the Canaanites (who had the same usage) that this had any special significance. Of another sort, there are descriptions of Wisdom which seem to suggest a second person within the Godhead, for example, "And thy wisdom with thee, which knoweth thy works, which then was also present when thou madest the world" (Wis. ix, 9). If this is no more than a way of saying that God was not without the attribute of wisdom at the time when He made the world, it seems a rather elaborate way of stating an obvious truth. To us who have heard Our Lord's explicit revelation, such things are full of suggestion. But they did not lead the Jews, nor were they of a sort inescapably to lead them, to the truth that God, remaining one, is yet in some mysterious way more than one. To a truth so astounding indeed, one must be led inescapably or one will not arrive there at all. It is not the sort of truth that one will leap to embrace on a mere hint.

Our Lord did not stop at a hint. As I have said, He insists on an element of plurality, returning to it again and again. There is of course no faintest mitigation of the utter monotheism of the Jews. Our Lord quotes God's own revelation to them: "Hear, O Israel: the Lord thy God is one God." But there is a new element of more-than-oneness, which does not contradict the oneness but somehow enriches it. Thus (John x, 30) He says "I and the Father are One." Here there is clearly a statement of two Who are yet one. In the last two verses of St. Matthew's gospel we find Our Lord saying: "Baptizing them in the name of the Father, and of the Son, and of the Holy Ghost." Here we have plurality again, this time three, yet the unity is stated in the use of the word "name," not "names."

This combination of oneness and plurality is most evident in Our Lord's discourse to the Apostles at the Last Supper. The whole of this discourse, from the fourteenth chapter of St. John to the seventeenth, should be read again and again: everything is in it. But for the moment our concern is with these two elements in what Our Lord has to tell us of the Godhead. In this discourse the special note is what can only be called a certain interchangeability. What I mean by this will appear from some examples. Thus in the fourteenth chapter we find Philip the Apostle saying to Our Lord: "Let us see the Father," and Our Lord answering him, "Whoever has seen me, has seen the Father."

We find this same notion, which I have been driven to call clumsily interchangeability, in what Our Lord has to say of answer to prayer, the sending of the Holy Ghost, God's abiding in our souls. Thus He says (John xvi, 23): "If you ask the Father anything in my name, he will give it to you." But he had already said (John xiv, 14): "If you shall ask me anything in my name, that I will do."

We have just heard Our Lord saying that the Paraclete, the Holy Ghost, is to abide with us forever; but a few verses later, in answer to a question of St. Jude, Our Lord says: "If anyone love me he will keep my word and my Father will love him and we will come to him and make our abode with him."

What Our Lord's first hearers, ignorant of the doctrine of the Blessed Trinity, made of His allusions to it we cannot know: we may guess that they were utterly puzzled. But there is a great profit for ourselves, knowing the doctrine, in listening to these same words of Our Lord. I shall not attempt any full treatment here, but shall indicate how the reader may go about it for himself.

Begin with the famous text Matthew xi, 27: "No one knows the Son but the Father, and no one knows the Father but the Son, and him to whom the Son shall reveal him."

Here we have two capital points of the doctrine: first, that it can be known only by revelation, the power of the human mind cannot reach it without the aid of God: second, that the central point of the mystery of the relation of Father and Son, that in which its being as a mystery can be summarized, is the knowledge each has of the other—which seems at least to suggest the first procession by way of knowledge.

Self-existence and the timeless present of eternity are in "Before Abraham was made, I am" (John viii, 58); equality of nature in "All things whatsoever the Father hath are mine" (John xvi, 15); distinction of persons and identity of nature in "I and the Father are one" (John x, 30); and that unsayable reality for which theologians have coined the word "circumsession" in "The Father is in me and I in the Father" (John x, 38).

Remembering that nature is the principle of operation—the person does what his nature allows—the identity of nature is asserted by Our Lord in an identity of operation: "My Father works until now and I work" (John v, 17); "Whatsoever things he (the Father) does, these the Son also does in like manner" (John v, 19).

Of the Third Person Our Lord says less; but it is enough. The Spirit is a person: "When *he,* the Spirit of truth is come, he shall lead you unto all truth" (John xvi, 13); He is equal to the Son, each is a paraclete: "I will ask the Father and he will give you another Paraclete" (John xiv, 16); He is equal to Father and Son: "baptizing them in the name of the Father and of the Son and of the Holy Ghost" (Matt. xxviii, 19). To see just what that phrase means as to the Godhead of the Holy Ghost, try substituting any other name, however mighty. "In the name of the Father and of the Son and of the Archangel Michael." The thing would sound ridiculous. With all possible respect to the Archangel, one would feel that the company was too exalted for him.

But there is another truth Our Lord makes clear: that though He, the Son, possesses the Divine Nature in total equality with the Father, it is still as a nature received: He is not the origin: "The Son cannot do anything of his own impulse, he can only do what he sees his Father doing" (John v, 19–23) because the Divine Nature in which He lives and moves and has His being is wholly received from His Father.

With this we may compare Our Lord's parallel phrase about

the Holy Ghost: "He will not speak of his own impulse, he will utter the message that has been given to him" (John xvi, 13). For the Holy Ghost, too, has received that Divine Nature which is totally His—received it not from the Father only but from the Son also, so that Our Lord can go on to say: "It is from me that he will derive what he makes plain to you."

This same truth about the procession of the Second Person from the First, and of the Third Person from the First and Second, is illuminated in another way as well. Our Lord speaks of Himself, the Second Person, as being "sent"—always by the Father. He speaks of the Third Person as to be sent—sometimes by the Father, sometimes by Himself. In this "sending" we must see no glimmer of subordination of the Son and the Holy Spirit. They come to us by the divine will, which is their own as totally as it is the Father's: but inasmuch as they received the nature in which that will is, they may be thought of as sent. That is why the Father, who possesses the Divine Nature as unreceived, is never spoken of as sent; that is why the Son, who receives the Divine Nature from the Father alone, is spoken of as sent by the Father but not by the Holy Ghost; that is why the Holy Ghost, who receives the Divine Nature from Father and Son, is spoken of as sent by the Father and by the Son. But it must be repeated, the sending is not to be thought of as a command imposed but as the free decision of a nature possessed in total equality by each.

TO GOD THE FATHER

GREAT GOD: within whose simple essence, we
  nothing but that which is Thy Self can find;
  when on Thyself thou didst reflect Thy mind,
  Thy thought was God, which took the form of Thee:
And when this God thus born, Thou lov'st, and He
  lov'd Thee again, with passion of like kind,
  as lovers' sighs which meet become one mind,
  both breath'd one Spirit of equal deity.
Eternal Father, whence these two do come
  and wil'st the title of my father have,
  an heavenly knowledge in my mind engrave,
That it Thy Son's true Image may become:
  incense my heart with sighs of holy Love
  that it the temple of the Spirit may prove.

LIFE AND THE FOOD OF LIFE

❧ WE COME to what our Lord regards as the supreme topic of His proclamation, and, indeed, as the very object of His coming amongst us and of His existence. He had said: "I am come to seek and to save that which was lost." But when you ask: "What will you do then? *For what* are you saving them?" He answers: "I am come that they might have life and have it more abundantly" (John x, 10). And if one asks: "What do you mean by *life?*" He replies (as by now you might expect): "*I* am the Life."

Now, to these words we have most emphatically to attach a meaning. Were you to say to anyone: "Christ is my life," or even, "Christ is Life," you would be thought a fanatic or mad. And you would indeed be hard put to it to explain what you did mean. Yet both those sentences would, on the lips of Christians, be perfectly sensible things to say, and, indeed, the only thing that a Christian in the last resort could say.

What do you mean, anyway, by "life"? Baffling question, if you really seek an answer. Word that is used by us all so glibly; that has entered into a thousand habitual phrases and even slang. "I want to see life," says the lad emancipated from his school and embarking on a tour round the world, or even round London after dark. "Music is my life!" cries the enthusiast, implying at least that every other mode of existence in which music played no part would be intolerable, and that without music she would at once commit suicide. "I have lived my life," sighs the elderly person who envies the opportunities and zest of youth; and the prize-fighter announces that life for him is over in his thirties. Moreover, life is dear. Again and again I have seen men in war-hospitals, of whom you honestly thought that it would be better that they should die—limbs shot away; face shot away. But they would say to one: "Life is very precious, Father." What could they mean?

Let us begin by acknowledging that we do see a difference between the most perfect imitation and the simplest living thing. Nay, you can have a silken flower or a waxen fruit that *would be* far finer specimens of what they represent than the actual tulip, the actual peach that is in your possession, *were they real*. They have not and cannot have that mysterious interior glow, pulsation, activity—that power of taking up other things and turning them into their living selves that is so different from mere absorption; that casting of their unity of Self-hood over what they assimilate, but, above all, that radiant Beauty which is proper to vitality and which we can never never make nor give. I confess that I am lost in worship before the simplest living thing, because by that fact of life I enter into all but direct communication with the Creator of all Life whatsoever. I know that even "lifeless" things possess reality and energy, and neither can these be created by me or by anyone else; but at least I can shift the earth about and remodel stones and interconnect them in such ways as they permit; but they do not grow; they do not develop; they are not alive, and while I can destroy life I cannot even seem to supply it.

Such life is not its own absolute justification. It is no sin to pick a flower and see it wilt when the due hours have passed. Nor yet to kill a bird, a rabbit. But I confess that when I see, for example, a shot pheasant, and in an instant its vivid black eye filmed, the glow and gloss gone in but a moment from its feathers, the thing *taken* that can never be given nor restored . . . I confess to feeling that I would hesitate long before doing any such thing as to kill. I frankly acknowledge this, alien as it is to our national instinct for "sport," and superficially similar as it seems to the doctrine of those who say you have no right thus to kill, which is false. But it remains that for no merely selfish reason would I ever wish to see dead that which is capable of life.

Now, if I can thus go to communion with God in the grass of the field, the least little living insect, what must I think when I come to man?

Human life can be a terrifying thing to think of. I don't mean the incidents or conditions of such or such a life, but the thing itself. Its egocentricity. By that I mean that each man is the centre of his whole world. He describes everything in terms of himself, so far as its position goes. Two men face one another, and one will say that a thing is on his left, while the other must needs say that it is on his right. Each occupies his little bit of space in this world, and while he is there no one else can be there, and from there he looks out at the entire universe. But what is his bodily position, despite its uniqueness, when compared with the lonely independence of his mind? Each man sees through his own eyes; each thinks his own thoughts, unshared by any other. For you may learn from your neighbour what he thinks, but you cannot think *his* thoughts, nor feel *his* feelings. Even when you know another well, and love him or her most intimately, and as it were live by that other's life and have one soul between you—all that is, after all, but a way of speaking, and for ever and for ever you are not that other, but your Self. Each person who reads this book is thinking special thoughts—isolated thoughts—about what is read; a barrier as of ice—impenetrable more than ice is, even though transparent, maybe, as purest ice—separates each reader from every other reader, and only by the bridge of words, or of imagination, or of guess, can any one soul communicate—and even then how partially—with any other soul! God-like and majestic uniqueness of each soul! And pathetic isolation of each soul—limitations of each soul—loneliness of each soul! Life itself is so marvellous that it may almost steal the worship due to God, and, indeed, in pagan ages the myriad phenomena of Life did so steal it. But when you realize the tininess of each human life, the small scope of its awareness, its wavering will, how tragic would be such a god-hood, if god-hood indeed it were! Enough. As Life it is amazing, and a contact with God, but how different from God—how much is it *not*, that God *is*.

II

Because, then, of the mysterious magnificence of this thing, and because of its insufficiency, Christ says that He means to give us more of it, and for that purpose has He come. The whole Gospel of St. John is occupied with this theme of Life—Life of which our Lord says to Nicodemus that it needs to be given to a man from God, for, how can a man bring himself alive? Yet we need to be "born anew." And, speaking with the Samaritan woman, He pictures it as a fountain leaping ever fresh within the soul. And then He works the "sign" that shall enable Him to speak still more definitely about it. He heals the paralytic man—restores him, as we might say, to life—and, when they stand astonished, He proclaims that greater works than this shall He show them, that then, indeed, they may marvel. For, as the Father can raise the dead and give life to them, so, too, the Son—whom He wills, them maketh He alive. "He," our Lord continues, "who hears My word and believes on Him who sent He *hath* eternal life . . . he has crossed over from Death into Life." We have to "hear Him," in a way that will mean more than merely listen to Him; "see Him," so that we are not just looking at Him; "come to Him," so that we somehow adhere to Him and are not just standing alongside of Him; "believe in Him" in a way that surpasses the mere regarding what He says as true; and then something will happen to us which is no more than palely shadowed forth by the restoration of paralyzed limbs to the ordinary energies of man, and what can but be described as a "making alive," as though all our earlier vitality had been but death.

Does our Lord, indeed, mean just physical resuscitation? Well, recall the incident of Lazarus. Lazarus had died and for four days had been buried. Our Lord raised him to bodily life again. That, surely, would be one of those "greater things" at which "indeed we might marvel"? Recall what had passed between our Lord and the dead man's sister, Martha. "Oh, if you had been here," the poor woman in her anguish cried to Him, "my brother had not died." "Thy brother," He answered, "shall rise again." "I know that he shall rise," she said, despondently, "at the last day." Ah, no! Even that, even that mysterious restoration to "life" that is to befall every one of us, is but a material affair, itself little more than a symbol of that Giving of Life that is the purpose of Christ amongst us. So you hear now from His lips the tremendous identification:

> "I am the Resurrection and the Life;
> He that believeth in Me, though he were dead,
> Shall live;
> And he that liveth, and believeth in Me
> Shall never die."

I cannot here rehearse the whole of the doctrine of Grace. I can only say that as a stone is not alive at all, and as a flower "lives," yet with how slender and semi-real a life compared to the meanest among animals, and as it would be death for a man were all that is peculiarly human in him—intelligence and freedom of will—to be stricken from him and he reduced to be but as the brutes are, so there is a yet higher life in store for men, a

supernatural life, a free gift from God and called, therefore,
"grace"—for that is what grace means. And the plan of God is
that we should acquire that life by incorporation with our Lord,
so that by His life we live. This is not altogether beyond our
imagination or understanding, because you may have experienced how you can actually absorb vitality from proximity to a
very vitalized and healthful person, and how exhausted you
can become by much dealing with a fatigued or bloodless person—someone who is, as they say, but half-alive—dead-and-alive.
And you can also recognize how great is our increase of vitality
by sheer social life, by incorporation with our fellows in a "side,"
a party, any group animated by one thought and will. A new
personality springs into being—the collective vitality of the
group, in which we share and which invigorates and reinforces
us. Dim, indeed, are these comparisons for the illustrating of
what happens when you come into contact—personal, vital, organic contact with Jesus Christ, our Life.

III

"Come to Me—I am the Bread. I am the Vine!" I remind you
briefly of the way in which our Lord made His great proclamation of Himself as our food (John vi). He led up to it, as ever,
gradually.

First, He worked the miracle of the multiplication of the
loaves, meaning to use that miracle as the taking-off point, so to
say, for His further spiritual doctrine. The crowds certainly
flocked together on the next day, but He had to rebuke them—
they had come out of astonishment, excitement—they did not
even see that the miracle was a "sign," that is, that it pointed
to something beyond itself. Unless they *could* get further than
this material food, and even than the exterior miracle, they need
not have troubled thus to throng to Him.

"Work not," He cried, "for the food that perishes,

But for the Food that endures unto Eternal Life—
The Food that the Son of Man is offering you:
For Him hath the Father sealed, even God."

"What are we to do," they answer, "that we may work
'Works of God'?"

"This is the Work of God—
To believe in Him whom God hath sent."

They realize that He is making the supreme claim to be the
Messias. In what sense would He work, or had He worked, a
"sign" that should convince them of that?

"What sign workest Thou, that we may see it,
And put Faith in Thee?
Our forefathers did eat the Manna in the wilderness—
'He gave them bread from heaven to eat . . .'
What workest Thou?"
"In solemn truth I tell you—
Not Moses gave you the real Bread from Heaven;
But my Father is offering you the Bread from Heaven—
The True Bread.
For the Bread of God
Is that which comes down out of Heaven
And gives life to the world."

The Jews do not immediately see that "That which came
down out of heaven" is one and the same thing as "He who
came down out of heaven"; and, half clumsily, like the woman
at the well, who asked our Lord to give her His mysterious
spring-water, so that she need trouble no more to come and
draw laborious pailfuls from this well, they cry: "Give us this
bread always!" He has to speak more clearly.

"I am the Bread of Life:
He who cometh unto Me
   Shall never hunger;
And he who believeth in Me
   Shall thirst no more at all."

And He repeats and insists that it is He who has come down from heaven, for no private purposes of His own, so to say, but to accomplish the Father's will, that is, the giving of life to a dead world. But now the Jews are indignant. They knew, said they, His parents. How, then, could He have come down out of heaven? Our Lord insists but the more:

"I am the Bread of Life.
   Your forefathers ate the Manna in the wilderness,
      And died.
This is the Bread that comes down out of heaven,
   That a man may eat of *that*
      And never die.
I am the Living Bread
   Which comes down out of heaven;
If a man eat of My Bread
   He shall live for ever.
And the Bread that I will give for the world's life
   Is My Flesh."

Observe the steps by which Christ has moved. Do not exhaust yourselves by working merely for this world's life. Work God's works, proper to a diviner life.—How can we do that?—By believing in Me.—What, then, are your credentials, your heavenly guarantee, equivalent to the manna given by Moses—"bread from heaven"?—That bread-from-heaven gave no real life. My Father is offering—is sending—a true Bread from Heaven, that Bread of Life. Come to Me—believe in Me—eat of it—eat of Me

—and live "eternally"! Yes—feed on *Me*. For that Bread is My Flesh.

Like Nicodemus, who, on hearing that men must be "born anew," asked "How can these things be?" the Jews wrestle with the problem: *"How* can this man give us His flesh to eat?"

Our Lord, with ever growing emphasis, repeats His assertion, in negative form at first, then, positive and triumphant.

> "In solemn truth I tell you—
> If you do not eat the Flesh of the Son of Man,
> And do not drink His Blood,
>   You have no Life in you.
> He who doth eat My Flesh
> And drink My Blood,
>   Hath Eternal Life . . .
> For My Flesh is a true food,
> And My Blood, true drink:
> He that eateth My Flesh
> And drinketh My Blood
> Abideth in Me,
> And I in him.

> As it was He, the Living Father, who did send Me,
> So he that eateth Me
> He shall live, too, by Me.
> *This* is the Bread that came down out of heaven:
> Not as your fathers ate,
>   And died,
> He who eateth *this* Bread
> Shall live for ever."

TEACHING UPON THE LAW

❧ CENTRAL in Our Blessed Lord's teaching, because central in the political and religious life of the little people whom He taught, was the question of the Law. It was the unique achievement of this little God-guided people that no other pre-Christian people, small or great, had explicitly and minutely based, as they had based, their social code on an ethical code. Not even Greece, of the golden age of Plato's Republic and Aristotle's Nicomachean Ethics, had attempted what the Jews before them had attempted and achieved. Indeed, far from seeking to measure the State by an immovable or absolute ethical code, these Greek thinkers were bewildered into finding the ethical absolute in the State itself. For the Greeks, with their merely notional acceptance of God and their very definite patriotic acceptance of Greece, the good man was the good citizen. On the other hand, for the Jew, with his concept of God clearer than even his clear patriotic concept of his nation, the good man, being God's man, would necessarily be the good citizen.

The Jewish law consisted of general precepts and of particular precepts.

The general precepts were a fundamental ethical code. They were called the Decalogue or Ten Commandments. By later writers they are called the Moral Precepts.

This fundamental ethical code of moral precepts contained only the general, as distinct from the particular, duties of man to God, and of man to his fellow-men.

To these general moral precepts were added particular precepts:

1. The ceremonial precepts dealing with man's duties to God; and

2. The social or judicial precepts, dealing with man's duties to his fellow-men.

We need not remark that the fundamental ethical code was unchangeable. But the ceremonial precepts, which were preparatory for the coming of the Messiah, were unchangeable only until He came. His coming would necessarily make their continuance an untruth.

Again, the social precepts, which were laws made for the civic life of the Jewish people, and therefore not adapted to every people, had neither the essential continuance of the moral precepts, nor the essential discontinuance of the ceremonial precepts, but might or might not be continued according to the will of a people.

As there was no direct effect of Our Blessed Lord's action that was not part of His plan, we now know that He was minded (1) to support the ethical precepts of the Law; (2) to abolish the (preparatory) ceremonial precepts of the Law; and (3) to leave untouched the social precepts of the Law.

Perhaps we have not yet recognized how Our Blessed Redeemer's support of the precepts of the Natural Law mark Him off from the few men whom many of their fellow-men look on as religious leaders. Men as strong-minded as Mahomet did not feel themselves strong enough to impose sexual ethics beyond the average of their contemporaries. On the other hand, Jesus found a level of morality which it would have been easy enough, and worldly-prudent enough, *not* to follow. For example, though there had been no legal repeal of the precept "Thou shalt not commit adultery," there was such a widespread practical repeal that the legal machinery for punishing adultery by stoning the adulteress had long since ceased to function.

Lesser moralists, such as the world has often seen, would have acted on the principle: "The precept has been universally denied in practice. Let us avoid hypocrisy—let us deny it in principle." Our Blessed Lord's avoidance of this wonted way of popularity for religious reformers argues a wisdom beyond that of the worldly-wise.

This reinforcement of the moral precepts of the Law made Him many friends, especially among the simple, God-fearing people. But it also made Him many and perhaps more enemies amongst those who, like the Pharisee of the parable, thought themselves God-fearing people. If not all of them felt the lash of His denunciation of fornication and adultery, they could not help feeling scourged with thongs of truth when He spoke of honouring father and mother, and pilloried those whose tithing of mint and cummin was a breach of "Thou shalt not steal."

But if Our Blessed Lord's reinforcement of the moral precepts of the Law recruited His enemies heavily from the wicked, His abrogation of the ceremonial precepts made many enemies even of the good. These good men could see only as Sabbatarians. Their Sabbath, with its elaborate ritual, was such a national, religious, historic, artistic social synthesis and symbol that any change in it was worse than sedition. Indeed, because whoever ventured to change an institution as divine as the Sabbath claimed to be divine, it seemed to follow that Jesus, by claiming authority over the Sabbath, was implicitly claiming to be equal to God. No wonder there is a note of understanding, if not sympathy, in Our Lord's words to His apostles: "The hour cometh when whosoever killeth you will think he offereth a sacrifice to God."

These good folk, with headlong zeal for the Sabbath, did not take time to realize that it was not the substance but the passing accompaniments of the ceremonial law which Jesus was minded to abrogate. It was not sacrifice, but the lesser sacrifices of living and lifeless beings, He was abrogating. Indeed, He was prepar-

ing to fulfil and perfect all local sacrifices by the unique self-
sacrifice of the Cross. So little of what was permanent was
ended that His Apostles have transmitted to all time the weekly
sacrifice, and have laid upon their followers the duty of assisting
at that weekly sacrifice under pain of grievous sin. It is even
arguable that if the Catholic obligation of presence at the weekly
sacrifice were to fail, the very notion of man's individual and
collective duty of sacrifice to God would perish in the world.
It was not then the substance, but some of the ceremonial
accompaniments of sacrifice that were set aside when Jesus
showed Himself Master of the Sabbath. But, as preparations for
the king's coming are set aside when the king has come, so were
the elaborate legal ceremonies preparatory to the coming of the
Messiah set aside when Jesus, the Messiah, had come.

If we have ventured to suggest that Our Blessed Lord's attitude to the moral precepts and the ceremonial precepts of the
Law argued, or at least evidenced, a more than human wisdom,
that wisdom is corroborated by His attitude towards the social
precepts of the Law. Circumstances which would have led any
other reformer into political action for the good of his religious
reform left Jesus untouched. The occupation of a religious
reformer's country by a foreign nation is an opportunity for
giving his reform the cutting-edge of patriotism. Even nowadays
moral reformers commonly denounce the immorality of their
country as a foreign import. The Roman occupation of Palestine gave Our Blessed Lord an unique opportunity of enlisting
the whole force of Jewish patriotism on the side of His religious
mission. What that patriotism was capable of could be measured by the battlings and victories of the Machabees. Even as
He went from hamlet to hamlet a group of His fellow-Galileans
—perhaps after hearing His words—had made an appeal to the
sword and had soon experienced the terrible Roman wrath,
the ruthless guardian of the Roman peace.

MATTHEW SPEAKS

I

His fame had spread through Syria like flame in dry grass,
From Galilee and the Decapolis and over Jordan the people came.
Crowds came out of Judea and out of Jerusalem.

In the hearts of the old men
hope for the race smouldered again:
"Oh, that Messiah were come to set us free!"
In the hearts of the women
hope for the children flickered with faint flame:
"Oh, that Messiah were come to set them free!"
The proud heart of youth blazed, suddenly on fire:
"Oh, for our own glory, in the glory of Messiah!"

I was afraid,
I, the tax-collector,
who had sat in the custom house.
I knew men through and through,
having got my living, as it were,
by other men's despair.

I knew the humiliated,
I knew the oppressed;

I knew the king,
whom they had crowned already
in their desire:
they had created him
out of their bitterness.

Out of their broken flesh,
out of their hunger and thirst,
out of their chains—
weaponless, they had forged him a sword;
ragged, they had woven for him
purple raiment and cloth of gold for a king:
out of the festering wound,
out of the conqueror's scorn,
in dreams, the son of the race was born—
Messiah, the Son of Dreams.

I knew it all.
How often I had sat in the market-place
and seen the women there, rocking to and fro,
like those who sit by the dead to weep—
rocking, rocking, rocking,
to and fro;
trying to rock the cradled nothingness
in the barren womb
to sleep.

As for the young,
they wanted a leader, whose power
would be in his lust for power,
one whose tongue
would utter their dumb pride
in song,
one in whose heart

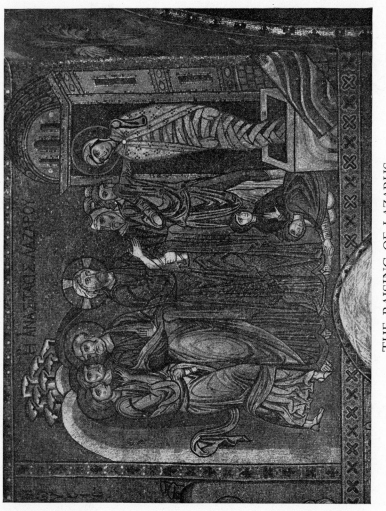

THE RAISING OF LAZARUS
12th Century Mosaic

their frightened hearts would beat
to the sound of drums.

II

I was afraid
that they would despair
when they saw the Lord.

He was very poor,
He had the chiselled features
of one who denies himself;
His hands
were the large hands
of an artisan—
and without a sword;
His eyes,
the eyes of pity and love;
His speech,
the broad, slow speech
of a countryman.

I was afraid,
But when He began to speak
it seemed to each who heard
that the word was spoken to him alone.

He dawned upon the people;
He did not take them by storm:
soft as the blown thistledown's sowing,
the seed of the Word was sown.

Each who heard
knew the light growing within him,
like morning,

slowly welling
and filling the empty sky
before the first song
of the first bird.

I understood,
when He began to teach,
why first
He had given light to blind eyes;
and to deaf ears,
the music of water and wind;
and to hands and feet that were numb,
the touch of the delicate grass and the sun;
and speech to the dumb.

For He spoke of the things
men see and taste and hold:
of salt and rock and light
and the wheat in gold;
of winds and wings and flowers
and the fruit on boughs;
of candle-light in the house.

They heard His voice,
Like the voice of a murmurous sea
a long way off, washing the shores of peace:
but each knew within him
a soundless music,
a voiceless singing,
saying:

"Feel the pulse of My love
with your finger-tips;
prove My tenderness

in the tiny beat
of the heart of the mother bird;
lay your hand on the hard bark of the tree—
know Me
in the rising sap
of the green life
in the dark.

"I have strewn the flowers
under your feet:
see if I love you:
see if My love is sweet!"

There was a thawing then,
like the melting of frost
when winter is done
and the warm sun
kisses the world.

There was a thawing then
in the hearts of the women,
and after the hard frost
of the hard years,
their unshed tears
were flowing.

They understood
how the Lord
takes the loveliest least
for His self-bestowing.

They would remember,
when they were baking bread,
how He had said

that His grace
works secretly in them,
like yeast.

When they sifted the ash
and blew the spark of the fire,
they would remember
the Breath of the Spirit
that fans the smoking flax.

He spoke of chastity,
the splendour of love;
of desire,
silver purified
in the heart of the fire;
of thought,
white linen spread
for the marriage feast.

Then
the men knew,
with a great sighing of joy,
that the dead bough
must fall from the living tree;
the fetid thought,
the furtive word,
the seeping lust,
the cloying grief,
the blight on the green leaf,
the hard fruit
with soft rot at the core,
would be no more,
no more.
But the heart would be born again

to a white maying and morning
and first falling in love.

III

Christ looked at the people.
He saw them assailed by fear:
He saw the locked door;
He saw the knife in the hand;
He saw the buried coin;
He saw the unworn coat,
consumed by moth;
He saw the stagnant water
drawn and kept in the pitcher,
the musty bread in the bin—
the defended,
the unshared,
the ungiven.

He told them then
of the love
that casts out fear,
of the love that is four walls
and a roof over the head:
of the knife in the sheath,
of the coin in the open hand,
of the coin given
warm with the giver's life,
of the water poured in the cup,
of the table spread—
the undefended,
the shared,
the given—
the Kingdom of Heaven.

Christ looked at the people.
He saw the hard years
graven upon their faces;
He saw the old clothes,
worn to the shape of their work;
He saw their unshed tears;
He saw the labourer's hands,
hollowed out by the tools
as His own were hollowed out
by the mallet to cup the nail.

He saw the crust of the will,
like the hard crust of rye;
He saw flesh and blood,
the sacramentals of love;
He saw the image of God,
the crystal in the rock.

He lifted
His large and beautiful hands
to bless.

TEACHING UPON POVERTY

I

⚞ THE SON OF GOD expected those who served His Father to welcome Him, and it was for them that He came. When He opened the prophecy of Isaias in the synagogue at Nazareth, He chose this passage: "The spirit of the Lord is upon me. Wherefore he hath anointed me to speak the gospel to the poor: he hath sent me to heal the contrite of heart. To preach deliverance to the captives and sight to the blind, to set at liberty them that are bruised, to preach the acceptable year of the Lord and the day of reward. And when he had folded the book he restored it to the minister and sat down. And the eyes of all in the synagogue were fixed on him." Then He spoke with authority, "This day is fulfilled this scripture in your ears."

When He had before Him the crowd of the poor, the crippled, the unfortunates of all sorts who had followed Him into His solitude, He raised His eyes to them, says St. Luke—we can imagine with what love—and cried out: "Blessed are ye poor." It was as though the whole meaning of His message lay in that: You have no idea how lucky you are! I have come to tell you, I have brought you the good news! At His birth, His first thought was for a group of poor men: He had sent an angel to the shepherds near by, to tell them from Him: "I bring you good tidings of great joy." And in case John the Baptist might be astonished

at His puzzling way of revealing Himself, instead of making the
glitter expected of the Messias, He answered His forerunner's
disciples: "Go and relate to John what you have heard and seen;
the blind see, the lame walk, the lepers are made clean, the deaf
hear, the dead rise again, to the poor the gospel is preached."
The sentence clearly rises past the raising of the dead to a climax,
to a kind of miracle still more amazing than those first mentioned. Does it not imply that it is even more extraordinary for
the poor to have the gospel preached to them than for the dead
to be raised again? I find it hard not to think so. In any case, the
last phrase is certainly not the once exception in a list made
up of miracles.

To announce the gospel to the poor is, surely, the hardest
thing of all, for it is making them see that for them happiness
consists in being poor.

Our Lord then preached by example. He chose to live in a
nation that had lost its heritage, during a tragic period of its
history. Christians do not give enough thought to the conditions
in which He lived. They picture the charming scenes at Galilee,
or the simplicity of His life with the fishermen of the lake, without seeing the darker colours of His country and His time.
Palestine cut a sad figure in human eyes beside Tyre and the
great empires nearby. And by the time God came to live there,
she had long been trampled underfoot by the nations. The
Syrians, the Egyptians, the Chaldeans, the Assyrians, the Greeks
and the Romans had all ravaged her. She was an occupied country and her conquerors were harsh.

What are the estimates of historians worth? One says: "If one
reckoned up all those who fell during the wars and revolutions
and added those assassinated by the orders of Herod and the
procurators, during that dreadful century, the total would be
at least two hundred thousand men—a terrifying number for so
small a country, and even more terrifying when one considers
that those who died on the battlefields were the physical élite of

the nation, and Herod's victims represented the intellectual élite."
It is hard to see how we can establish even an approximate
figure, but the impressions of the scholars do call up a picture
of the misery and suffering in which Christ chose to live His
life so totally. That was the context—it was to those men at that
time and in that country that He was preaching the blessedness
of poverty, and of tears, of gentleness and peace. And that is the
tone of the Gospel.

How great was Christ's personal poverty in this impoverished
time? The indications given us by the Gospel are like the
remains of a very old painting; men who cannot understand
them tear them apart wondering how they can be compatible,
never realising what the atmosphere of those early days was really
like. On one side you have the birth in the stable, then later
the accusation that He loves good meat and good wine, an accusation which must have had some sort of basis; and at the heart
of everything the frightful abjection of His Passion and Cross.
I know that mediocre men will always explain the Gospel according to their own mediocre ideals; they see Jesus leading a
simple life of moderate means, with certain privations and trials,
no doubt, but on the whole realising an average degree of comfort, without excess in either direction until the Passion. On the
other hand there are tormented imaginations which see it all
as tragic. Examine the facts carefully, hear what the exegetes
have to say, try to bring the whole thing alive—you can do this
because of the "sense of Christ" Our Lord inspires in the faithful through the Church—and you will not be able to accept
either interpretation. You must somehow unite them—going
further in both directions!

For the compass of Christ is always a union of extremes. We
can never exaggerate the position the Cross held in His mind.
It obsessed Him all His life with a strength that was the strength
of His love. A single glimpse of the "furnace" that His heart was,
and of the wealth of the suffering He chose to undergo, makes

it clear that even when His way of living looked like any other man's the work of the Spirit must have been intense. If He was placing Himself within our limits, He was doing so with an infinite ardour. As His Transfiguration manifested for a moment the glory whose splendour was always with Him, so the astonishing destitution He underwent revealed His passionate thirst for poverty. But while the Transfiguration was a single incident, which He showed to only three witnesses, He continually and openly suffered extreme humiliations because He had become man, and must touch the depths of man's miseries. However low we fall, we will always find Him lower. But with His immense liberty of soul, He would not be restricted to one single line. He took advantage of riches where He found them, visiting Levi, Zachaeus, and Simon, honouring their meals by the very sharing of them. He was too utterly poor to consider poverty an absolute value: He was detached even from poverty. Possessing every perfection, He must have been able to say with even more right than His apostle: "I have learned in whatsoever state I am to be content therewith. I know both how to be brought low, and I know how to abound (everywhere and in all things I am instructed): both to be full and to be hungry: both to abound and to suffer need" (Phil. iv, 11–12). St. Paul concludes: "I can do all things, in him who strengtheneth me." How much more, then, was Christ Himself, the Author of that strength, wholly independent alike of possessions and privations.

He was born in a stable, and while we must see all that centuries of Christian meditation have seen in the fact, we must also realise that this solitary and sheltered place was far less painful than the crowding, the vulgarity, the noise of the caravanserai, where His parents could find no room. Nazareth was thought a wretched little place; its name appears neither in the Old Testament nor the rabbinical writings, and we find it said, "Can anything of good come from Nazareth?" Its houses were rather hollowed out of the crumbling rock than built up from

without, and the air in them was the air of a cellar. But the
earth was fertile, the harvests yielded a hundredfold, there was
abundance of olive oil, and Joseph the carpenter cannot have
had much trouble in making a living for himself and his family.
The people were slow-witted and violent. As in our own lives,
bitter and sweet were mixed inextricably in everything. You
have not got to see the picture as one of unrelieved blackness.
Tragedy lives far below the outer crust of experience.

Just before Our Lord began His ministry, the devil tempted
Him to turn His spiritual wealth to material profit: to turn
stones into bread. He replied, as He was so often to insist later,
that God's word was enough—so much so that by a sort of over-
measure or "bonus" it even sustained physical life. But this trust
in God's help remained within the framework of the needs God
willed and never became rash or presumptuous. "It is written:
thou shalt not tempt the Lord thy God." And lastly, He refused
the earthly power and glory offered Him. He triumphed by abas-
ing Himself to adore God.

We see Him next as a preacher, and He shows at once the
selflessness of the apostle. Now this was more than just a necessary means, something called for by the very nature of apostle-
ship. Our Lord parted company with His mother. She hastened
the hour of parting herself, by asking Him to perform His first
miracle, at Cana. He showed that He was God, Lord of the
elements. He left her, denied Himself her companionship, because He had a task to perform as the Word of God. And when
she followed Him (perhaps because the anguish became too
keen, or perhaps giving way to the entreaties and complaints
of His cousins), He seemed absolutely to repel her. Mary then
disappears from the gospel, and we do not see her again till
Calvary, where she completes her sacrifice with her Son's.

He tramped the roads. He often spent whole nights in prayer
in the wilderness. He had no home, "Nowhere to lay his head."
One day He had no money to pay the tribute for Himself and

Peter, and the only thing to do was to perform a miracle to get the drachma they needed. However, do not let us exaggerate. The apostles had a purse which Judas had charge of, and it must generally have been full, since Judas found in it something to steal, and when they were in unfriendly country, they did not depend on what they were given, but bought food. There were holy women, some of them rich, who devoted themselves to Christ and His disciples and helped them. He took pleasure in being entertained in at least one household—Bethany; there they went to such trouble for Him that He begged for more simplicity: "One dish is enough" (that was the immediate meaning of the "one thing necessary"—surely so homely a phrase never had such spiritual resonances!). He opened His heart quite naturally to friendship.

These very human characteristics, together with those mentioned earlier, take on fullness of meaning when we remember that Our Lord came to give us an example of detachment, when we know that He knew "what was in men's hearts," when we see everything, as we must, in the light of the Passion. He saw every detail of it with His divine knowledge, His own prophetic sight of the future, and the writings of the prophets who had announced His coming. Towards the Passion He went with an anguish that made Him groan, and yet with an unutterable longing (John xii, 27). That was why He was here. "But for this cause I came unto this hour." During this "hour" His actions had a redemptive power, not so much because they were what they were as because He offered them for us with infinite love. He could have saved the world by any one of them, but Eternal Wisdom willed this frightful overabundance of suffering and humiliation; the reason, I suppose, was to give this love full scope for its ardour, and to bring men to realise the near frenzy of it. It was suffering indeed, and Christians should strive to understand it, though they can never see it clearly or sorrowfully enough. But it was even more a stripping off of everything—

utter abandonment. The Passion was the collapse of the great hope, a failure made shameful by the gibes of men. It was a tearing away of everything even down to His clothes, in Latin, *habitus,* what we *have,* what is most clearly ours, the last thing left us as long as anything is left us at all. When we reach the point of losing even our clothes, then we have certainly lost the most fundamental of the gifts we *can* lose, our dignity. We are brought down to our very essence. But Christ knew the most mysterious dereliction of all. He was betrayed by His friends, reduced to the state of a criminal slave, "delivered into the hands of men"—and nothing could be more terrible than that: in the instability of the world today, when no barrier seems to stand against human cruelty, we begin to see what it means to be delivered into the hands of men. Men, furious at the disappointment of their hopes, made a mock of Christ, cast Him out of their world, thrust Him up towards Heaven on a cross.

II

St. Paul says that for *us* Christ, who was richness itself, became poor (1 Cor. viii, 9). Christ's teaching—being at once extreme and moderate—is as complex as His example. We can only realise its perfect oneness by an impulse of the Holy Ghost. Anyone with no sense of eternal life will find it contradictory.

There are critics who see in it two irreconcilable doctrines. Men who can see no further than this world are short-sighted, and cannot see into the distance where they meet. On the one hand, they see Our Lord violently condemning riches, on the other simply giving in to the accepted state of things in a world founded on them.

"Woe to you that are rich. . . ." "It is easier for a camel (or a cable, says another translation), to pass through the eye of a needle, than for a rich man to enter into the kingdom of heaven." Money is called "the mammon of iniquity." In this regard, Jesus, usually so gentle, appears far harsher when it comes to the point than His terrible cousin, John the Baptist. The precursor, when it came to practical questions, was quite moderate. He shook the crowd by the force with which he spoke, but when they asked in fear and trembling, "What then? . . . What must we do?", he simply replied that they must share out their goods, so that what the rich had above their needs might be given to those who had needs to fill. Dealing with the publicans and soldiers—both of whose jobs involved extorting money—he did not even order them to right the wrongs they had done; he simply said to them: "Do nothing more than that which is appointed you. . . . Do violence to no man. . . . Be content with your pay." Whereas Jesus answered: "Go sell what thou hast and give to the poor." He snatched the tax-collector away from his counter. And if anyone objected: "How then is a man to live?", His answer, at least as some have seen it, was: "Only the baser sort worry about that."

And yet, it has also been argued that He was willing to accommodate Himself to the conventions of property as they were seen by the world of His day. So much so that a whole system of conservative morality has been formulated from the gospel; more or less like this: (1) It is not indispensable for the rich to give away all their goods (Matt. x, 42). (2) Property must be respected (Luke xvi, 11; xx, 14; xv, 12). (3) It is perfectly legitimate to let out to rent, to trade, to lend at interest, to make money (Matt. xxv, 16). (4) A certain prudent self-interest is praiseworthy (Matt. xiii, 44; xviii, 34; xxv, 14). (5) Christ promised material riches to all who believed (Luke xviii, 29).

Looking at these two groups of facts and teachings, the modern man who wonders whether Christ was a capitalist or a communist comes to the conclusion that there is simply no way of reconciling His teachings.

Loisy finds his own way out: he thinks that Our Lord expected the world to end very shortly, and therefore thought that none of it mattered very much. All He thought necessary was a sort of "interim morality."

Now we know that Christ founded His Church to last for all
the centuries, and we also know that during all those centuries,
material realities have been enormously important, their influence truly immeasurable. How? Beyond our line of vision. And
not in their own right, but rather because of the heart that is
fixed on them.

What Christ is really saying is that riches and poverty have
no value in themselves. What matters is how we treat them.
We have got to use our earthly life to get beyond this earth. We
are at work to establish the Kingdom of God here as far as we
can, which means that the realities of this world must be transfigured, but first we must, so to speak, turn them round. Our
point of view is divine, our object is divine, but our material is
the realities of this world. It is a carrying-on of the law of the
Incarnation.

SONNET

 Almighty God, whose justice like a sun
Shall coruscate along the floors of Heaven,
Raising what's low, perfecting what's undone,
Breaking the proud and making odd things even.
The poor of Jesus Christ along the street
In your rain sodden, in your snows unshod,
They have nor hearth, nor sword, nor human meat,
Nor even the bread of men: Almighty God.

The poor of Jesus Christ whom no man hears
Have waited on your vengeance much too long.
Wipe out not tears but blood: our eyes bleed tears.
Come smite our damnéd sophistries so strong
That thy rude hammer battering this rude wrong
Ring down the abyss of twice ten thousand years.

THE RIDDLES OF THE GOSPEL

WE HAVE ALL heard people say a hundred times over, for they never seem to tire of saying it, that the Jesus of the New Testament is indeed a most merciful and humane lover of humanity, but that the Church has hidden this human character in repellent dogmas and stiffened it with ecclesiastical terrors till it has taken on an inhuman character. This, I venture to repeat, is very nearly the reverse of the truth. The truth is that it is the image of Christ in the churches that is almost entirely mild and merciful. It is the image of Christ in the Gospels that is a good many other things as well. The figure in the Gospels does indeed utter in words of almost heartbreaking beauty his pity for our broken hearts. But they are very far from being the only sort of words that he utters. Nevertheless they are almost the only kind of words that the Church in its popular imagery ever represents him as uttering. That popular imagery is inspired by a perfectly sound popular instinct. The mass of the poor are broken, and the mass of the people are poor, and for the mass of mankind the main thing is to carry the conviction of the incredible compassion of God. But nobody with his eyes open can doubt that it is chiefly this idea of compassion that the popular machinery of the Church does seek to carry. The popular imagery carries a great deal to excess the sentiment of "Gentle Jesus, meek and mild." It is the first thing that the outsider feels and criticises in a Pietà or a shrine of the

Sacred Heart. As I say, while the art may be insufficient, I am not sure that the instinct is unsound. In any case, there is something appalling, something that makes the blood run cold, in the idea of having a statue of Christ in wrath. There is something insupportable even to the imagination in the idea of turning the corner of a street or coming out into the spaces of a market-place, to meet the petrifying petrifaction of *that* figure as it turned upon a generation of vipers, or that face as it looked at the face of a hypocrite. The Church can reasonably be justified therefore if she turns the most merciful face or aspect towards men; but it is certainly the most merciful aspect that she does turn.

And the point is here that it is very much more specially and exclusively merciful than any impression that could be formed by a man merely reading the New Testament for the first time. A man simply taking the words of the story as they stand would form quite another impression; an impression full of mystery and possibly of inconsistency; but certainly not merely an impression of mildness. It would be intensely interesting; but part of the interest would consist in its leaving a good deal to be guessed at or explained. It is full of sudden gestures evidently significant except that we hardly know what they signify; of enigmatic silences; of ironical replies. The outbreaks of wrath, like storms above our atmosphere, do not seem to break out exactly where we should expect them, but to follow some higher weather-chart of their own. The Peter whom popular Church teaching presents is very rightly the Peter to whom Christ said in forgiveness "Feed my lambs." He is not the Peter upon whom Christ turned as if he were the devil, crying in that obscure wrath, "Get thee behind me, Satan." Christ lamented with nothing but love and pity over Jerusalem which was to murder him. We do not know what strange spiritual atmosphere or spiritual insight led him to sink Bethsaida lower in the pit than Sodom. I am putting aside for the moment all questions

of doctrinal inferences or expositions, orthodox or otherwise; I
am simply imagining the effect on a man's mind if he did really
do what these critics are always talking about doing; if he did
really read the New Testament without reference to orthodoxy
and even without reference to doctrine. He would find a number
of things which fit in far less with the current unorthodoxy than
they do with the current orthodoxy. He would find, for instance,
that if there are any descriptions that deserve to be called realis-
tic, they are precisely the descriptions of the supernatural. If
there is one aspect of the New Testament Jesus in which he
may be said to present himself eminently as a practical person,
it is in the aspect of an exorcist. There is nothing meek and
mild, there is nothing even in the ordinary sense mystical, about
the tone of the voice that says, "Hold thy peace and come out
of him." It is much more like the tone of a very business-like
lion-tamer or a strong-minded doctor dealing with a homicidal
maniac. But this is only a side issue for the sake of illustration;
I am not now raising these controversies; but considering the
case of the imaginary man from the moon to whom the New
Testament is new.

Now the first thing to note is that if we take it merely as a
human story, it is in some ways a very strange story. I do not
refer here to its tremendous and tragic culmination or to any
implications involving triumph in that tragedy. I do not refer
to what is commonly called the miraculous element; for on that
point philosophies vary and modern philosophies very decidedly waver. Indeed the educated Englishman of today may be
said to have passed from an old fashion, in which he would not
believe in any miracles unless they were ancient, and adopted
a new fashion in which he will not believe in any miracles
unless they are modern. He used to hold that miraculous cures
stopped with the first Christians and is now inclined to suspect
that they began with the first Christian Scientists. But I refer
here rather specially to unmiraculous and even to unnoticed and

rather inconspicuous parts of the story. There are a great many things about it which nobody would have invented, for they are things which nobody has ever made any particular use of; things which if they were remarked at all have remained rather as puzzles. For instance there is that long stretch of silence in the life of Christ up to the age of thirty. It is of all silences the most immense and imaginatively impressive. But it is not the sort of thing that anybody is particularly likely to invent in order to prove something; and nobody so far as I know has ever tried to prove anything in particular from it. It is impressive, but it is only impressive as a fact; there is nothing particularly popular or obvious about it as a fable. The ordinary trend of hero-worship and myth-making is much more likely to say the precise opposite. It is much more likely to say (as I believe some of the gospels rejected by the Church do say) that Jesus displayed a divine precocity and began his mission at a miraculously early age. And there is indeed something strange in the thought that he who of all humanity needed least preparation seems to have had most. Whether it was some mode of the divine humility, or some truth of which we see the shadow in the longer domestic tutelage of the higher creatures of the earth, I do not propose to speculate; I mention it simply as an example of the sort of thing that does in any case give rise to speculations, quite apart from recognised religious speculations. Now the whole story is full of these things. It is not by any means, as baldly presented in print, a story that is easy to get to the bottom of. It is anything but what these people talk of as a simple Gospel. Relatively speaking, it is the Gospel that has the mysticism and the Church that has the rationalism. As I should put it, of course, it is the Gospel that is the riddle and the Church that is the answer. But whatever is the answer, the Gospel as it stands is almost a book of riddles.

First, a man reading the Gospel sayings would not find platitudes. If he had read, even in the most respectful spirit, the

majority of ancient philosophers and of modern moralists, he
would appreciate the unique importance of saying that he did
not find platitudes. It is more than can be said even of Plato.
It is much more than can be said of Epictetus or Seneca or
Marcus Aurelius or Appollonius of Tyana. And it is immeasurably more than can be said of most of the agnostic moralists
and the preachers of the ethical societies; with their songs of
service and their religion of brotherhood. The morality of most
moralists, ancient and modern, has been one solid and polished
cataract of platitudes flowing for ever and ever. That would
certainly not be the impression of the imaginary independent
outsider studying the New Testament. He would be conscious
of nothing so commonplace and in a sense of nothing so continuous as that stream. He would find a number of strange claims
that might sound like the claim to be the brother of the sun and
moon; a number of very startling pieces of advice; a number of
stunning rebukes; a number of strangely beautiful stories. He
would see some very gigantesque figures of speech about the
impossibility of threading a needle with a camel or the possibility of throwing a mountain into the sea. He would see a
number of very daring simplifications of the difficulties of life;
like the advice to shine upon everybody indifferently as does the
sunshine or not to worry about the future any more than the
birds. He would find on the other hand some passages of almost
impenetrable darkness, so far as he is concerned, such as the
moral of the parable of the Unjust Steward. Some of these
things might strike him as fables and some as truths; but none
as truisms. For instance, he would not find the ordinary platitudes in favour of peace. He would find several paradoxes in
favour of peace. He would find several ideals of non-resistance,
which taken as they stand would be rather too pacific for any
pacifist. He would be told in one passage to treat a robber *not*
with passive resistance, but rather with positive and enthusiastic
encouragement, if the terms be taken literally; heaping up gifts

upon the man who had stolen goods. But he would not find a word of all that obvious rhetoric against war which has filled countless books and odes and orations; not a word about the wickedness of war, the wastefulness of war, the appalling scale of the slaughter in war and all the rest of the familiar frenzy; indeed not a word about war at all. There is nothing that throws any particular light on Christ's attitude towards organised warfare, except that he seems to have been rather fond of Roman soldiers. Indeed it is another perplexity, speaking from the same external and human standpoint, that he seems to have got on much better with Romans than he did with Jews. But the question here is a certain tone to be appreciated by merely reading a certain text; and we might give any number of instances of it.

The statement that the meek shall inherit the earth is very far from being a meek statement. I mean it is not meek in the ordinary sense of mild and moderate and inoffensive. To justify it, it would be necessary to go very deep into history and anticipate things undreamed of then and by many unrealised even now; such as the way in which the mystical monks reclaimed the lands which the practical kings had lost. If it was a truth at all, it was because it was a prophecy. But certainly it was not a truth in the sense of a truism. The blessing upon the meek would seem to be a very violent statement; in the sense of doing violence to reason and probability. And with this we come to another important stage in the speculation. As a prophecy it really was fulfilled; but it was only fulfilled long afterwards. The monasteries were the most practical and prosperous estates and experiments in reconstruction after the barbaric deluge; the meek really did inherit the earth. But nobody could have known anything of the sort at the time—unless indeed there was one who knew. Something of the same thing may be said about the incident of Martha and Mary; which has been interpreted in retrospect and from the inside by mystics of the Christian contemplative life. But it was not at all an obvious view of it; and

most moralists, ancient and modern, could be trusted to make
a rush for the obvious. What torrents of effortless eloquence
would have flowed from them to swell any slight superiority
on the part of Martha; what splendid sermons about the Joy
of Service and the Gospel of Work and the World Left Better
than We Found It, and generally all the ten thousand platitudes
in favour of taking trouble—by people who need take no trouble
to utter them. If in Mary the mystic and child of love Christ
was guarding the seed of something more subtle, who was likely
to understand it at the time? Nobody else could have seen Clare
and Catherine and Teresa shining above the little roof at
Bethany. It is so in another way with that magnificent menace
about bringing into the world a sword to sunder and divide.
Nobody could have guessed then either how it could be fulfilled
or how it could be justified. Indeed some freethinkers are still
so simple as to fall into the trap and be shocked at a phrase so
deliberately defiant. They actually complain of the paradox for
not being a platitude.

But the point here is that if we *could* read the Gospel reports
as things as new as newspaper reports, they would puzzle us
and perhaps terrify us *much* more than the same things as
developed by historical Christianity. For instance; Christ after
a clear allusion to the eunuchs of eastern courts said there
would be eunuchs of the kingdom of heaven. If this does not
mean the voluntary enthusiasm of virginity, it could only be
made to mean something much more unnatural or uncouth. It
is the historical religion that humanises it for us by experience
of Franciscans or of Sisters of Mercy. The mere statement standing by itself might very well suggest a rather dehumanised
atmosphere; the sinister and inhuman silence of the Asiatic
harem and divan. This is but one instance out of scores; but the
moral is that the Christ of the Gospel might actually seem more
strange and terrible than the Christ of the Church.

I am dwelling on the dark or dazzling or defiant or mysterious

side of the Gospel words, not because they had not obviously
a more obvious and popular side, but because this is the answer
to a common criticism on a vital point. The freethinker frequently says that Jesus of Nazareth was a man of his time, even
if he was in advance of his time; and that we cannot accept his
ethics as final for humanity. The freethinker then goes on to
criticise his ethics, saying plausibly enough that men cannot
turn the other cheek, or that they must take thought for the
morrow, or that the self-denial is too ascetic or the monogamy
too severe. But the Zealots and the Legionaries did not turn the
other cheek, any more than we do, if so much. The Jewish
traders and Roman tax-gatherers took thought for the morrow
as much as we do, if not more. We cannot pretend to be abandoning the morality of the past for one more suited to the
present. It is certainly not the morality of another age, but it
might be of another world.

In short, we can say that these ideals are impossible in themselves. Exactly what we cannot say is that they are impossible
for us. They are rather notably marked by a mysticism which,
if it be a sort of madness, would always have struck the same
sort of people as mad. Take, for instance, the case of marriage
and the relations of the sexes. It might very well have been true
that a Galilean teacher taught things natural to a Galilean envi-
ronment; but it is not. It might rationally be expected that a man
in the time of Tiberius would have advanced a view conditioned
by the time of Tiberius; but he did not. What he advanced was
something quite different; something very difficult; but something no more difficult now than it was then. When, for instance, Mahomet made his polygamous compromise we may
reasonably say that it was conditioned by a polygamous society.
When he allowed a man four wives he was really doing something suited to the circumstances, which might have been less
suited to other circumstances. Nobody will pretend that the
four wives were like the four winds, something seemingly a

part of the order of nature; nobody will say that the figure four
was written for ever in stars upon the sky. But neither will anyone say that the figure four is an inconceivable ideal; that it is
beyond the power of man to count up to four; or to count the
number of his wives and see whether it amounts to four. It is
a practical compromise carrying with it the character of a particular society. If Mahomet had been born in Acton in the nineteenth century, we may well doubt whether he would instantly
have filled that suburb with harems of four wives apiece. As he
was born in Arabia in the sixth century, he did in his conjugal
arrangements suggest the conditions of Arabia in the sixth century. But Christ in his view of marriage does not in the least
suggest the conditions of Palestine in the first century. He does
not suggest anything at all, except the sacramental view of marriage as developed long afterwards by the Catholic Church. It
was quite as difficult for people then as it is for people now. It
was much more puzzling for people then than to people now.
Jews and Romans and Greeks did not believe, and did not even
understand enough to disbelieve, the mystical idea that the man
and the woman become one sacramental substance. We may
think it an impossible or incredible ideal; but we cannot think
it any more incredible or impossible than they would have
thought it. In other words, whatever else is true, it is not true
that the controversy has been altered by time. Whatever else is
true, it is emphatically not true that the ideas of Jesus of Nazareth were suitable to his time, but are no longer suitable to our
time. Exactly how suitable they were to his time is perhaps suggested in the end of his story. . . .

The truth is that when critics have spoken of the local limitations of the Galilean, it has always been a case of the local limitations of the critics. He did undoubtedly believe in certain
things that one particular modern sect of materialists do not believe. But they were not things particularly peculiar to his time.
Doubtless it would be nearer still to the truth to say merely that

a certain solemn social importance, in the minority disbelieving them, is peculiar to our time. He believed, for instance, in evil spirits or in the psychic healing of bodily ills; but not because he was a Galilean born under Augustus. It is absurd to say that a man believed things because he was a Galilean under Augustus when he might have believed the same things if he had been an Egyptian under Tuten-kamen or an Indian under Genghis Khan. It is enough to say that the materialists have to prove the impossibility of miracles against the testimony of all mankind, not against the prejudices of provincials in North Palestine under the first Roman Emperors. What they have to prove, for the present argument, is the presence in the Gospels of those particular prejudices of those particular provincials. And, humanly speaking, it is astonishing how little they can produce even to make a beginning of it.

So it is in this case of the sacrament of marriage. We may not believe in sacraments, as we may not believe in spirits, but it is quite clear that Christ believed in this sacrament in his own way and not in any current or contemporary way. He certainly did not get his argument against divorce from the Mosaic law or the Roman law or the habits of the Palestinian people. It would appear to his critics then exactly what it appears to his critics now; an arbitrary and transcendental dogma coming from nowhere save in the sense that it comes from him. I am not at all concerned here to defend that dogma; the point here is that it is just as easy to defend it now as it was to defend it then. It is an ideal altogether outside time; difficult at any period; impossible at no period. In other words, if anyone says it is what might be expected of a man walking about in that place at that period, we can quite fairly answer that it is much *more* like what might be the mysterious utterance of a being beyond man, if he walked alive among men.

I maintain, therefore, that a man reading the New Testament frankly and freshly would *not* get the impression of what is

now often meant by a human Christ. The merely human Christ
is a made-up figure, a piece of artificial selection, like the merely
evolutionary man. Moreover there have been too many of these
human Christs found in the same story, just as there have been
too many keys to mythology found in the same stories. Three or
four separate schools of rationalism have worked over the ground
and produced three or four equally rational explanations of his
life. The first rational explanation of his life was that he never
lived. And this in turn gave an opportunity for three or four
different explanations; as that he was a sun-myth or a corn-
myth or any other kind of myth that is also a monomania. Then
the idea that he was a divine being who did not exist gave place
to the idea that he was a human being who did exist. In my
youth it was the fashion to say that he was merely an ethical
teacher in the manner of the Essenes, who apparently had nothing very much to say that Hillel or a hundred other Jews might
not have said; as that it is a kindly thing to be kind and an assist-
ance to purification to be pure. Then somebody said he was a
madman with a Messianic delusion. Then others said he was
indeed an original teacher because he cared about nothing but
Socialism; or (as others said) about nothing but Pacifism. Then
a more grimly scientific character appeared who said that Jesus
would never have been heard of at all except for his prophecies
of the end of the world. He was important merely as a Millen-
narian; and created a provincial scare by announcing the exact
date of the crack of doom. Among other variants on the same
theme was the theory that he was a spiritual healer and nothing
else; a view implied by Christian Science, which has really to
expound a Christianity without the Crucifixion in order to explain the curing of Peter's wife's mother or the daughter of a
centurion. There is another theory that concentrates entirely on
the business of diabolism and what it would call the contemporary superstition about demoniacs; as if Christ, like a young
deacon taking his first orders, had got as far as exorcism and

never got any further. Now each of these explanations in itself seems to me singularly inadequate; but taken together they do suggest something of the very mystery which they miss. There must surely have been something not only mysterious but many-sided about Christ if so many smaller Christs can be carved out of him. If the Christian Scientist is satisfied with him as a spiritual healer and the Christian Socialist is satisfied with him as a social reformer, so satisfied that they do not even expect him to be anything else, it looks as if he really covered rather more ground than they could be expected to expect. And it does seem to me that there might be more than they fancy in these other mysterious attributes of casting out devils or prophesying doom.

We should have a worse shock if we really imagined the nature of Christ named for the first time. What should we feel at the first whisper of a certain suggestion about a certain man? Certainly it is not for us to blame anyone who should find that first wild whisper merely impious and insane. On the contrary, stumbling on that rock of scandal is the first step. Stark staring incredulity is a far more loyal tribute to that truth than a modernist metaphysic that would make it out merely a matter of degree. It were better to rend our robes with a great cry against blasphemy, like Caiaphas in the judgment, or to lay hold of the man as a maniac possessed of devils like the kinsmen and the crowd, rather than to stand stupidly debating fine shades of pantheism in the presence of so catastrophic a claim. There is more of the wisdom that is one with surprise in any simple person, full of the sensitiveness of simplicity, who should expect the grass to wither and the birds to drop dead out of the air, when a strolling carpenter's apprentice said calmly and almost carelessly, like one looking over his shoulder: "Before Abraham was, I am."

WILLIAM LANGLAND

POVERTY AS THE BEST LIFE

I MOVE THIS MATTER most of all for poor folk,
For in their likeness our Lord often has been discovered.
Witness in the Pascal Week, when he walked to Emmaus.
Cleophas did not recognize Christ before them
Through his poor apparel and pilgrim garments,
Till he blessed and broke the bread that they were eating.
They were aware by his works that he was Jesus,
But they could not tell him by his talk and clothing.

All this was in example to us sinful people
That we should all be lowly and loving in our speaking,
And not apparel us over proudly, for we are pilgrims together.
God has many times been met among needy people
In the apparel of a poor man and in a pilgrim's likeness,
But never a soul has seen him in the sect of rich folk.

Saint John and other Saints were seen in poor clothing,
And were pilgrims praying for men's almsdeeds.
Jesus alighted upon a Jew's daughter of gentle lineage,
Yet a pure and poor maid, and wedded to a poor man.

Martha moved a complaint against Mary Magdalene
And said such words to our Saviour himself:

*Domine, non est tibi curae quod soror mea reliquit me solam
     ministrare.*
God answered hastily that he followed either,
Both Mary's way and Martha's way, as Matthew bears witness,
But God put poverty first and praised it more highly.
Maria optimam partem elegit, quae non, etc.
All the wise men that ever were, by aught that I can witness,
Praise poverty as the best life, if patience follow it,
As by far the more blessed and better than riches.
Although it is sour to suffer, sweet comes after,
There is a rough rind around the walnut,
But after that bitter bark has been shelled away
There is a kernel of comfort which conduces health—
So after poverty or penance patiently suffered;
For that makes men mindful of God, and more truly willing
To weep and to pray well, whence mercy arises.
And thus Christ is the kernel and comfort of the spirit.
The poor man sleeps more soundly and safely than others.
He dreads death, darkness and robbers
Less than he who is rich, as reason witnesses:
Pauper ego ludo, dum tu dives meditaris.

SON OF MAN

⯈ THE FORM UNDER WHICH the testimony of Jesus is offered must remain enigmatic, and even incomprehensible, to anyone who does not recall the restless, wholly material and national, even chimerical character of the hopes of Israel at that time. Apart from this setting, how can we explain the safeguards, the qualifications, the reticence, or (to use the word adopted by the ancient Fathers in this connection) the economy, employed by Jesus in the affirmation of his mission and the revelation of his dignity?

The whole Jewish world was then expecting a Messias, and this expectation had, on the showing of pagan historians, overflowed through all the East and beyond. How simple it would have been to say: "I am he!"

But in place of that categorical assertion, what do we see? The Master imposes silence on those possessed with spirits who proclaim him "the Holy One of God" (Mark i, 25), the "Son of God" (Mark iii, 11-12), "Jesus, Son of the Most High God" (Mark v, 7), etc. We hear him forbid his disciples to make him known as the Messias (Mark viii, 30; ix, 8); he avoids the eagerness of the crowds (Mark i, 36-38; viii, 10; John vi, 14-16); and he deliberately extinguishes the fame of his miracles (Mark i, 41-44; v, 43; vii, 32-36). Finally we see him, while proclaiming the advent of the Kingdom of God, at times eluding, as a distasteful subject, direct questions concerning his own part in the establishment of this Kingdom. At this point the reader of the Gospels is tempted to share the feeling expressed by a group of impatient hearers: "How long wilt thou hold our souls in suspense? If thou art the Christ, tell us so openly!" (John x, 24).

But Jesus had at least two reasons for not so acting, the first unconnected with the second. Let us recall the characteristics by which we have already described the Herodians on the one hand and the Zealots on the other; let us realise what was the situation in Palestine. In those divided, stormy surroundings, in which the watchword of one party was "Above all, no connection with Rome!", and in which the feverish expectation of the others anticipated the coming of a warrior-king who would drive the Gentiles from the Holy Land, a resounding Messianic claim on his part would have aroused their fears and galvanized their hopes. Thence would spring troubles and violent repressions, which Jesus did not wish to break out until the hour fixed by Providence: nor was it the object of his mission to quell them by force of miracles. Even as it was, in spite of the "economy" he used, the Master had more than once to flee the indiscreet enthusiasm of the people. Did they not talk of taking him and proclaiming him king? . . .

That is why Jesus, faithful to the idea of the Kingdom which he was to describe in the parables of the leaven and of the mustard-seed, adopted a rigid economy in the statement of his personal message. Following the footsteps of the ancient prophets and of John, he began by stirring up in men of good will, who were already moved by the Baptist's preaching, that uneasiness, that fruitful disquiet, that compunction, that hunger and that thirst for justice which, according to the Scriptures, was to mark the dawn of the Kingdom of God. For pictures of prosperity, of revenge, and of external glory, he substituted more humble, more intimate, more personal views, an indispensable prepara-

tion for the understanding of and inclination to accept the
Gospel. Meanwhile, from the very beginning of his preaching,
the Master performed those works of kindness, of deliverance,
and of power, foretold by the great seers of the past. In view of
these works and of the attitude of John the Baptist, to which
we have drawn attention, the words of Andrew and Simon Peter
could not but mount spontaneously to the lips of those who with
uprightness and simplicity awaited the Hope of Israel: "We
have found the Messias!" (John i, 41). Thus were fulfilled the
descriptions in *Isaias:*

> The spirit of the Lord is upon me.
> Wherefore he hath anointed me to preach the gospel
> to the poor:
> He hath sent me to preach deliverance to the captives and
> sight to the blind,
> to set at liberty them that are bruised,
> to preach the jubilee year of the Lord.
> (Luke iv, 18–19; Is. lxi, 1 ff.).

Had not this jubilee year of the Lord arrived? The poor were
evangelized, the sick healed, devils expelled, spirits set at liberty by the fall of the literalist burdens of human origin which
weighted the yoke of the Law. Jesus had only to let the facts
speak: but while he guided the minds of his hearers towards the
complete truth, he avoided premature declarations, repulsed the
unworthy homage of impure spirits, and tried the growing faith
of his apostles, which for some time yet was to waver between
eclipse and sudden brilliance.

But the Master needed, in this progress towards the light,
some name which should indicate him without compromising
him, which should stimulate minds without misleading them,
and whose Messianic character should be real but not provoking.
Through the Gospels we know that he chose that of "Son
of Man." It is, as a matter of fact, certain that the Saviour habitu-

ally, and, as far as we can judge, from the beginning of his ministry, used this title, or if you will (to avoid prejudging anything) this designation, when speaking of himself. Persevering efforts have been made in recent times to eliminate this unusual phrase from Jesus's vocabulary, or at least to restrict and postpone its use. But the facts are opposed. We need only recall the chief ones: this expression, which (with one exception, which confirms the rule) is always put in the Master's own mouth, abounds in all the Gospels, *John* as well as the Synoptists, and in every part of them. It then disappears from the New Testament, only appearing once in the *Acts,* when the dying Stephen sees "the heavens opened and the Son of man sitting on the right hand of God," and in the Johannine *Apocalypse,* in two analogous visions. Then its character is so clearly Semitic that St. Paul is compelled to give it a hellenistic transcription; and all ancient Christian tradition substitutes clearer and more explicit designations, such as "Lord," "Son of God," and even "Son of David" and "Servant" or "Child of God." All this proclaims its authenticity as an archaic and obscure term, and one which, far from offering a temptation to introduce it into the texts, has to be explained or even replaced by other expressions.

This fact once placed beyond doubt, it remains for us to discover the meaning given by Jesus to the expression. "Son of Man" is the exact equivalent of "man," and its use is no doubt due to the strict laws of Hebrew parallelism. Three times it is found in the Scriptures with this meaning. In *Ezechiel* it recurs, employed in the vocative, over and over again with a shade of pity, accentuating "the contrast between the majesty of God who is speaking, the fragility of the instrument he uses, and the grandeur of the part which that instrument is called upon to play." (E. Tobac, *Les Prophètes d'Israël.*)

When the expression reappears in the celebrated passages of *Daniel* it takes a vaguer sense, strictly that of a being having the figure of a man, at least a man in exterior aspect. The second of these passages brings on the scene the archangel Gabriel under human form, appearing and acting as a "son of man," that is to say as a man. There remains, then, the first, which, by reason of its greater importance, must be transcribed in its context.

In the first year of Baltassar, king of Babylon, the prophet dreams a dream which he puts briefly into writing. The great sea stretches in front of him, and from the four cardinal points, "the four winds" which stir up the ocean, four powerful Beasts rise up in the shape of·a winged lion, a bear, a panther with four wings, and finally a horned monster which changed its appearance. Then thrones are set and God, the Eternal, the Ancient of Days, surrounded by an imposing array, takes his place. The Beasts are judged; the fourth is condemned and cast into the flames, the others, their power taken away, survive for a time. Now while Daniel "considered these visions of the night,

> lo, one like a son of man came with the clouds of heaven. And he came even to the Ancient of Days; and they presented him before him. And he gave him power, and glory and a kingdom: and all peoples, tribes, and tongues shall serve him. His power is an everlasting power that shall not be taken away: and his kingdom that shall not be destroyed."
>
> (Dan. viii, 13–14)

One of those standing by then explains to the prophet that the four Beasts represent four empires, and that to their rule should succeed the sovereignty of the Most High and of his saints, which shall never fail:

> "the kingdom and the power, and the greatness of the kingdom under the whole heaven, may be given to the [people of the] saints of the Most High. Whose kingdom is an everlasting kingdom."
>
> (Dan. vii, 27. The words within brackets are disputed.)

This vision outlines in a striking picture the ancient prophetic scheme of Messiahship. The principal figure in the picture, whose function is to represent the visible element by means of which the eternal sovereignty of Jahveh will be exercised, is presented to the seer "like a son of man." . . .

IV Esdras, an apocalypse which reflects with rare breadth of view the feelings of the Israelites who were not converted to Christianity, after the ruin of Jerusalem in 70, shows us a human figure who gloriously accomplishes the work of the Messias emerging from the sea and coming "with the clouds of heaven," with an appearance which indubitably identifies him with Daniel's "son of man." Later rabbinical tradition, which is meagre enough—and with good reason, for the text of Daniel had become common ground for Christian apologetics—is none the less clear in the same sense. . . .

The name "Son of Man" was capable of a Messianic sense through its use in the prophecy of Daniel and in some interpretations of later literature, but in no way by its actual form. It was closely related to the phrase familiar in the prophets, especially from Ezechiel onwards: "Son of man!"—that is, "Man born of woman! man whose life is a breath!" Thus it was of itself alone a sort of parable, an enigma, a mashal of a type of which Hebrew tradition offers many examples. It raised problems, even if it did not of itself solve any; for Jesus used it to arouse the attention of the hearers and not to satisfy their curiosity. While effectively uniting the person and the mission of Jesus with the highest Messianic prerogatives of the universal Lord and Judge, it also brought out in relief those characteristics of apparent weakness, of gracious brotherhood, of redemptive suffering, and, in a word, of humanity, which must in reality mark the Master's life.

GOD THE SON

I

⚡ It is evident that, since Jesus refers Daniel's prophecy of the Son of man to himself, his consciousness transcends all bounds of human possibilities and his claims reach up to the clouds of heaven, to the right hand of God himself.

Indeed, they reach still farther. It is highly significant that Jesus' conception of himself as the Son of man is by no means coincident with Daniel's prophecy, nor exhausted by it. So exalted, so profound, so rich is the reality which lives in him that it goes far beyond Daniel's picture and gives the old phrase *Son of man* a deepened sense and a new import. When, that is to say, Jesus calls himself the Son of man, he is by no means only looking, as in Daniel's prophecy, to the coming end of time and its glory. Not one half of his declarations about himself as the Son of man have reference to the last judgment. For the most part they apply to his work of redemption in the present, quite in accordance with that fusion of the now and the hereafter, of time and eternity, which characterizes his preaching of the kingdom. When Jesus sets the present with its distress and sin in the clear, dazzling light of his last judgment and in the glory of the new kingdom, he knows himself to be the one who shall take away the distress and the sin, who shall redeem mankind for the new kingdom. As the Son of man he is judge and Saviour in one. Hence his message even as it applies to the present is an evangel. "Blessed are the eyes which see the things that you see. For I say to you that many prophets and kings have desired to see the things that you see, and have not seen them" (Luke x, 23 sq.). Since he, the Son of man, will hereafter be Lord and King of the Kingdom of God, he is already in the present the source of salvation. "Come to me, all you that labour, and are burdened, and I will refresh you" (Matt. xi, 28). His eschatological task presupposes the Messianic. Or better still they postulate one another. Jesus is therefore fond of using the term Son of man when he is speaking of his redemptive work in the present. "The Son of man is come to seek and save that which was lost" (Luke xix, 10). "The Son of man" is he who sows the good seed, the children of the new kingdom (Matt. xiii, 37). It is the right of the Son of man to liberate man's ethical and religious endeavour from all extraneous bonds, even a law so venerable as the law of the Sabbath. "The Son of man is Lord also of the Sabbath" (Mark ii, 28). Further, the "Son of man" does even what God alone does, what to many of the Jewish scribes exceeded the power of the expected Messias. He forgives sins. "That you may know that the Son of man hath power on earth to forgive sins [he saith to the sick of the palsy] I say to thee, Arise, take up thy bed, and go into thy house" (Mark ii, 10–11). There is the same claim in his words to the sinful woman: "Thy sins are forgiven thee" (Luke vii, 48). In the forgiving of sins the redeemership of the Son of man, which embraces the present world, reaches its apex, and his Messianic claims their strongest and most emphatic expression. Here Jesus attains not only to the right hand of God, but into his heart.

Since he is filled with the awareness that it is the will of the Father that the redeemership of the Son of man should be consummated in suffering and the Cross, that the Lord and king of the new kingdom must win for himself his own by shedding his own life's blood for them, he always calls himself the Son of man when he speaks about his Passion. Again and again, when predicting his Passion, he emphasizes the fact that "the Son of man must suffer." "The Son of man is not come to be ministered to but to minister and to give his life a ransom for many." To Jesus when saying this the picture Isaias draws of the suffering servant of God and Daniel's prophecy of the Son of man blend into a single majestic vision. He who, with a self-confidence which has no parallel, sees himself at the end of time as judge of the world and Lord of the new kingdom, at the same time knows himself to be the one whom Isaias foretold, who "hath borne the sins of many, and hath delivered his soul unto death" (Is. liii, 11 sq.). In the one little phrase, Son of man, the homeliest thing which he could tell us of himself, in the term "man" are concealed the most tremendous contrasts in this consciousness he had of himself. Jesus knows himself to be exalted to the heavens, and he sees himself thrust down into the slime of the earth. He is come to rule; he is come to minister and to die. King of the kingdom is he, and yet man, indeed the slave of men.

We can now understand why Jesus took by preference the name Son of man that by its simple symbolism he might indicate what he intends to be for man: a man among men and yet their king, their judge, and their Saviour, a man from heaven. From this that other term by which his contemporaries expressed their belief in the king of the last age, namely the Mashiah, that is the anointed, the Christ, took on a new meaning. Whereas the Jews, when in their eighteen-clause petition they prayed for the coming of the Christ, had in mind a restoration of the glories of the kingdom of David, Jesus saw this "Christ" only as the coming Son of man, as the saviour and judge of the world. It was in this sense that he took Peter's confession, "Thou art the Christ" (Mark viii, 29; Luke ix, 20), and because of its mysterious depth he attributed it to an inspiration from on high. "Flesh and blood hath not revealed it to thee, but my Father who is in heaven." It was in this sense that the first Christians took it over from

Peter, and since that day there has been no sweeter name in heaven or on earth than "Jesus Christ." If the expression "Christ" had hitherto been cumbered by Jewish conceptions that the expected Messiah would be of earthly stock, it henceforth turned men's hearts to the Son of man, to the right hand of the Ancient of Days, to the Saviour of the present, the king and judge of the future.

This was the novel and revolutionary element in the claim of Jesus. It stands in the most direct contrast with what the Jews of his time, under the spur of their selfish nationalistic instincts, believed and hoped of their expected Messias. In this too is to be sought the determining cause of the drama of Golgotha. Had Jesus claimed to be a Christ in the Jewish nationalistic sense of the term, he would not have been crucified, even though his claim had been disputed and disallowed. For according to the law applicable to the case, such a claim, even though baseless, was not blasphemy against God, and was therefore not a capital offence. It was only when Jesus in that grave hour not merely gave assent to the high-priest's question, "Art thou the Christ, the Son of the Living God?", but with that serene truth which was of his essence, added the further confession: "And you shall see the Son of man sitting on the right hand of the power of God, and coming with the clouds of Heaven"—it was only then that he gave unequivocal meaning and an unequivocal answer to the equivocal question of the high-priest, for this it was when regarded in connection with Jewish Messianic ideas. In his fetters he sees himself at the right hand of the power of God. Arraigned before an earthly judge, he knows himself to be on the judgment seat of God. Could there be a greater paradox, and a more atrocious offence? "Then the high-priest rent his garments, saying: He hath blasphemed, what further need have we of witnesses? Behold, now you have heard the blasphemy: What think you? But they answering said: He is guilty of death. Then they did spit in his face, and buffeted him."

Jesus died, Jesus had to die, because men were too petty, too
narrow, too abject and too obtuse to comprehend his sublimity
and his divinity. He died for these base men because he was
the Son of man.

II

Jesus had sent out the seventy-two disciples to preach the
gospel of the kingdom all over the country. They returned
rejoicing with the news that evil spirits had been subject to them.
And Jesus tells them that they should rather rejoice because their
names were written in heaven. And "in that same hour he
rejoiced in the Holy Ghost and said: I confess to thee, O Father,
Lord of Heaven and earth, because thou hast hidden these
things from the wise and prudent, and hast revealed them to the
little ones. Yea, Father, for so it hath seemed good in thy sight.
All things are delivered to me by my Father, and no one knoweth
who the Son is but the Father; and who the Father is but the
Son, and to whom the Son will reveal him. And turning to his
disciples, he said: Blessed are the eyes which see the things that
you see. For I say to you that many prophets and kings have
desired to see the things that you see and have not seen them;
and to hear the things that you hear, and have not heard them"
(Luke x, 21 sqq.).

Jesus speaks here with a joy and a triumph past measure. The
success of the seventy-two has proved to him that the Messianic
seed is germinating, that belief in his mystery is awakening.
Precisely in the fact that it is the "little ones" who believe in
his name he sees a special sign of God's graciousness and compassion. And so, overcome by this love, he draws from the welling riches of his own nature, where this love has proved itself
more creative than it has anywhere else. There are three glories
with which the Father has invested him. "All things are delivered to me by my Father"—all things, all honour and greatness,
all authority and power, mankind and all the angels. There is

literally nothing which is held by the Father alone, nothing which does not belong also to Jesus. These words quoted by Luke, span infinities upon infinities. John explains and supplements them by other sayings of Jesus. "All things whatsoever the Father hath are mine" (John xvi, 15). "All my things are thine and thine mine" (John xvii, 10). "As the Father raiseth up the dead, and giveth life; so doth the Son also give life to whom he will. For neither doth the Father judge any man: but hath given all judgment to the son. That all may honour the Son, as they honour the Father" (John v, 21 sqq.). "Thou hast given him power over all flesh, that he may give eternal life to all whom thou hast given him" (John xvii, 2).

And the second glory lies yet deeper. It is properly the source of the first. "No one knoweth who the Son is but the Father: and who the Father is but the Son." The Son has a reality to which, in its ultimate depths, no one has access save the Father alone. Conversely, the reality of the Father is revealed to the Son alone. Thus Father and Son stand in a wholly unique, exclusive communion, in which no one else has any part. And the uniqueness of their communion lies in the fact that they are Father and Son. Jesus here paraphrases his essential relation to the Father, making use of conceptions native to the Jewish people and to Hellenistic mysticism beyond their borders. According to them no perfect knowledge of God is possible to man. Only God can have such knowledge of himself. Man can only be known by God (cf. I Cor. viii, 1 sqq.; Gal. iv, 9). Quite otherwise, as Jesus here emphasizes, is his own relation to God. He and he alone has the same perfect knowledge of the Father as the Father has of him. And this knowledge is his because he and he alone is the Son. On the other hand, to men the reality of the Son is no less mysterious than that of the Father. So hidden and so inaccessible is it, that only One knows it, and this because he is the Father. If we strip this self-revelation of Jesus of its mystical covering, we find the kernel to be nothing but a clear, unequivocal attestation to the unique, essential relation of his person to the Father and of the Father to him. They alone know and possess and permeate one another down to the very depths of their being, because they alone stand in the relation of Father and Son to one another. What Jesus here reveals with sublime simplicity is congruent with those self-revelations of Jesus which St. John, the evangelist of the interior life, relates. "Do you not believe that I am in the Father and the Father in me?" (John xiv, 10). "Philip, he that seeth me, seeth the Father also" (John xiv, 9). "Neither me do you know, nor my Father: If you did know me, you would know my Father also" (John viii, 19). "I know mine, and mine know me, and I know the Father" (John x, 14 sqq.). "Believe the works: that you may know and believe that the Father is in me and I in the Father" (John x, 38).

The third glory follows directly from this oneness of being which united the Father and the Son. It was given definitive expression in the same discourse in which Jesus bore witness to himself, when he said, "No one knoweth who the Father is but the Son, and to whom the Son will reveal him." In its deepest sense his teaching and that of the Christian religion is therefore summed up in the words, "through the Son to the Father." There is no other way to the Father but by the Son. Here, too, we catch in the synoptic account the voice of the Johannine Christ, a clear proof that St. John, the beloved disciple, has faithfully preserved and handed down to us the inmost thoughts of Jesus and the manner in which these were communicated to his disciples. To the question of Thomas, "Lord, how can we know the way?" Jesus answered, "I am the way, the truth, and the life. No man cometh to the Father but by me" (John xiv, 6). "Just Father, the world hath not known thee: but I have known thee: and these have known that thou hast sent me" (John xvii, 25).

With this the last veils have fallen from the mystery of Jesus.

Proceeding from his purely human, mental and moral nature, through his religious interior life, we have found our way to his supernatural mystery; to the Divinity of his nature, to the Son of man as the judge and Lord of the future and the Saviour of the present. We have seen that what was earthly in him was based upon the superterrestrial, and that only from this standpoint could his human life be made historically intelligible. His superterrestrial nature is in turn revealed to us as the mystery of his Sonship, as the one direct sharing in the nature of the Father, as a oneness with him. The enigma of his historical appearance has been resolved in his own words: "No one knows the Father but the Son"; "I and the Father are one."

At these words thoughts fail and our tongue stumbles. The conception they express is staggering. Once upon a time, within historical memory, there lived a man, thoroughly sound in mind and body, who was gifted with unusually lucid insight into the facts of existence, into the greatest as well as the least, and with extraordinarily keen understanding. He was a man who was more selfless and unself-seeking than anyone who has ever lived, and whose life was devoted to the service of the poor and the oppressed. And this healthy, clear-sighted, selfless man, from beginning to end of his life, knew himself to be the unique well-beloved Son of the Father, to be one who knew the Father as no other man could. More than this, there was once a man, within historical times, who, as a child of the Jewish people, knew of only one God of heaven and earth, of a unique Father in heaven, and stood in reverential awe before this heavenly Father: a man whose meat was to do the will of this Father, who from his earliest youth in good days and bad had sought and loved this will alone, whose whole life was one prayer; a man, further, whose whole being was so firmly united with this Divine will, that by its omnipotence he healed the sick and restored the dead to life; a man, finally, who was so intimately and exclusively dedicated to this will, that he never swerved from it, so that not even the slightest consciousness of sin ever oppressed him, so that never a cry for penance and forgiveness passed his lips, so that even in dying he begged pardon not for himself but for others. And this man from the intimacy of his union with God could say to afflicted mortals, "Thy sins are forgiven thee." And it was this holy man, utterly subject as he was to God throughout his whole life, absorbed as he was in God, awestruck as he stood before him, who asserted, as if it were the most natural and obvious thing in the world, that he was to be the judge of the world at the last day, that he was the suffering servant of God, nay more, that he was the only begotten Son of God and consubstantial with him, and could say of himself, "I and the Father are one."

Can we, may we, dare we give credence to this man? We are asked to believe in the Incarnation of God, that is to say, we are asked to accept the fact that God so humbled himself as to "empty" himself, to use St. Paul's words, of his Divine majesty (Phil. ii, 7). Is it not our duty to conclude that a man was mistaken, though he were the holiest who ever lived, rather than to believe that God would humble himself so immeasurably? Is not a man here rising up against God? Is it not in the last resort unbelief, if we believe? Does not our vigilant, reverent sense of God's uniqueness and eternal majesty actually oblige us to refuse our assent and either, like Caiaphas, to rend our garments and to cry out "He hath blasphemed," or with his kindred to lament his madness? Must we not, with Chesterton, rather "expect the grass to wither and the birds to drop out of the air, when a strolling carpenter's apprentice says calmly and almost carelessly, like one looking over his shoulder: 'Before Abraham was, I am.' 'I and the Father are one'"?

We can only say that a man who at this point, when confronted with the paradox of God the all-perfect, all-holy, eternal, becoming a man, a carpenter, a Jew haled before the court and crucified, shrinks away, can go no further, and breaks down, may be actually less remote from a living piety than one who coolly accepts all this and glibly repeats his Credo, or indeed than one who does homage to the noble humanity of Jesus yet has the temerity to pooh-pooh what Jesus said of himself as harmless rhetoric, the innocent exaggerations of a pious eccentric.

And yet, in this question of all questions, has man, for all his faith and his conception of God, really the last word? What does "conception of God" mean? Is it not itself man-created? Is not God greater than man's conception of God? Is not the wisdom of man folly in God's sight? How, if God willed to prove himself God and to reveal the infinity of his omnipotence and the measurelessness of his love by becoming for our sakes a creature, a man who allowed himself to be crucified? In the infinite possibilities of God all conceivable possibilities are included, even the possibility of a Bethlehem and a Golgotha. What if God demands of man precisely this belief in the unbelievable? Suppose it was in this unbelievable way, and in no other, that it was his will to break down our human pride, to shatter all our human standards of what is possible, and to bring our minds and being into subjection to himself, and to himself alone? We cannot ignore Jesus. He is a possibility of God's. And given the possibility that God appeared on earth, we can see clearly that the humanity of Jesus was the right, true, unique place for his theophany. For nowhere else do there appear all the attributes of God, his majesty and omnipotence, his compassion and grace, so purely and continuously as here. If God appeared on earth in the form of man, he can only have appeared in Jesus. Nor is this all. The Divine is shown in Jesus with such overflowing richness, such impressive force, such evident clarity that we should have to close our eyes to the evidence and impugn the possibility of a fact attested by history, if we would deny the Divinity of Jesus.

III

From Palm Sunday to Pentecost

"Who gave himself for us, to ransom us from all
our guilt, a people set apart for himself."

(Titus ii, 14)

NARRATIVE

I

⟨ WE ARE NOW at the last week before Our Lord's death. The Pharisees were determined to kill Him, and He met them head on. Because His popularity was too great for a public arrest, their plan was to take Him by night; but each night He left the city—on the Saturday, Sunday and Monday nights He went to the Lazarus, Martha and Mary household at Bethany; the Tuesday and Wednesday nights He passed on Mount Olivet; and on Olivet He was taken on the night of Thursday, by the temple guard, brought there by Judas. It is interesting to note how decisive a part is played by the family at Bethany. It was the raising of Lazarus from the dead that finally decided the rulers to kill Him: it seems to have been the anointing of Christ's feet with precious ointment by Mary—on this last Saturday night —that decided Judas to betray him: for Judas was furious at the waste of money and Our Lord rebuked Him. It was on the Wednesday after that he asked the chief priests what they would give him to betray Christ.

In between, everything had happened to steel their resolve. The whole town was thronging about the man who had raised Lazarus from the dead, and His teaching in those days was at its starkest in emphasis upon the truths they found intolerable —that the Jewish race had forfeited its priority and that they themselves were evil.

As He was coming in from Bethany on the Sunday, the crowds went out of the city to meet Him and strewed palms in His way and hailed Him as the Son of David. As He continued on His way, and Jerusalem came into view, He wept over it. All that day He was healing in the Temple. He spoke again of His own death and had a foretaste of the agony in the garden— "Now is my soul troubled. Father, save me from this hour. But for this cause I came unto this hour."

On the Tuesday His teaching is at its strongest and most terrible. He told the chief priests and the scribes that tax-gatherers and harlots should go into the Kingdom of Heaven before them; in the parable of the Wicked Husbandmen He told, in language wholly unveiled, how the Chosen People would kill God's own son and how their inheritance should be taken from them and given to the Gentiles. A curious alliance of Pharisees and Herodians tried to catch Him with a question about tribute and received the answer: "Render unto Caesar the things that are Caesar's and to God the things that are God's." The Sadducees tried conclusions with Him on the resurrection of the body and were reduced to silence. Then comes the most terrible of Our Lord's utterances, His long attack upon the hypocrisy of scribes and Pharisees—"You serpents, generation of vipers, how will you flee the judgment of hell?" He tells the parable of the Widow's Mite, followed by a prophecy of the destruction of the Temple; after which Our Lord went out of the city to Mt. Olivet and there told His apostles of the destruction that awaited the City, of the end of the world and the last Judgment, with heaven for the loving and hell for the un-loving.

On Wednesday Christ told the apostles that in two days He must die and Judas arranged with the authorities to betray Him.

II

On Thursday He ate the paschal supper prescribed by Jewish law with His apostles, told them of the sacrifice that by His

death He was to offer His Father for the redemption of mankind, and made them the priests of the Eucharistic meal whereby
until the end of the world men should receive His own Body
and Blood.

Matthew and Mark and Luke each give their account of
this; so does St. Paul (I Cor. xi). Here is St. Luke's (xxii, 19).

"Then he took bread and blessed and broke it, and gave it to
them, saying, This is my body which is to be given for you; do
this for a commemoration of me.

"And so with the cup, when supper was ended, This cup, he
said, is the new testament, in my blood, which is to be shed
for you."

Our Lord has much to say to the Apostles by way of preparation for the role that must be theirs when He is gone from them
and they must carry on His work. He tells them with no apparent anger that they are all about to desert Him and that Peter
will deny Him thrice that night. "It was I that chose you. The
task I have appointed you is to go out and bear fruit, fruit which
will endure." But all this they shall not do in their own power,
but in the power of the Holy Spirit. It is indeed necessary that
Our Lord go to the Father in order that the Holy Spirit may
come to them. There is a great deal about the Holy Spirit; and
it is natural, therefore, that Our Lord should give His most
extended teaching on the Blessed Trinity.

And in terms of the Blessed Trinity He uttered the life-
formula of the Atonement—"I am in my Father and you in me
and I in you."

From the supper room Our Lord went as on the two previous
nights to Mt. Olivet, to a garden called Gethsemani. And there
"he grew sorrowful and dismayed; My soul, he said, is ready to
die with sorrow. He fell upon his face and said, My Father, if
it is possible, let this chalice pass me by; only as thy will is, not
as mine is. And in his agony his sweat fell to the ground like
thick drops of blood."

Then Judas came with a band of soldiers and betrayed his

Master with a kiss. Jesus was dragged from court to court that night—two appearances before the Jewish Sanhedrin, and two before the Roman Governor Pilate, separated by an appearance before Herod. In their own court, the Jews accused Him of calling Himself the Son of God, and His admission settled the matter for them: He must die. Before Pilate they accused Him of sedition—"forbidding to give tribute to Caesar and saying that He is Christ the King." As the night proceeded and merged into the day, He was mocked and spat upon, thorns were twisted into a rough wreath and pressed upon His head, He was scourged. Finally He was made to carry His own cross to Calvary, a hill outside the city. There He was nailed to His cross and so hung between two thieves, one of whom repented and was promised Paradise. At the end of three hours He died and His body was laid in a tomb nearby. This was on the Friday. On Sunday morning He rose again from the dead. In between, as St. Peter tells us, "in his spirit he went and preached to the spirits who lay in prison"—that is, to those who had died in a state of grace and were awaiting the redemptive act which should open heaven to them.

III

For forty days after His resurrection He was upon earth, in repeated though not continuous contact with His followers, completing their preparation for the work He had given them. He gave them power to forgive sins or withhold forgiveness, re-affirmed Peter's supremacy (he was to be shepherd of the whole flock), gave them the commission to carry His doctrine and His sacraments to all nations to the end of time. But none of this activity was to begin until the Holy Ghost had come upon them. After forty days He ascended into Heaven, to the right hand of the Father; and ten days later, in that same upper room where so much had happened, the Holy Ghost descended upon them and their mission was begun.

The Resurrection was not simply a convenient way for our Lord to return to His apostles and give them final instructions, nor His Ascension simply a convenient way of letting them know definitely, beyond question or peradventure, that He had left this world. Resurrection and Ascension belong organically to the Sacrifice He offered for us. The Sacrifice, insofar as it is the offering to God of a victim slain, was complete upon Calvary. But in the total conception of sacrifice, it is not sufficient—as Cain found long before—that a victim be offered to God; it is essential that the offering be accepted by God: and given that the nature of man requires that sacrifice be an action externally visible, it belongs to the perfection of sacrifice that God's acceptance should be as externally visible as humanity's offering. It is in this sense that Resurrection and Ascension belong organically to the Sacrifice. By the miracle of the Resurrection, God at once shows His acceptance of the Priest as a true priest of a true sacrifice *and* perfects the Victim offered to Him, so that whereas it was offered mortal and corruptible it has gained immortality and incorruptibility. By the Ascension God accepts the offered Victim by actually taking it to Himself. Humanity, offered to God in Christ the Victim, is now forever at the right hand of the Father.

PALM SUNDAY

ANYBODY WOULD HAVE TOLD YOU, if you had asked in Jerusalem on the first Palm Sunday, that Jesus of Nazareth was at the height of his popularity. It even looked as if his reputation was destined to go beyond the limits of Palestine. Some Greeks, who had come up to Jerusalem for the feast, expressed a desire to see him. If we may use a modern comparison without irreverence, he was in the position of some popular leader nowadays when the foreign journalists begin to take notice of him. What was the "interview" he gave them? A curious one. "The hour is come for the Son of Man to be glorified. A grain of wheat must fall into the ground and die, or else it remains nothing more than a grain of wheat; but if it dies, then it yields rich fruit."

Our Lord Jesus Christ did not come to earth to share our crowns. The pageantry with which he rode into Jerusalem was not what it looked like, a bid for popular leadership. Rather, it was a kind of satire on worldly success; he would heighten the contrast between that whirl of popularity in which he lived, and the lonely contempt in which he died, by a dramatic gesture. Those palms should lie trodden in the dust for days afterwards, to remind the world how brief are its triumphs. He had come to earth to die. His human body should be lodged in the earth like a grain of wheat, to yield the splendid harvest of his Resurrection. And it was our Resurrection, as well as his; we

were to see with our eyes, handle with our hands, the mystery
which still baffles our understanding, the law of death in life
and life in death.

It would not be difficult to illustrate that moral by an allusion
to those many countries in the modern world which lie dead,
awaiting their Resurrection. But perhaps the best way of keeping
a day of intercession is to look beyond the immediate prospect
which drives us to our knees. Holy week should be a week of
holydays—holidays from the problems and fears which occupy
our thoughts. Your soul is a grain of wheat which must fall
into the ground and die, on pain of sterility; only by a death to
self and a Resurrection into the world of grace can it become
fruitful for God. We must enter into the joys of Easter by entering into the sufferings and the death of Christ. Entering into
them, not by way of artistic appreciation, not by merely feeling
sorry about it. We were buried with Christ in our baptism;
we are dead, and our life is hidden with Christ in God. Our
business in Holy week is to associate ourselves with Christ's
Passion, to unite ourselves with Christ's Passion, to unite ourselves with the dispositions of will and purpose with which he
emptied himself, annihilated himself, in our name. Self has
to be dragged out and crucified.

THE LAST SUPPER

⤷ IN HIS LAST DISCOURSE to His disciples, Jesus let fall a statement which the instinct of mankind has seized upon as being
the most perfect and most appropriate rendering in words of the
devotedness of the highest friendship: "Greater love than this,"
He said, "no man hath, that a man lay down his life for his
friends." There is a profound pathos attaching to these words on
His lips at the moment of their utterance, for He knew as He
said them that in a few hours they were to find their most
complete exemplification in His own case. He would die and
His death would be the *supreme proof* of His love for His
hearers and for all mankind. Before it should come to pass,
however, He has still to give them the *supreme expression* of
that love He bore towards all. His charity for the sons of Adam
called upon the Omnipotence of God to express that love, not
in words merely, but in a *fact* which should be worthy of the
exercise of that Omnipotence. The response of the Omnipotence
was the Blessed Eucharist. These two facts, the laying down of
His life for His friends as testimony of His love for them, and
His giving Himself to them in the Blessed Eucharist as the
most perfect mode of expressing that love, are as it were but two
aspects of one complex reality. The Passion is directed towards
the Blessed Eucharist: it leads up to it, in the order of causality,
and makes it possible. It is only because the Body of Jesus has
been broken and mangled on the Cross that it can become our

spiritual food; it is only in virtue of the shedding of His Precious Blood, that It in turn can become our spiritual drink. Hence Our Lord said: "Take ye and eat, this is my Body which is given for you"; "This is the chalice, the new testament in my blood, shed for you." It is to be noted that the body that the apostles are given to eat is a body described as "given" or "offered in sacrifice," or, as another reading has it, "broken"; that is, in sacrificial death: likewise the blood that is handed them to drink is blood that is poured out in death. It is a body and blood that has been sacrificed that the apostles are bidden to consume. At the Last Supper, and at every Communion table since, the disciples of Christ are gathering the fruits of Calvary: their banquet is on the Body and Blood of their God, offered in sacrifice on their behalf. In that supper chamber for the first time are verified the words He had spoken to them long before: "Except you eat the flesh of the Son of Man, and drink his blood, you shall not have life in you." As the apostles took the divine gift from the hands of the Master they scarcely realised that their access to this life-giving food was through the death of Him Who was giving them Himself to eat at that moment. . . .

There is in all these texts a strange conjunction of life and death. The death of "Life" itself was the life of those who were dead. Christ's death is the life of His followers, because it is only by His Cross and Passion that their spiritual death is taken away and that they are restored to supernatural life. To administer spiritual food to the spiritually dead would be vain and useless; one must be living with the life of grace before it becomes possible to partake of and to profit by the heavenly nourishment. It is in Christ's death we are baptised to the new-ness of that life which is nourished by the Eucharist. The Blessed Sacrament is indissolubly linked with the death of Jesus. Hence the joy with which the Church celebrates the memory of this act, which has left her in unending possession of her Spouse on earth, is deeply tinged with sadness. The chants of Holy

Thursday are sombre and full of pathos. The Church cannot but exult in the stupendous act of love, but its exultation does not allow it to lose sight of what that act of love cost Jesus. The same thought haunts St. Paul, and for him another element of sorrow is added to the memory of the great event. There is deep feeling in the words with which he prefaces the history of the Last Supper: "The Lord Jesus, the same night in which he was betrayed. . . ." The night on which was given His greatest gift to men was the night also which witnessed His betrayal to death by His own. The same note of intense though restrained emotion is discernible in the narrative of the Evangelists as they unfold the wonderful events that took place in the Supper Room on Jesus' last night on earth.

The Pasch had been consumed according to the ancient rite; the table was cleared of the remains of the Feast of the Passover; and thus disappeared for ever the figures of the Old Law. Some loaves of unleavened bread were then placed before the Saviour. All eyes were fixed on Him. A sense of impending disaster weighed on the minds of the apostles. They were filled with a vague foreboding, for their Master's words had become more and more explicit and signified all too clearly that a crisis that augured ill for their earthly aspirations was swiftly approaching. At the same time they were filled with an eager expectancy. Everything pointed to the accomplishment of the promise He had made months before that He would give them His flesh to eat. Their hopes had been stirred to the highest pitch by the assurance that had been vouchsafed them that this divine nourishment would impart to them everlasting life— a life wholly different from that ministered by that other heavenly food which their fathers had eaten in the desert, and which nourished only for a time. Their souls were awakening to a sense of the supernatural; the extraordinary and elaborate preparations that they had made under the directions of the Divine Master, had betokened that the Pasch that was about to take place was one which was to be carried out on a plane infinitely higher than that in which the old rite was to be accomplished in the other houses in Jerusalem that night. . . .

The moment had come when Our Lord was about to perform that great act which was to perpetuate His presence amongst men until the end of time. "With desire," He said to them, "I have desired to eat this pasch with you, before I suffer." As other men pursue pleasures and satisfactions, Our Lord sought for sacrifice, not, indeed, for its own sake, but as the price of the salvation of men. "I have a baptism," He had said previously, "wherewith I am to be baptised: and how am I straitened until it be accomplished." That hour of His baptism in blood was eagerly sought for, because His death was the condition of His being able to give His great Gift to men—the Gift of Himself. . . . He raised His divine eyes towards Heaven and thanked His Father for the power that was given Him to do what He was about to do. He took the unleavened loaf in His hands, blessed it, pronounced those words which, instinct with the Omnipotence of God, effect what they signify: "This is My Body." And at once the most wondrous thing creation had ever witnessed took place in the awe-stricken silence of that upper room. Only the words of God broke that tingling silence, and as their sounds died away one substance had become another. The substance of bread had become another substance—and that, the substance of the Body of Jesus Christ— united with His soul and Divinity! Similarly He took the chalice. Again the silence was broken: "This is My Blood of the New Testament"—and where there had been wine, there was now the Blood that was to flow so profusely from His veins a few hours later.

In this dual consecration, in which there is a seeming separation of Body and Blood, was set forth in vivid symbol the death to which He had submitted Himself and which was to take place on the following day. The institution of the Blessed Eucharist is intimately bound up with the sacrificial death of Christ. The mysterious change having taken place,

Our Lord said: "Take ye and eat," and the wondering apostles, one after the other, communicated at the hands of their Divine Master. It was their first communion. They received with a childlike faith and simplicity, realising that now there was accomplished in a mysterious manner that saying of His which had so scandalised His incredulous followers some months previously. The apostles had not trusted to their own human views according to which it would be impossible for Jesus to give them His Flesh to eat; they had trusted in His Omnipotence and now that trust was rewarded; though as yet they understood but little, for the Holy Ghost had not yet descended upon them. Jesus had wrought a wonder surpassing the wonders of creation.

Again Our Lord raised His hands over the apostles, His lips moved in prayer, and He then said: "Do this in commemoration of Me"; and the great mystery that He had just accomplished is perpetuated, is made possible to the end of time. The Holy Ghost descended invisibly upon the followers of Jesus, and they received the stupendous power to do as He Himself had done, and to transmit to others that same power. The Catholic Priesthood was inaugurated. By this act Our Lord made possible for all time His stay on earth amongst men, whom He loved to such an excess. And yet He knew with His Divine foresight what that meant for Him. Though He saw that His Body and Blood would be treated with reverence by a multitude of devout souls, yet He realised full well that in many and many an instance in the course of ages He would be placing Himself at the mercy of unworthy and sinful priests who would treat Him with irreverence and sacrilege. He saw in vision all the profanations, outrages and, what was more painful still to His loving heart, the cold indifference that He was to endure from tepid and careless Christians. . . . Love, especially Divine Love, does not halt to calculate and weigh advantage and disadvantage in the balance. He risked all to serve some, whom He aimed at drawing into close intimacy with Himself.

IMMOLATION

❧ On taut air—bells; lifted, adoring eyes;
and, sinner, seraph, God, look upon God.

PRAISE OF ANGELS AND PEOPLE

Honour to Thee and praise!
Love unto Thee and praise!
Honour and love to Thee, O Lord, and praise.

Christ, star-told in the east,
Christ, lover of "these least,"
Christ of the marriage-feast
in this White Host.

Christ by the kings adored,
Christ come to bring the sword,
Christ the Incarnate Word
in this White Host.

Christ of the uncast stone,
Christ in the Garden prone,
Christ agonized, alone,
in this White Host.

Christ with ensanguined cheek,
Christ from the scourging weak,
Christ with his mockers meek
in this White Host.

Christ of the supper room,
Christ of the empty tomb,
Christ of the Day of Doom
in this White Host.

Who was, before the Sun,
Who lived, ere Life begun,
Who shall, when Time be done,
in this White Host,

Who dreamed this realm of earth,
Who called the seas to birth,
Who made the stars for mirth,
in this White Host.

Who Glory is and Light,
Who Majesty and Might,
Who Fulness of Delight,
in this White Host.

Who dread Divinity,
Who One in Trinity,
Who is Infinity,
in this White Host.

Jesu, with Magdalen I join my plea,
with him who craved remembrance from the tree,
with drowning Peter: "Lord deliver me"
by this White Host.

THE SACRIFICE OF THE SACRED COMMUNITY

IF OUR LORD JESUS CHRIST has desired to eat this Pasch, it is as the bridegroom desires to eat the wedding feast with the bride. Out of mankind the God-Man is drawing those men whom He will build up into a society, the Church His Bride. Then, as the husband pours his life into the wife, thus making a child in her, so into the Sacred Community will Christ pour His life, so that she gives birth to His children by the sacrament of Baptism. As the Father by the hands of the mother feeds his children, so by the hands of Holy Mother Church will Christ feed *His* children, with His own most precious Body and Blood. Not to the individual only, to Peter and John and the rest, but to the Twelve as a group, to the Sacred Community—the Woman clothed with the Sun—does the Sun of Justice say: "With desire I have desired to eat this Pasch with you."

They have eaten the Pasch, the type, having with them the anti-type. They have eaten the spotless male lamb, which was emptied of blood and roasted with fire: a type to be fulfilled on Calvary, when all the precious Blood of the Lamb of God shall have been spilled and all His Flesh burned up in the fiery furnace of His pain. They have eaten bread and drunk wine: how shall that type be fulfilled? How, indeed, shall both types be *completely* fulfilled? For the lamb was not only slain, and bled, and roasted, but eaten also; the first part of the type is answered by Calvary indeed, but not the eating. Unless Christ be truly received in the Sacrament, the last part of the type remains unfulfilled.

Both types are fulfilled by the joining together of the two in one, and of both with the anti-type. Thus is fulfilled the prophetical action of Melchisedech and the prophetical word of Malachi. Jesus, Who on Calvary is Isaac, in the Cenacle is Melchisedech, offering the clean sacrifice of bread and wine. He takes bread, and lifting up His eyes to the heavenly Father, He blesses, breaks and gives it to the Apostles, saying: "Take ye and eat: for this is My Body which is being given for you."

Taking also the chalice, in like manner, He blesses and gives to them, saying: "Drink ye all of this: for this is the chalice, the New Testament in My Blood, which shall be shed for you and for many, to the taking away of sin."

If this is not sacrifice, it is nothing. If it is not the sacrifice of Christ's Body and of Christ's Blood, not in mere figure and symbol but in fact, then Christ has lied.

He Who speaks is the Divine Word, by Whom all things were created, in Whom they were given their nature—made to be the kind of thing they are. He spoke, and all things were created; He speaks again, and of all things He created, two change their nature, and at His word are re-created—changed into Him. The Word created bread and wine, and the Word made Flesh re-creates them to be His Body and His Blood. As into the racial framework He has inserted the whole reality of Godhead, so that what appears to be man only is in very truth God made Man: so into the ritual framework of the Pasch He inserts the full reality of Godmanhood, so that what appears to be bread and wine is in very truth Himself, both God and Man living in flesh and blood.

THE ENTRY INTO JERUSALEM
Mosaic

The Body is being given *now*, the Blood is being shed *now*, in this chalice.

The Sacred Community in Abraham, the Church of the Old Law, is made holy to God in the sprinkling of the blood of animals, oxen, sheep and goats: the blood of testament—the witness, that is, to the union between God and man; that as man offers sacrifice of animals now, so will he lay down his own life rather than offend God. The Sacred Community in Christ, the Church of the New Law, is made holy to God in the sprinkling of the blood of Christ, the Lamb of God unspotted and undefiled. This Blood is the blood of testament, the witness to the union between God and man in Christ; as Christ offers sacrifice now of His own Manhood, laying down His life for sin, so that union is to be forever. This union of God and man in Christ is first the God-Man, then the Sacred Community His Body; and as it is impossible that the Holy Manhood should sin and so be separated from God, so it is impossible that the Church should so fall into sin as to fall away from Christ. Hence there can never be question of setting up a new Church, under any pretence whatever of fidelity to tradition or of a need for reform. This Blood is the chalice of the new *and eternal* Testament.

If this language be not the form of a sacrifice in a sacrament, it is nothing.

This Sacrament is the testament of Christ: the witness of Christ's last wish. It is His last will, by which He shows to the Father His dying wish that He should remain forever with his Bride, the Church. "Entreat Me not to leave her, nor to cease from following after her; for whither she goes I desire to go too, that You, my God, may be her God." It is impossible that Christ, the acts of Whose human will are always guided by the light of the Beatific Vision, should have a wish not pleasing to the Trinity; hence His prayer is granted, and He remains with the Church under the appearances of bread and wine.

"Eat—take—do this."

They come forward, believing, loving, adoring, and looking into His eyes, from His hand they receive His very Self.

"Do this in commemoration of Me."

He is about to leave the world, taking His visible Presence out of space and time as He goes to the Father; but the Church remains in the world. So, not for this night only, but for all nights He provides; and all power having been given to Him in heaven and earth, power even to make bread and wine Himself, He gives that power to the Church. Even as He reigns in power in the kingdom given Him by His Father, so do His Twelve reign.

"Increase and multiply," said God to Adam and his wife, putting into them the power not only to have children themselves, but to pass on to those children the same power, that they themselves might increase. So by the one word humanity lives on and grows.

"Do this," says the Word, putting into His priests not only the power to heal the sick, to raise the dead, to cast out devils, but to do greater things also: to make bread and wine His living Body and Blood, and not only to do this, but to pass on that same power to others, that they themselves might also consecrate. So by this one word of the Word, the Church lives on and grows, even to the end of the world.

So the types and shadows have ending, and the new rite of faith prevails. By that light of faith the Twelve see where they stand: on Sinai; and moved by no daring, but by the grace of God, they seek the consummation of Sinai.

"Lord, show us the Father."

So Moses prayed: "Show me Thy glory." And the Word, Who is the likeness of His Father, replied: "Thou canst not see My face; for man shall not see Me and live."

Impossible for the creature to bear the weight of glory, the sight of the Increate! But there was a hollow in the rock where the creature might lie, sheltered by a hand; and as the Godhead passed on, and that Hand was drawn away, so the eyes of flesh and blood looked out upon the showing of spirit, of Him Who Is: in a glory of blinding light, brighter than the sun, the back of a mighty Man walking on under that cloud of night which veiled the theophany from all eyes save those of Moses.

Now, men ask to see as Moses saw: "Lord, show us the Father, and it is enough for us."

And He replies: "So long a time have I been with you, and you know Me not? Philip, he that sees Me sees the Father."

They have looked on, and received into themselves, the full Christ, in Godhead as well as Manhood. But he who receives one Person of the Trinity must of necessity receive all three. God, the divine Being, is not divided into parts. The Father does not have one slice of the Divine Being, the Son a second and the Holy Spirit a third, but the Father, being the whole of Godhead, all the divine Life, gives the whole of that Life to the Son; and the Father and the Son breathe forth the whole of that Life as the Holy Spirit. Hence those who in this Sacrament receive the Son, the Divine Word, receive also the Father and the Holy Spirit.

So the cycle of being is closed: Increate Spirit is united with dead matter.

God, He Who Is, is present in every part of His creation. For a spirit is where it acts; and were God not acting on His creation to keep it in being, it would fall back into the stuff of which it was made: nothing. God is further present in man, not simply by preserving man, but by giving man supernatural life and by dwelling in man as in His temple. Above all, God is present in man by being Himself made Man. By being both God and Man Christ unites in one Person non-living matter (for Adam's body was made of the dust of the earth); sensitive matter, as in plants; self-moving matter, as in animals; created spirit; supernatural life; and the Divine Indwelling.

Now, at this Last Supper, as man binds together the two halves of creation, spirit and matter, so the God-Man binds together Spirit and all its creation: making very God to be present, under the appearance of bread and wine, non-living matter drawn from plant life, and received by men in the bodily animal way of eating and drinking.

He Who hates nothing that He has made has gone down into the very deeps of His creation. He descended among men that He might raise them up as the sons of God; He descended into the lower parts, that He might bring out the souls of the just who died before His death, and lead them to heaven. He has descended into the depths of that Nature which has not sinned against Him, that He might raise it also.

For Adam, man, was created in a certain setting, and was to glorify it and raise it up; but when he fell, he drew down all his world with him. Christ raises up human nature and with it all the nature of which it is Lord, as a man lifting one link of a chain lifts all the chain by that one link, that He may raise both man and nature to the very throne of God. As He is the new Adam, He is to have a new world: having overcome by the victory of the cross, He shall possess these things; and make of them a new heaven and a new earth. The divine Word, issuing from the Father and from whom all created things issue in turn (for in Him were all things made; and without Him was made nothing that was made) as man will lead all things back to God.

"And He that sat upon the throne said: 'Behold I make all things new . . . I am Alpha and Omega, the beginning and the end.'"

IN THE UPPER ROOM

WHAT DID YOU hear last night, your head on His breast
   there?
It was Peter in the dark supper-room
Asking of John,
Who with Mary, His Mother, was just returned
From burying Him.

I heard His blood moving like an unborn child,
And His Heart crying.
I heard Him talking with His Father
And the Dove.
I heard an undertone as of the sea swinging, and a whispering
   at its centre.
I listened, and all the sound
Was a murmuring of names.
I heard my own name beating in His Blood,
And yours, Peter,
And all of you.
And I heard Judas,
And the names of all that have been
Or shall be to the last day.
And it was His Blood was calling out these names,
And they possessed His Blood.

Did you hear my name?
Asked a woman who was sitting at His mother's feet.
I heard your name, Mary of Magdala, and it was like a storm
    at sea
And the waves racing.

I heard Peter's name,
And the sea broke, I thought, and ran over the world.

You heard then the name of Mary, His Mother, Peter said
    quietly, as he wept there kneeling.
I did, and it was like the singing of winds and they moving
    over an ocean of stars, and every star like a hushed child
    sleeping.

Again Peter—
What of Iscariot?
I heard the tide come in, and I felt the tide go out,
And I saw a dead man washed up on the shore.

And then John fell to weeping, and no one there could com-
    fort him but only Mary, the Mother of Jesus, and he could
    tell them
No other word.

GETHSEMANE

THERE IS a startling paradox in this, that he who came, as he said, to give life to men, to fill up the measure of their joy, to show them the way back to the wonder and peace of living in God, he who is known by names that are radiant with joy, light, life, love, is known also as "the Man of Sorrows." At first sight one would be tempted to say that he had fallen in love with our suffering. He made himself subject to our limitations—to discomfort, poverty, hunger, thirst and pain. He chose to experience fear, temptation, failure. He suffered loneliness, betrayal, injustice, the spurning of his love, mockery, brutality, separation, utter desolation of spirit, the sense of despair, and death.

But it was not with our suffering that Christ fell in love; it was with us. He identified himself with our suffering because he identified himself with us, and he came not only to lead his own historical life on earth, but to live the life of every man who would receive him into his soul, and to be the way back to joy for every individual. He took our humanity in order to give us his, and since guilty man must, as a very condition of his own ultimate joy, and even for his fullest measure of earthly joy, "make" his soul through expiation, through personal atonement, Christ chose to atone for mankind as each man must do for himself: through suffering. "He who was without sin was made sin for us."

Christ is "the Way." He taught the way to wholeness, showed it in his historical life, and he *is* the Way in the life of every individual who does not refuse his destiny of Christhood.

Christ, who knew everything that is necessary to man, and that only what is real is necessary to him, knew that the most profound secret of psychological healing for guilty men is to know the Eternal Father: "Eternal life is knowing thee, who art the only true God; and Jesus Christ, whom thou hast sent" (John xvii, 3). The gospel is woven together from beginning to end by Christ's continual awareness of the Father and his continual awareness of his own sonship.

He used everything around him to try to make men realize the Father's love for them. Everything should remind them of his tenderness, even the sparrows and the daisies and the grass. In that wonderful discourse before his death, in the hush of the Cenacle, he makes it clear that being at one with God is the utmost happiness man can know, and that it is his own happiness and glory.

Just as he spoke continually of his Father to make him known and loved, he continually reiterated the fact that his human will was wholly surrendered to him. His work in life was to do his Father's will: "I came not to do my own Will but the Will of him who sent me." Every act of his was done through him by his Father's Will: ". . . and the Father, who dwells continually in me, achieves in me his own acts of power" (John xiv, 10).

Every word that he spoke was a word that it was his Father's will to utter through him: ". . . it was my Father who sent me that commanded me what words I was to say, what message I was to utter. And I know well that what he commands is eternal life; everything then, which I utter, I utter as my Father has bidden me" (John xii, 49, 50).

It was this surrender to the divine Will that allowed the Holy

Spirit to sweep him on to his Passion and the consummation of
his love.

It is in the garden of Gethsemane that the surrender of
Christ's own human will comes to its climax; here too, that the
drama of the culmination of his fight with the shadow, a fight
that had been going on all through his life, comes to the final
crisis; and here that in Christ the struggle every man is faced
with is fought out, ending in his accepting the suffering of the
guilt of mankind.

In Gethsemane Christ faced the crisis which so many millions
must face when they are challenged by love—will they be
stripped of all pretence, and be naked, themselves, before love?
Will they consent to the revelation of the secret of self, and the
mystical death of Love? Will they take up the cross of daily
hardship and poverty and sacrifice of self, and carry the burdens
of life, for love of others? This is the challenge which comes in
turn to everyone—"Can you drink the chalice that I must drink?"
It came to Christ in Gethsemane, and his consent led on to the
consummation of his love on the Cross.

Above all, it is in Gethsemane that we see the climax of
Christ's acceptance of guilt, which began with the first pulsation of his human heart, and dimly, from ages and ages away,
realize what mental suffering it involved him in. "My soul, he
said, is ready to die with sorrow" (Matt. xxvi, 38). For he was
seeing what he was to take upon himself—the guilt of the whole
world. He saw all the sin of the world for all time in all its naked
evil, and he saw all the results of sin on the soul and body of
man, and all the results of it in suffering.

He saw all the disease and corruption, and festering and
swarming and seething of sin. For the second time in his human
life he saw "all the cities of the world and the glory of them"—
the blasphemy of luxury side by side with slums, the rat-infested
brothels hidden away in mean streets in London, flaunted almost
on the steps of the Shrine of the Blessed Sacrament in Mont-

martre. He saw the black industrial cities with their back-to-back houses, and the stunted and twisted little children forced into the factories; he saw all the battlefields of the world with all their mutilation and suffocation and agonized dying, he saw all the secret dungeons and prisons where men rot away, and all the concentration camps with their starvation and corruption and their piles of corpses and their gas chambers. He saw all the persecutions that would destroy the souls and bodies of men: the persecution of Christians by heathens, of Catholics by Protestants, of Protestants by Catholics, and, most bitter of all to the breaking heart of Christ, the persecution of Jews by Christians, carried out in his own name.

All this and more and more and more. And incomparably more terrible than any of it, the sheer elemental evil that was the cause of it all.

But worst of all he felt himself to be bearing the guilt of it all, felt, as he lay there on the ground exposed to the eye of God, that all the guilt was on him.

Adam was the first sinful man, and he tried to repudiate guilt; Christ was the first sinless man, and he accepted the guilt of all sin. Adam was the first man to hide from God; Christ was the first man to expose his soul, covered in the wounds and ugliness inflicted by guilt, to the fierce blaze of God's light.

His human will shrank from this, and from the death that measured evil hung up naked in the sight of God, covered from the crown of his head to the soles of his feet with the blood and the filth and the spitting of sin.

"When he had gone a little further, he fell upon his face in prayer, and said, my Father, if it is possible, let this chalice pass me by; only as thy will is, not as mine is" (Matt. xxvi, 39).

As he prayed, in agony of mind, Christ experienced in himself the struggle of our whole race—with the accumulation of guilt from which nearly every individual, except the saint, tries to escape, and for which nearly everyone repudiates all personal responsibility. There was no escape for Christ. For the last time his human will surrendered to the will of God, and the man who had a few moments before been lying on his face on the ground, oppressed by all the fear and dread and depression of all mankind, was comforted by an angel, and rose up, self-possessed, majestic, to go out to the consummation of love.

A PLACE CALLED GETHSEMANE

⚥ "HE BEGAN TO BE SORROWFUL: he began to be afraid." We live today in a world so haunted by fear that this story of Christ's agony must be very close to us. Anxiety lies heavy on the hearts of men; and on the lips of philosophers the very word has become a commonplace. But it is not only fear that we share with this figure in the garden. The most fearful thing about the world's fear is its hopelessness, its sense of futility, a futility reflected again by those philosophers for whom anxiety is an anguish from which there is no issue. Here, in the garden, he began to be afraid and it was indeed a dread of the torments to come; it was indeed the burden of loneliness; it was the terrible sense of defilement, the even physical horror of the black waters of evil overwhelming him; but, added to all this there was the knowledge that it would all to some extent be in vain, to some extent be futile.

If we search for a solution to the problem of pain we can hope to find it only in the divinity of Christ, only in the tears of God. God so loved the world that he was willing to allow the horror of sin and the suffering that comes of it—why? Because then by becoming man he could share in the suffering and thereby could reveal to us the richness of reality, the deep mystery of love in a way he could never otherwise have done; and so in the end we in our turn could become something deeper and richer than we should ever otherwise have been. And in this scene, which is ultimate love unfolding itself in what seems like ultimate tragedy, that answer is given, that love is given; and yet he was despised and rejected, he *is* despised and rejected; and for many it is as though it had never been, and for many of us Christians it is in practice as though it had never been.

Yet, though the sense of futility is woven into the texture of the agony, the agony itself is still only a moment in the Passion; and he approaches it not with hopelessness but with joy, and it ends not in hopelessness but in the ringing triumphant cry, *Consummatum est,* the perfect work is achieved; and there follows not darkness and emptiness but the spearpoint of light of resurrection, the new day. Nor is it merely that joy succeeds sorrow as sorrow had succeeded joy; this sense of futility is creative of what is to come. Without it the Passion would not have been so perfect: for love is greatest when it is stripped of all sense of achievement, all return, and is sheer naked self-giving. That is what we watch in the garden: the divine self-emptying which alone could annihilate the self-centredness of man. He was despised and rejected and left utterly alone, that his acceptance of his lovelessness and his loneliness might deliver us from ours.

And as from the darkness of the garden there comes the light of universal deliverance, so it can be in our own souls. Watching with him we can teach ourselves first a sense of sin, a sense of the reality of the evil that is in us. But we must not stop there. We take our sorrow for it not to an implacable judge but to the prodigal father of the parable, to the God who says, No matter when you come back, nor even why you come back, provided only you come back in the end, there will be the music and the lights and the feasting to welcome you. So out of the sorrow is born a deeper love; and Christ is comforted not only by an angel, not only by the love of those who have never rejected him, but by the sorrow of those who have, but who have then returned to him in greater love. . . .

They came to a garden, and it was night. The little walled enclosure, remote from the city, the silvery olive trees, the disciples sleeping: everything is still. Stillness is the womb of all great achievement: the immobility not of inaction but of intense energy. It was wisely said: "Nobody but a fool would mistake silence for emptyheadedness; nobody but a fool would confuse the immobility of the monk with aridity and death of soul." But stillness is something that has to be achieved. We tend nowadays to think of silence as the privation of sound; in fact it is noise that is the privation of silence. If we want to watch with Christ and live with Christ we must first learn to be still. Throughout the Passion there are these enclaves of silence against the background of noise and tumult; and the sound and the fury signify nothing but death, produce nothing but futility: it is silence that is creative of life. Christ had commanded the waves, Be still, and they obeyed him; man refuses to obey, and is lost in a whirlpool of noise and commotion that lead only to chaos. If we are to be saved from our futility we must recover the faculty of being still: we must make an enclave of silence within our own souls.

He said to them, Watch and pray. We shall never live in that other dimension which is our true element unless we learn to be still, in that state of awareness we call prayer. Sometimes indignation is aroused by the suggestion that if we want to heal the world's evils we should pray: to sit still and do nothing, we are told, is simply to invite the evils to overwhelm us. But prayer, even the prayer of petition, is not asking God to do something for us while we remain idle; it is not the negation of activity; it is the essential condition of the only kind of activity that can ever drive out evil. Without it we can never hope to acquire either wisdom or love; and without these, activity is futile. The sense of futility is indeed the price we pay for having lost not only the power to be still but even the desire to be still.

There are some again who see in this story a proof not of the power but of the purposelessness of prayer. Christ, they say, prayed that the cup might pass from him, and prayed in so great an agony of earnestness that his sweat fell to the ground like thick drops of blood; but his prayer remained unanswered. But this is to misunderstand the nature not only of Christ's prayer but of all prayer. He prayed, but conditionally, as we always must: Not my will but thy will be done. And the prayer was heard. St. Luke tells us that after his first prayer an angel came to strengthen him; and you can see the change wrought in him if you read in St. Matthew's Gospel the different words of his second prayer: not now the simple cry of anguish, Let this cup pass from me, but the fuller, readier acceptance: If this cup may not pass from me, but I must drink it, thy will be done. So in the stillness of prayer strength comes to him; so it will come to us if we watch and pray with him; and in that stillness too, and only there, humanity as a whole will find new heart.

TRIAL AND DEATH

They took Jesus first to the house of Annas, once the high priest and now the father-in-law of the high priest Caiaphas. No doubt the cultured cleric of the metropolis thought that a few leading questions to this village Carpenter would yield matter for a capital charge. He began to question the world's Redeemer about His followers and His teaching. Quietly the eternal wisdom showed the cultured cleric's folly even to himself. Jesus had not been summoned to give an account of His sayings and doings. He had been arrested because they thought there was *prima facie* evidence that His sayings and doings were a breach of the ecclesiastical, and therefore of the civil, law. The Prisoner —for He was now a prisoner—had not to answer questions but to confront and refute witnesses. This Greater than Solomon in wisdom urges His right to be confronted with witnesses for the charge. These witnesses should have been easy to find because, as He said: "I have spoken openly to the world. I have always taught in the synagogue and in the Temple." To this answer there was no answer in law. There was only the answer of force and this was given Him. A servant of Annas struck Him a blow. Then God struck back, aiming His blow not at man's body but at man's mind: "If I have spoken evil, give witness to the evil: if well, why strikest thou me?"

To Annas, with his long experience of law pleadings, the Prisoner's answers unveiled a legal flaw which he had not wish

or authority to settle. He washed his hands of all responsibility
by sending the bound Prisoner to the High Priest Caiaphas.
Only the High Priest with his council, the Sanhedrin, had the
supreme authority, by Rome's permission, to deal authoritatively
with a capital charge, made under such questionable conditions.

Meanwhile, the one whom Jesus had chosen to be the Rock,
whose strong faith was to strengthen his brethren, was proving
himself less than a reed. His Master might well have called upon
him to give witness in His defence. But this witness was perjur-
ing himself by denying that Jesus was his Master. Earlier in the
night, Peter had, with a seaman's oath, sworn that he would
stand by Jesus, even if he stood alone. Now He denies that he
even knows Him; and again with seaman's oaths he deepens his
lie and his denial.

Three years of fellowship with the Lamb slain "from the beginning of the world" had not hardened the rock against fear!

Caiaphas, the High Priest, wielded the divine authority which
the Son of God came not to destroy, but to fulfill. Never had that
Son been disobedient to any lawful authority in any of its
lawful commands. As this was the first, and last, time that He
stood before the religious authority which His Heavenly Father
had commissioned, it was the most dramatic and momentous
issue He had yet faced.

Caiaphas had made no mistake about the gravity of the issue.
He had summoned the Sanhedrin for an early morning session
in order to condemn and punish the Prisoner before sunset had
brought in the death-restrictions of the Sabbath.

Witnesses were called and heard. But their witness being at
cross-purposes was incapable of supporting a charge and especially a capital charge. At last some witnesses accused Him of
saying: "I will destroy this Temple made with hands, and within
three days I will build another not made with hands." It was a
garbled witness to a prophecy. But a false prophecy was hardly

enough to justify a death sentence. And it was a death sentence that was sought.

The Word made flesh met this garbled testimony with silence, and uttered no word. The High Priest exercised his divinely given authority and, in presence of the Chosen People's Official Council, asked the official question he had a right and duty to ask: *"Art thou the Christ—the Son of the Blessed God?"*

To that question of questions the Word made flesh had a divinely given duty to reply: He said: *"I AM."*

He added, prophetically: "You shall see the Son of Man sitting on the right hand of the Power of God and coming with the clouds of heaven."

The poor manacled and helpless Prisoner was in such violent contradiction with His words that the High Priest seemed to give the only judgment that could be given: "What need ye any further witnesses: You have heard the blasphemy. What think you?"

They all condemned Him to death.

A day had not passed since He sought to prepare His disciples for their life's work by the prophetic words: "The hour cometh when whoever killeth you will think that he doth a service to God."

Once condemned—and condemned for blasphemy—He became as a worm and no man. The crowd, following, as usual, the way of their leaders, condemned Him, and began at once to carry out the condemnation: They struck Him. They spat on Him. They mocked Him, saying: Prophesy. Poor, blinded children of men, they did not know that when He said *"I AM"* He fulfilled all prophecies already given, and when He foretold His coming with the clouds He gave the greatest prophecy that could be given.

As the world's Redeemer was to die, not only for the Jews but for the Gentiles, it was necessary that not only Jews but

Gentiles should be found consenting to His death. Countless prophecies of the chosen people were fulfilled when, in the early morning of Good Friday, a poor Galilean, manacled and wearied, was brought to the gates of the stronghold to be condemned to death by that foreign power which was slowly putting the Jewish kingdom to death.

Pontius Pilate, our Gentile representative on that day of the world's redeeming, was not admittedly a weak governor. Already he had not hesitated to massacre what were accounted a group of fanatical Galileans. It may have predisposed him against mercy that the Prisoner, whom an official group from the Sanhedrin brought before him, was a Galilean.

The charges brought against Jesus if proved were more than enough to bring the desired death sentence, which no one was desiring more than was the quiet, manacled Prisoner. Pilate was told that by the court of the Sanhedrin the Prisoner had been found guilty of stirring up the people—of refusing to pay tribute to Caesar—and of calling Himself the Messiah, that is the promised King of the Jews.

Pilate's official duty, as an official of the Roman Emperor, was to ask the Prisoner if He claimed to be the King of the Jews. Jesus' official duty, as a subject of the Emperor, was to give a plain answer to the question. He answered: "I am." But it was also His duty to explain, as He did explain, that His Kingdom was not of this world. The Kingdom of men's souls which He was bringing in for the whole world would not aim at destroying even the worst realm in the world. But, whilst resisting rulers when they were unjust, His kingdom would support them, even at cost of life, where they were just.

Pilate's wife had warned her husband, what she had been warned in dream, that Jesus was a just man who was better left alone. This warning became effective when Pilate heard that Jesus was not a Judean, but a Galilean who had come up to Jerusalem from Galilee for the Passover. As Herod, Governor of Galilee, was also in Jerusalem for the same purpose as this poor, wearied Galilean, Pilate sought to end an old-standing feud with Herod by sending him "the King of the Jews."

Herod had reasons for wishing to speak with the prisoner. One day, some three and thirty years before, his father, Herod the Great, had heard from three eastern travellers that they had seen the star telling the birth of the King of the Jews and they came to adore him. Herod, whom history strangely calls Great, may have been one of those men who think that, as the welfare of the kingdom is the welfare of the king, any challenge to the kingly power must be put down even by bloodshed. And the one Babe of Bethlehem, who had been born to die, but not to die by Herod's sword, now stood a manacled, silent Prisoner before Herod's son.

Before the son of the king who had sought the life of the Child this Child, who was the Word made flesh stood—and stood dumb. Had He sought life, now was the hour when He had but to ask this new-found friend of Pilate as a pledge of friendship to ask for the release of his fellow-Galilean. But it was His Father's will and therefore His own that He should die. To Herod and Herod's court the Prisoner's silence betokened a fool who did not realize that He was to die if He did not at least by a word show that He wished to live. In fool's white they sent Him back to Pilate, who might serve out life or death to One who seemed almost too witless for the trouble of putting to death!

But the dumb lips unlocked when Pilate spoke as one having an authority not found in Herod. Perhaps the human heart of Jesus was touched that it was this stranger alone who was making an effort to defend Him. Even the cruel Roman scourging and crowning with thorns was Pilate's last despairing effort to still the blood-lust of the fanatics.

But on that day of days, when God would not spare His Son, mercy had little hold on the hearts of men. The sight of a fellow-man, purpled in His blood and crowned with thorns, drove mercy farther from their minds and they cried "Crucify Him." When Pilate, perhaps despising the cowards and rabble before him, said "Crucify Him, you. I find no cause in Him," truth came unbidden from the throats of the crowd: *He ought to die, because He made Himself the Son of God.*

At that cry from the blood-lusting hearts of the crowd Pilate feared, because the fear of the Lord is the beginning of wisdom. He asked in fear: "Whence art Thou?" It was a question to be put, not by the civil, but by the religious authority. The Eternal Wisdom could fitly answer it only by silence. Then Pilate, stung by the seeming ingratitude of the Prisoner he sought to save, said: "Wilt Thou not speak to me? Knowest Thou not that I have authority to crucify Thee and I have authority to release Thee?"

The dumb lips opened for the last time in what we death-dreading mortals might call self-defence. The words spoken to this representative of the Roman Empire were spoken, not just to Pilate, the Roman representative of Rome's authority, nor yet to Rome, the seat and source of that authority, but to all rightful authority wherever found and whether wielded in the sphere of man's body or of man's soul.

"Thou shouldst not have any authority over me unless it were given thee from above. Therefore he that delivered me to thee hath the greater sin."

All authority is from a higher, and the sins of the highest authority are the worst. Such was the quiet, unruffled judgment of the Son of Man Who would one day come with the clouds to judge all the Pilates, and Herods and Kings and Kingdoms and Authorities that have come and gone amongst men.

When the crowd had answered Pilate's further appeal for release by telling Pilate that he was no friend of Caesar, Pilate's kindling fear of God and of his conscience gave way to his fear of men. The last cry of the crowd: "We have no king but Caesar" broke the last defence of his conscience. Seated in the judgment seat of ultimate justice he delivered over to die One Whom he had judged not guilty of any word or deed worthy of death!

Thus God, Who orders all things well, had arranged that the greatest of human empires should not only register the Redeemer's birth but should register and testify to the innocence of the Redeemer's death.

Thus, too, was the world's Redeemer put to death by the whole world of Jew and Gentile. And if both these worlds sinned by the part they took in their Redeemer's dying, they had the greater sin who had the greater light and greater authority.

The human bodily strength of Our Lord was so plainly ebbing that they did not let Him bear the Cross alone, but gave Simon of Cyrene immortality by constraining him to lend a helping hand. It was the only help the Redeemer had in His solitary work of Redemption. But Simon's help was neither sought nor could it be refused when offered, and, humanly speaking, it may have enabled the weakening limbs of Jesus to climb the hill of His crucifixion.

On that day, when pillars fell and veils were rent and values reversed, courage seemed to have found sanctuary only with the weaker sex. A group of women wailed this widow's Son, bound for death in the very summer of His life. With kingly courtesy, He bade them stay their tears for Him, but to weep for the doom that was upon them today and would be upon them and their children tomorrow.

No disciples stood round Him as they once stood around Him to keep those mothers and their little ones from drawing near this widow's Son. His hands could not touch and bless them as on the day when another group had been beckoned to Him, and touched and blessed.

But it was to these women from the crowd, whose tears unlocked His heart, that He gave His last merciful warning. Not
for them alone, but for the world was His warning given, because these mothers were even then carrying the world of
tomorrow in their arms.

Never had the words of Mary's Son been more charged with
the directness and drama of the people's speech. He bade them
weep for the days when the fruitful womb and the milk-full
breast would be accounted almost a curse, but the barren womb
and the milk-dry breast would be accounted a blessing. In that
day all the glory that was Israel would be as a flower trampled
in the mire. Men and women alike would ask the mountains to
fall on them and the hills to cover them. By their own doing
they would have brought about such a state of things that life's
chief occupations, activities, pleasures, would seem but an
escape from life.

No words of greater doom had ever passed these lips that once
and again uttered the terror-striking "Woe! Woe!" But now that
the death He has desired with desire is awaiting Him on the
neighbouring hill, the voice of this Son of Mary has the tenderness of a mother clasping and soothing her hurt child; for "God
shall wipe away all tears from their eyes and death shall be no
more."

It was not a poor, death-shrinking criminal who at last stood
on the hill of Calvary. It was the Good Shepherd laying down
His life for His sheep. It was the One High Priest offering up,
not now in symbol but in reality, the world's One Redemptive
Sacrifice on the altar of the world. . . .

The Cross of Calvary, on which Jesus was at once the world's
Priest and the world's Victim, was also the Chair of the World's
Teacher. As all His deeds were gifts, so, too, all his words were
truths, indeed fundamental truths, to be believed by our mind
and lived in our life.

Hardly had He been nailed to the Cross and the Cross fixed on the hill-top than they heard Him cry, saying: "Father, forgive them; for they know not what they do." Only the Redeemer's love could have uttered this cry, which even today seems to belie His claim to be God's very Truth. This pleading that the men who put Him to death knew not what they did adds only another mystery to the essential mysteriousness of the Word made flesh.

Some of the magistrates wrought the unpardonable thing of mocking a dying man, saying: "If Thou art the Elect of God, save thyself." Cruelty and callousness could go no farther. One of the poor wretches crucified by His side took up the crying: "If Thou art the Christ—save Thyself and us." He was chid by his fellow-thief, who uttered the memorable cry: "Lord, remember me when Thou comest into Thy kingdom." To discern a King in the poor scourged Prisoner by his side betokened the living faith that moves mountains of past sin. Then the King said courteously to His new-found subject: "This day thou shalt be with Me in Paradise." In the great doings of mankind's redemption the Redeemer does not overlook the individual soul.

At the foot of the Cross there stood a little group with fearless loyalty. Among them was the Apostle who, perhaps first of the frightened eleven, had mastered his fear. Perhaps his love, not only of Jesus, but of the Mother of Jesus had brought John as her guardian to the hill of death.

When Jesus saw this disciple whom He loved and the Virgin Mother whom He loved still more, He said: "Lady, behold thy Son!" To the disciple He said: "Behold thy mother." From that hour all men are empowered to say to her: "Lady, thou art God's mother—and ours." After the kingdom of grace and everlasting bliss this was God's greatest gift to men.

When He had given men His mother He cried out "I thirst," as if some life-stream had been drained from His veins. His love was suffering the pangs of having nothing more to give!

In His sacred Manhood He had nothing further to give—nor indeed in His sacred Godhead, for it is not the Son who gives the Father. It is the Father who gave His only-begotten Son.

But he could and did express the Father's temporary withdrawal from the Son's manhood in the mystic cry: "My God, my God, why hast Thou forsaken me?"

This was the cry of One who is not merely obtaining the forgiveness of our sins by His merit, but is obtaining the forgiveness of our sins by satisfaction. Who merits the forgiveness of a debt rests on the love of the one who forgives for the one who merits. But who satisfies for a debt does not rest on the love of the one who is paid for the one who pays. But the one who satisfies, as our Redeemer satisfied for others to His Father, shows His love for either or both of those to whom and for whom He satisfies.

From the first moment of His created human will Jesus merited the Redemption of all sinners from all sin. But only in His natural death did He satisfy for, as well as merit, the forgiveness of man's sin. And as this unselfish satisfaction did imply His love for the Father and for us, but did not imply or demand the Father's love of Him, He expresses this unselfish satisfaction in the mystic cry: "My God, My God, why hast Thou forsaken Me?"

This is taken to mean that every human faculty suffered all it could. If the cry "I thirst" is the body simply expressing the redemptive pain it was allowed to suffer, this mystic cry expressing an alienation from God expresses that darkness of mind and heart now allowed to settle upon the Crucified.

Yet, of course, the sinless soul of Jesus, either in the Garden or on the Hill, could not swerve from full acceptance of the Father's will. The Father had sent Him to die, and the Father's will was the life of His human life. He uttered the heroic cry: "Father into Thy hands I commend my spirit."

On the day when Jerusalem heard Him saying that He was

the Good Shepherd who would lay down His life for His sheep He had also spoken of the Father: "Therefore the Father loveth Me, because I lay down My life, and I take it up again." Two supernatural works had made the Passion possible: The first was that all the supernatural, divine strength of His divine person was prevented from preventing His suffering; the second was that just enough strength was given to His soul that the bodily and mental sufferings did not part body and soul in death.

St. John, the beloved disciple, who was close to His Master in this hour of world-redemption, almost proudly says that the Son Who had come into our midst to do His Father's will and work by dying for us said: "It is finished." And only then did He bow His glorious head and give up the life He had taken up in obedience and love.

A little later soldiers came to end the life of the three men on the hill by breaking their legs. But seeing that the Man in the midst of the three was already dead, Rome made His death, as it had once made His birth, officially certain. Not a bone was broken, lest prophecy should be broken: but a lance pierced His heart. And from that love-broken heart, as if to make that love divinely certain, there gushed forth not blood only, but water and blood.

The great contemplatives whom we call doctors of the Church tell us the meaning of the water and blood. They remind us that the Redeemer's chief aim in life and death was to bring redemption to all mankind unto the end of the world by the Sacraments. And some are sacraments bringing grace to the sin-dead soul; and some are sacraments bringing further grace to the soul in grace. Now the Sacraments of the dead were symbolized by the water, and the Sacraments of the living were symbolized by the blood. Deo Gratias.

When Jesus, the victorious Captain, routed the enemy of man, His last words were a mighty shout. As if recognizing and answering the word of Him who made it with a word, the earth rocked with a great earthquake, which tore in twain the veil of the Temple Holy of Holies. A great darkness was upon the City of God's death. But it was the darkness that heralds dawn.

When the Roman soldiery—who were experts in death!—had certified that the Galilean was dead, two men, whose names still "smell sweet and blossom in the dust," Joseph and Nicodemus, wrapped the body of the Dead in linen clothes made sweet with spices, and laid Him in a tomb nearby in which no one had yet been laid.

That night the city was keeping a memory of Israel's deliverance from Egypt's thraldom by slaying and eating the Paschal Lamb.

But at noon the Lamb of God had been fixed on the Cross. There He had stayed, fastened not by nails, but by love, until He died. And not Israel merely but all men were by His death delivered from a doom worse than Egypt's thraldom, the yoke and debt and doom of sin.

THE CROSS SPEAKS

🖋 IT WAS LONG AGO,   I yet remember,
that I was hewn down   at the wood's end
torn from my place.   They took me there, strong foes,
they set me up as a gazing-stock,   bade me lift on high their
    felons.
Men bore me on their shoulders,   till on a hill they set me,
many foes fastened me there.   Then I saw mankind's Lord
swiftly come with courage,   for He willed to mount on me.
Then dared I not,   against the Lord's word,
bend or break,   when I saw
the earth trembling.   I might there
have felled all my foes,   but I stood fast.
Then He stripped Himself, the young Hero,   that was God
    Almighty,
strong and firm-hearted   He mounted the mean gibbet;
noble-hearted in the sight of many   He would set free man-
    kind.
I shook when the Prince clasped me,   but I durst not bow
    to earth,
fall to the ground,   but must needs stand fast.
A rood I was raised aloft,   I lifted the mighty King,
Lord of Heaven,   I durst not bend.
They drove me through with dark nails,   on me the marks
    are plain,

wide wounds of hate.   I durst not harm any of them.
They mocked us both together.   I was all wet with blood
poured from the Man's side   when He had sent forth His
     soul.
There on the hill   I underwent
many bitter things.   I saw the God of Hosts
sorely stretched out.   Darkness there
had wrapped in clouds   the Ruler's Body,
its fair radiance.   A shadow went forth
wan under clouds.   All creation wept,
bewailed the King's death,   Christ on the rood.
But there came from afar   eager nobles
to Him all alone;   I beheld all that.
Sore was I troubled with sorrows,   but I bent down to the
     hands of the men
humbly, with hearty will.   There they took Almighty God,
lifted Him down from the heavy pain.   They left me stand-
     ing
wet with blood;   I was all wounded with shafts.
They laid Him down, limb-weary;   they stood at His body's
     head;
they gazed on Him, Heaven's Lord,   and He rested there
     awhile,
tired from the great strife.   They began to make His grave
in the sight of His foes.   They carved it from the bright stone.
they laid in it the Lord of Hosts.   They began to sing a
     sorrow-song
alone in the evening tide.   Then they went away,
weary away from the great crowd.   With a few He rested
     there.

                                        From *The Dream of the Rood.*

THE OBJECTIVITY OF THE GOSPELS

❧ READ THE STORY of the crucifixion as if you were reading it for the first time. "Father, forgive them; for they know not what they do." Has human passion ever found so divine expression? "My God, my God, why hast thou forsaken me?" Is there anything like that in human tragedies before or since? Does Sophocles strike this note? Does Shakespeare?

And mark how loveliness is married to sorrow even in the closing movement of the final act. How beautiful upon the mountains are the feet of him that bringeth good tidings even when those feet are climbing the mount of Calvary. "Father, forgive them. . . . Today shalt thou be with me in Paradise. . . . Then said he to the disciple, Behold thy mother. . . ." Can these sayings be matched in all the masterpieces of men?

Read the story of Christ's appearance before Pilate. How immeasurably the story would have lost had Pilate been shown, as a writer of fiction would probably have shown him, as a callous and unimaginative procurator only too ready to hand over a troublesome fanatic to his troublesome foes. How the story gains when we begin to understand the impact of Jesus on his judge, on a man very like you and me, a man who had felt the magic of Jesus as so many who disown him have felt it, but who had not the courage to fall down and worship.

Pilate's distaste for the role which had been assigned to him is obvious from the first. I see him as a Roman, characteristic of his age, an age which had lost its faith in the gods, but which was still susceptible to superstition. Pilate reflected, as so many moderns reflect, "There may be something in it after all." He had nothing but contempt for the fanaticism of the Jews, and he faces, with Roman disdain, the angry priests who are demanding death for a man of whose immeasurable superiority he is uneasily aware. He explores every avenue for compromise. He is superstitious, for superstition flourishes in a time of religious decay, and he is sorely troubled by his wife's dreams. "Have thou nothing to do with that just man: for I have suffered many things this day in a dream because of him."Surely authentic history speaks in that verse.

As for poor Pilate, he becomes more hot and bothered as the hours pass. Desperately he tries to escape. He offers the angry crowd the ultimate choice, Jesus or Barabbas, and they choose Barabbas. Still Pilate persists, but his courage fails when he hears that terrible cry, "If thou let this man go, thou art not Caesar's friend: whoever maketh himself a king speaketh against Caesar."

Pilate "took water and washed his hands before the multitude, saying, I am innocent of the blood of this just person: see ye to it."

Do you think that a simple Jew could have invented this touch?

Pilate gives in, but not without one last kick. The Jews have beaten him, but Pilate is determined to spoil their triumph. Let Jesus hang on the cross, but let the cross fling a Roman taunt to the Jews whom the Romans despise. With his own hands Pilate writes, Jesus of Nazareth the King of the Jews," and this insult to all Judea is nailed to the cross. "There hangs your king," says Pilate in effect. Back stream the angry priests, but Pilate has had enough. There is a vivid French phrase which expresses that exasperated fedupness which differs in kind and not only in degree from ordinary boredom—*J'en ai soupé*. Pilate *en a soupé,* and he silences the Jews with a remark which men have quoted ever since to express unyielding finality. With the words, "What I have written I have written," he makes his exit from the stage.

Pilate stands as a type, for all time, of those who reject Christ's claims but profess to admire Christ's character. Christ has been patronised and praised in one book after another from the pens of wistful agnostics. Writers such as Matthew Arnold, Renan and Middleton Murry say, as Pilate said, "I find no fault in him." They all assume, as Pilate assumed, that they are "innocent of the blood of this just person," and, like Pilate, continue to ask, "What is truth?" in the presence of living truth. It is Catholic doctrine that Christ is crucified by those who reject him. Those who repudiate Christ, whether they reject him with honest and uncompromising hostility or with patronizing condescension, share the guilt of Pilate. For every man is faced by the choice of Pilate, there is no *via media* between worship and crucifixion.

The attention of one who was reading the Gospel for the first time would be focussed so intensely on the central figure that he would find it difficult to spare a thought for the lesser miracle of the biographers. Who were these men? What were these men?

That they were not creative artists, finished masters of the written word, this is certain. Nothing could be more certain. The effect which they produce is due to the theme, not to the artistry with which that theme is presented. It would make too great a demand on our credulity to credit the artlessness with which the tale is told, artlessness which has its own literary appeal, to conscious art. The Evangelists make all the mistakes that a conscientious beginner, tutored by modern handbooks on the writer's craft, would avoid. They spoil some of their most effective scenes by the failure to bring down the curtain. Their scenes often fade into one another by awkward transitions. The stories often begin and end abruptly. They report the most bewildering sayings without the least attempt to explain them, thus

CHRIST BEFORE PILATE
Jerome Bosch

violating a canon of sound fiction which ordains that every problem raised should have its solution, and that characters should
run strictly true to type. But the aim of the Evangelists is not
artistic fiction, but history. They are ambitious to report what
Christ said and what Christ did, and these unsolved conundrums
fall into place as the recollections of men who were often mystified by their Master. The Gospels are full of loose ends, of incidents which remain unexplained. Indeed, the cheerful casualness
with which the Evangelists leave unsolved even those problems
to which they could supply an answer, proves how far their
treatment is removed from the treatment of a modern biographer
or a modern novelist. Consider, for instance, the last Scene in
the Garden of Gethsemane. The disciples have forsaken Christ,
and the darkness is lit only by the torches of the guard. One
young man still continues to follow the soldiers, and the guard
turns on his heel with an angry exclamation, so one reconstructs
the scene—as if his nerves had been frayed by vague rumours
that the populace might attempt a rising in support of Jesus.
The guards lay hold of the young man. The linen cloth wound
round his naked body comes away in their hands, and the naked
man escapes into the darkness. The modern biographer, if he
recorded this strange incident, would speculate on the identity
of the young man, would, at least, attempt to explain his singularly inadequate wardrobe. If tradition be true, St. Mark had
good reason to know the answer to this riddle, St. Mark was
the young man in question, but he throws no beam of light
across the darkness into which the young man has fled.

If the Evangelists make many mistakes which a conscientious
beginner would avoid, it is no less true that they avoid most of
the mistakes which a beginner would make. The surest sign of
immaturity in a young writer is a certain weakness for labels.
He wishes to convince you, we will suppose, that his hero, Sir
Harry Tremayne, was famous for his caustic wit. So he labels
him. Instead of allowing us to infer from witty dialogue that Sir

Harry is a wit, he tediously insists that his *bons mots* were quoted from one end of Mayfair to another. The experienced writer avoids labels. He does his best to convince you with his dialogue, and allows us to infer wit from the remarks which he reports. He does not tell us that his hero is brave, but he shows his hero proving his courage in action.

One of the first facts about the Gospels which strikes anybody who has ever tried to write, is the remarkable absence of labels. The Evangelists do not try to describe Christ, they show Christ in action, and report what Christ said. Seldom do they add a comment of their own, as if they realised that although a biographer might try to interpret a human subject, biographers of Christ would do well to confine themselves to what Clough calls "the mere it was."

Interpretations of Christ from those who did not know him in the flesh may be forgiven, for it is a natural instinct which makes the Christian seek to expand the meaning of Christ's words, and to illustrate them in relation to modern problems. But the men who were fortunate enough to walk with Christ were too modest to believe that their readers would be interested to learn what they felt or what they sought. Their sole concern was to provide the world with an authentic record of what Christ said and what Christ did. Their theme was so tremendous that they dared not intrude their own poor comments into the divine tragedy. To quote Francis Thompson with due alteration, they feared

> "To mar immortal melodies
> With broken stammer of the Earth."

Men who have passed through supreme experiences are drained of emotion. Words are poor things to describe what they felt, so they content themselves with reporting what they saw and what they heard. Thomas Herbert, who accompanied his royal master, Charles I, to the scaffold, has left a record of those last hours as moving as it is simple. On the way to the scaffold, Charles handed Herbert his watch, "which Mr. Herbert keeps accordingly." Nothing more. What more is there to say? Is it really necessary to add that Herbert never looked at this watch without a poignant memory of the master he had loved so dearly and served so faithfully? "Which Mr. Herbert keeps accordingly," tells us all that we need to know.

The iron objectivity of the Gospels is more impressive, for their theme is infinitely more tragic than the execution of a king. Read the story of the crucifixion and remember that familiarity with the subject inclines us to forget that it hurts to be crucified. How easily this record might have degenerated into sentimentalism. To quote only one incident, it must have been difficult to resist the temptation to describe what the mother of Jesus felt during those long hours when she watched the slow agony of her Son. Yet how pitiably inadequate any words must be to express so terrible a grief. "Now there stood by the cross of Jesus his mother and his mother's sister." Nothing more, and for nineteen centuries Christians have been trying to find words to translate and art to represent what his mother and his mother's sister felt.

The engraver's knife moves across the plate. A few sharp lines, and the picture has taken shape. No dry point burr softens the hard outline which emerges.

"And they crucified him . . . and sitting down they watched him there. . . . I thirst . . . and straightway one of them ran and took a sponge . . . but when they came to Jesus, and saw that he was dead already, they brake not his legs. . . ."

Those who believe that religion should never degenerate into sentimentalism or emotion into emotionalism will find support in this conviction in the bleak poignancy of the crucifixion story.

That the Gospels are the work of eye-witnesses is indicated not only by the things which they record, but by the things which they do not record. The Gospels are full of homely details which an eye-witness would have recorded, and are full of gaps which a fiction writer would have filled in. Read the most perfect short story in literature, the story of the woman taken in adultery. The great masters of the short story might have invented that sublime touch, "Jesus stooped down, and with his finger wrote on the ground," but they would not have been content to leave us ignorant of what Christ wrote. It is contrary to the canons of fiction to arouse the reader's expectations without easing his curiosity. Had Tolstoy invented this touch, Christ would have written something very telling in the dust, something very telling indeed, but nothing half so telling as the silence of St. John.

Reticence is the keynote of the Gospels. The Evangelists record unadorned fact. They never point a moral or adorn the tale. They give us Christ's word of condemnation, and leave it at that. "Ye serpents, ye generation of vipers, how can ye escape the damnation of hell?" Christ said that, and down it goes in the record, but St. Mark makes no comment. *Deus locutus, causa finita.* Man need not endorse the verdict of God.

They add no words to condemn when they record the betrayal, and no words to condone when they report the denial. Every word tells but every word records a relevant fact. "He then having received the sop went immediately out: and it was night." Twelve words enough to tell us what the twelve felt. The door opens. The shadowed figure shows up against the stars, and Judas passes out into the darkness. *And it was night.*

They are no less reticent when they describe the denial. St. Mark is supposed to have written at St. Peter's dictation (*Petro narrante et illo scribente*). He tells the story of the denial without wasting a word. The chapter ends with a verse as simple as it is tragic. "And the second time the cock crew. And Peter called to mind the word that Jesus said unto him, Before the cock crow twice thou shalt deny me thrice. And when he thought thereon, he wept."

He wept. That is all, and that is enough.

It is possible that St. Peter's defection was not unrelated to his sudden attack on the Chief Priest's servant. He had cut off Malchus' ear, and escaped into the darkness. Only one person appeared to have guessed his identity, a servant of the High Priest and a kinsman of the luckless Malchus. He certainly had his suspicions. "Did I not see thee in the garden with him?" It was this question, according to St. John, which provoked Peter's second denial. It was, perhaps, the presence of Malchus' kinsman which was responsible for the first denial. If this be so, it is easy to understand St. Peter's failure of nerve. A homicidal attack on the servant of the Chief Priest was an offence which was probably punishable by death. St. Peter could hardly be expected to hand himself over to the officers of justice by confession. This much might be urged in St. Peter's defence, but not by St. Peter.

The old Apostle dictates the story to St. Mark, and he neither defends nor reproaches himself. Why should he? Is it really necessary for him to insist that he should not have denied his master? Would anything be gained by a pen picture or a psychological analysis of his subsequent remorse?

The fisherman who had followed Christ was not concerned with the impression which history might produce on the reader. He did not measure life by the verdict of men. He was not therefore tempted either to explain his defection, or to impress upon the reader the sincerity of his remorse. He who had foreseen his weakness had also foreseen his strength. He who had foretold the denial had also foretold the cross outside the walls of Rome on which the chief of the Apostles was to reaffirm his faith.

"Jesus saith to Simon Peter . . . Verily, Verily, I say unto thee,

When thou wast young, thou girdest thyself, and walkest whither thou wouldest: but when thou shalt be old, thou shalt stretch forth thy hands, and another shall gird thee, and carry thee whither thou wouldst not. This spake he, signifying by what death he should glorify God."

THE VETERAN OF HEAVEN

O CAPTAIN OF THE WARS, whence won Ye so great scars?
  In what fight did Ye smite, and what manner was the foe?
Was it on a day of rout they compassed Thee about,
  Or gat Ye these adornings when Ye wrought their overthrow?

" 'Twas on a day of rout they girded Me about
  They wounded all My brow, and they smote Me through the
    side:
My hand held no sword when I met their armèd horde,
  And the conqueror fell down, and the Conquered bruised
    his pride."

What is this, unheard before, that the Unarmed makes war,
  And the Slain hath the gain, and the Victor hath the rout?
What wars, then, are these, and what the enemies,
  Strange Chief, with the scars of Thy conquest trenched about?

"The Prince I drave forth held the Mount of the North,
  Girt with the guards of flame that roll round the pole.
I drave him with My wars from all his fortress-stars,
  And the sea of death divided that My march might strike its
    goal.

"In the keep of Northern Guard, many a great daemonian sword
  Burns as it turns round the Mount occult, apart:
There is given him power and place still for some certain days,
  And his name would turn the Sun's blood back upon its
  heart."

What is Thy Name? Oh, show!—"My name ye may not know;
  'Tis a going forth with banners, and a baring of much swords:
But My titles that are high, are they not upon My thigh?
  'King of Kings!' are the words, 'Lord of Lords!';
  It is written 'King of Kings, Lord of Lords.'"

"WHY HAST THOU FORSAKEN ME?"

PEOPLE HAVE FOUND difficulty in the mysterious cry of Christ upon the Cross: "God, my God, why hast Thou forsaken me?" Unbelievers have argued that it proved that Christ gave way to despair, and was thus obviously merely human. Believers have sometimes been puzzled as to what was the meaning of these words, and have sought an explanation in the supposition that Christ's human vision of God was obscured or overclouded, or that Christ bore the sins of all men, and thus realized Himself as the bearer of all iniquity, and as such forsaken by the Father.

Unbelievers are easily answered by a reference to the fact that Christ's words were clearly the first verse of the 21st Psalm, and that for the meaning of those words they must read through the Psalm referred to. They will see that the Psalmist does not voice despair; that the Psalmist does not suppose that he is forsaken by God in the sense of God having withdrawn His divine favour and grace, but only in the sense of abandoning him to the fury of his foes. They will see that it is a loving expostulation to God in the midst of the mocking, jeering crowd who are causing the agony of the Sufferer. They will see that the predominant note of the Psalm is one of complete trust in God, a tender clinging to His infinite goodness, and towards the end a peal of triumphant joy. The word "Why" with which the Psalm opens is the natural cry of a human soul in great distress, surrendering indeed to God's blessed will, but wondering at the mysteriousness of God's plans and the strange ways of Providence that should require or allow so unexampled and unmerited pains in the hearts of those that love God. If the Psalmist was not in despair when he began his Psalm, why should Christ have been?

The whole tenour of the Gospels is against such an idea, for Christ is represented as full of the utmost confidence in God, and often rebuking His followers as men of little faith; and only the evening before His death bidding His disciples to be of good cheer, as He had overcome the world. Nothing can be more historically certain than that the authors of the Gospels who recorded the words in question did not see in them a cry of despair.

They make Christ threaten His persecutors with His return on the clouds of heaven only a few hours before; they make Christ promise Paradise in His company to the penitent thief on the Cross; they make Christ commend His soul to His Father, and proclaim that all is fulfilled, and they make Him utter a mighty cry in dying, clearly as a sign of His power, though all the forces of His body had ebbed away. The evangelists make it plain that they saw in the details of the Passion the minute fulfilment of the prophecies. They actually quote Psalm 21 as being fulfilled; when therefore they put the first words of that Psalm on Christ's lips, we may rest quite certain that it never occurred to them that these words implied despair, or lack of trust in God.

Therefore it is historically unsound to give those words a meaning which they did not convey to His own most intimate friends. Let this suffice for Jews and infidels.

Christians, however, have also searched with all reverence into the meaning of these great words of sorrow. Sometimes they have sought an explanation in the suggestion that Christ as God allowed in His human soul the vision of God to become clouded and overcast, that He in His human soul voluntarily passed through a time of darkness. Sometimes they have made the strange suggestion that, as Christ carried on His shoulders the sins of all the world, as the Great Substitute for sinners, for whom He made atonement, He allowed Himself to feel the pain of the loss of God, as if He were alienated and separated from His heavenly Father.

Such suggestions, however well meant, are most dangerous, because almost indistinguishable from a great misunderstanding. Christ even as man could not err. Never; and one might almost add, least of all on the Cross. A feeling of alienation or separation from God would in Christ's soul have been a terrible illusion, if we understand it as a feeling that He was really separated from God, or that His divine Father was angry with Him. Such a thing would be inconceivable and blasphemous, for Christ even in His agony knew who He was, and His soul was God's own soul, and He ever saw the face of His Father who was in heaven. "This is my dearly beloved Son in whom I am well pleased" was as true of Christ passing through the waters of death as of Christ standing in the waters of the Jordan, or being transfigured on Mount Thabor.

Christ was utterly innocent, and He knew that sin was intrinsically impossible to His innermost being. The guilt of sin cannot be transferred from one soul to another. Not even in the divine Atonement could the guilt of men's sins be transferred, for this would be not so much a blasphemy as an absurdity and palpable impossibility. Imprudent people have used such extravagant expressions as that Christ, willing to undergo the uttermost penalty of the sinner, allowed His soul to feel, as it were, the torments of hell.

They are strange and dangerous words, barely safeguarded by the expression "as it were." The essence of the torments of hell consists in the knowledge of alienation from God, but Christ's soul was never alienated from God, nor could He think that it was. Christ felt an unspeakable sadness, loathing and horror, at the innumerable sins of men, because of their intrinsic heinousness and ugliness, which revolted His God-owned soul and because of the punishment and degradation which they involved for His fellow-men, His own kith and kin according to the flesh, whom He loved with immeasurable love. He felt this most of all because they offended His Father, whom He loved and adored with all the might of His being. No calamity ever so cast down a human soul as the fact of sin cast down the soul of Christ and steeped it in the deepest depth of bitterest sorrow. Christ on the Cross so profoundly deplored sin that His mental agony must have far exceeded all bodily pains, and must have been the real cause of His death. On entering Gethsemane, He had protested that His soul was sorrowful unto death, and He entered then into an agony which would have ended in His death in the Garden but for direct divine intervention. On the Cross after His cry: "O God, my God, why hast Thou forsaken me," the sorrow of His soul actually caused His bodily death.

We cannot easily realize that any one should thus sorrow about another's sin, but sometimes even amongst mere men, people have been known to die out of sorrow for others. History may give us but few examples, yet there are some. A mother may pine away and die because of the disaster that befell her children; a husband may die because of the calamity that met the wife he loved. The contemplation of the pain of our fellow-men fills us all with sadness. How much more would the sight of the evil of sin and plight of His fellowmen fill Christ with sadness, as He alone fathomed the depth of that evil and He alone loved His fellowmen to the uttermost. His dread and revulsion, His supreme repudiation of sin, His indescribable sorrow and sadness, His cry of pity to His Father, His desire to make amends for the sins of His brethren and sisters according to the flesh, His willing death in their stead on the altar of divine justice; all these things constitute the Atonement.

But all this is surely totally different from any imagined undergoing of quasi-torments of hell, or illusion that the wrath of God rested on Him. Christ redeemed us precisely because He bore our punishment but not our guilt. *Christus innocens patri reconciliavit peccatores.*

How could Christ undergo this desolation, this lonesomeness or this abandonment and unutterable grief, if He were conscious of His personal union with God, who is everlasting happiness and bliss?

A complete answer we cannot give, for no man but Christ experienced personal union with God. However, men have been in union with God through sanctifying grace, and many saints have been in union with God through supernatural revelation. God has given great graces and illuminations to certain mystics, by which they were lifted to the third heaven like St. Paul. Such people, though their souls were flooded with supernatural happiness, have at the same time known great sorrows.

Martyrs on the eve of their supreme sacrifice, when their soul was in closest union with God, and when therefore they possessed that inward peace which surpasses all understanding, have none the less passed through long hours of deepest darkness of soul. Blessed Margaret Clitheroe showed a steadfastness in the faith, a completeness of self-surrender, a patience during incredible torments, which excite our amazement. Her love for God made her abandon her husband, her home, and her children, rather than be unfaithful to God. On the eve of her cruel martyrdom—she was bound in a sack and crushed to death at York for having harboured priests—this Margaret passed the night in an agony of sorrow and dread, which must have been fearsome to behold. Prostrate for hours on the floor of her dungeon, she groaned in anguish and sorrow. Yet she knew that a word of apostasy from her lips would have restored her to her most happy home. If she did not say it, it was because her soul was so firmly rooted in God, so close in the embrace of His sweet grace, that she preferred to die rather than lose His love.

She knew, moreover, that after a few hours of martyrdom, how-ever fierce, she would forthwith be rewarded with the happiness of the Saints in heaven. Yet nothing of all this prevented her agony of dread which was some faint renewal of the agony of Christ in the Garden.

Blessed Margaret has not left us a description of her state of soul previous to her martyrdom, but many saints tell us that in their mystic states they combined unutterable happiness with unutterable sorrow. They could have died for sorrow, had not God prevented it, although they never lost that happiness which only God can give.

Such considerations may perhaps help us a little in our en-deavour to understand Christ's blessed soul during His passion. United as it was with the person of God the Son, it always possessed supernatural joy, yet this in no sense lessened the reality and fulness of its sorrows. Christ's soul has been com-pared to a high mountain, whose peak is in the still glow and glory of everlasting sunshine, while its base is beaten by the blackest storm.

As far as we can see, to some people death is easy, to some it is very hard. Christ determined that He in His humanity would know the sum of all human sorrows, hence He deter-mined that His death should be hard, that thus all should be helped by His example. The greatness of His agony He man-ifested in the words: "O God, my God, why hast Thou for-saken me?"

CHRIST TELLS OF HIS PASSION

ALONE was I born,
a comfort to my folk;   with their hands they enfolded Me,
wrapped Me in poor weeds   and laid Me in shadowy places
in swaddling-bands.   Lo! For the world I suffered it.
Little seemed I to the sons of men;   and I lay on the hard
    stone,
a young child in the Crib;   so would I drive death from
    thee,
and hot hell-bale,   that thou mightest shine holy,
happy in eternal life.   For that lived I in pain.
'Twas not high-mindedness   that I in my youth
bore impious scorn   and body-soreness,
but that through it   I might be like thee,
and that thou mightest   be made like Me,
like to my face,   set free from sin.
For love of mankind   my head suffered
the blows of hate;   my face bore pain.
It was often stained   with coarse spittle
from the wicked mouths   of evil-workers.
They blended for Me   bitterly together
an unsweet drink   of gall and vinegar.
Before the people   I bore the wrath of foes;
they filled me with blows,   reckless with hate
and struck me with scourges.   Sorely for thee

I suffered that   with humble heart,
scorn and hard words.   A sharp crown
about my brows   they bound hard,
pressing down the pain.   It was wrought with thorns.
Then was I hung   on a high beam,
fastened to the rood;   straightway they poured
with a spear-thrust   blood from my side,
gore on the ground;   thus from the power
of cruel devils   thou art delivered,
since I without blame   suffered pain
and hard evils,   till forth from my body
I sent all alone   my living spirit;
see now the death wounds   that they made long ago
on my hands   and on my feet,
by which I hung   hard-fastened.
Here mayest thou see   plainly yet
in my side   the bleeding wound.
How uneven   is the reckoning between us!
I took thy soreness   that thou, in bliss,
might possess   my kingdom in joy,
and by my death   I bought dear
long life for thee,   that beautiful in light
thou mightest dwell   without a stain.
My flesh-house lay   beneath the earth
hidden deep   in the dark grave
—it had harmed no man—   that thou mightest be brought
to the skies above,   mighty among angels.
Why didst thou leave   that shining life
that for thy love   I bought for thee
with my own body,   to help thee, cast down?
Thou art so witless   that thou didst not thank
thine own Ruler   for thy redemption.
I claim nought now   for that most bitter
death of mine   that I suffered for thee;

but give Me thy life   that thou with sin
hast wrongly slain,   to thine own shame.
Why hast thou besmutted   by thine own will,
through the wicked lusts   of foul sin
that chosen place   that I blessed in thee,
hallowed as a house   for my own delight?
Yea—that body   that I bought for myself
from the grasp of foes   and forbade it to sin
thou hast defiled   with shameful guilt.
Why hast thou hung Me heavier   on the rood of thy hands
than when I hung of old?   Lo, this is harder,
against my will fastened   on the rood of thy sins
than that other was,   when, fixed with pain,
I mounted up   on the cross-beams
by my own will,   when thy strong woe
moved my heart   and I drew thee from hell.

From the description of the Last Judgment in the poem *Christ*.

SUFFERING REDEMPTIVE

To the Christian, suffering is not a problem to be explored by the human mind, but a mystery to be experienced by the human heart. A mystery, the catechism tells us, is "a truth which is above reason, but revealed by Jesus Christ."

Christ's revelation about suffering is woven all through the gospels. Sometimes His words are puzzling, as if He wants us to ponder them and discover our grain of truth through a certain effort; growing in the effort, expanding our souls for the joy that they are going to receive. "Ask," He says, "and you shall receive, seek and you shall find, knock and it shall be opened to you."

At first sight there is much to puzzle. Suffering, He says, is a blessed thing. Blessed to be poor, to mourn, to be reviled and persecuted. He even warns those who enjoy the opposite. "Woe to you rich—woe to those who laugh now"—or so on.

Suffering, or at all events our willingness to risk it, is the one condition He makes for His friendship. Never once did He ask of those who wanted to join the motley little company of His friends if they were virtuous, sober, honest, and respectable; never once did He attempt to persuade or charm anyone to His service with fair promises of happiness. On the contrary, with uncompromising honesty He said: "If any man will come after me, let him take up his cross daily." "And whosoever doth not carry his cross and come after me, cannot be my disciple."

You might suppose that, longing for love as He did long for love, He would at least have encouraged those who ran to Him with ardent enthusiasm, but no, to the young man who said "I will follow Thee whithersoever Thou goest," He answered in the loneliest words that any man has ever uttered, "The foxes have holes and the birds of the air their nests, but the Son of man has not where to lay his head." As if to say, if you want to come with me, you must live my life, and my life is a life of sorrow, of homeless, wandering sorrow.

This warning of Christ's was no mere test, it was not like the traditional trial of love in the fairy stories, something that would evaporate as soon as the right answer was given: no, of those who accepted His challenge one died by his own hand in despair, all the others were put to death, saving one only, the most loved and most loving, John, who lived on and on for nearly a hundred years and suffered the more terrible martyrdom of not being able to lay down his life for Christ, of living out the years of loneliness without the sight of the divine Face that once his eyes had seen, without the closeness of the human Heart on which he had once laid his head.

Yet Christ, Who had made this demand of His friends, was always trying to alleviate suffering. He could not bear to see the widow woman weeping for her dead son, so He gave the boy back to her alive. He was always healing, forgiving, going about doing good to everyone. He wept openly when He saw Mary Magdalene weeping for her dead brother, although He knew what he would do, knew that in a few moments she would be overjoyed. He broke down at the sight of a merely passing grief.

But there is no occasion when Christ called into His own fellowship one whom He had cured of blindness, lameness, sickness or death.

What a number of contradictions is raised in all this! Christ bids everyone to try and ease suffering. He does so Himself. It seems that He can hardly endure the sight of it, yet He offers it as the only inducement to His friends and He says that it is blessed. Later, the same contradiction is visible in His Passion. At the beginning He says that the hour has come in which He will be glorified, yet He shrinks from it and even asks to be let off! And when He has endured everything, all temptation, the sight and sense of all sin and guilt, the injustice of the condemnation, the betrayal by His friend, the stripping of His garments, the hour in which He was forsaken by God, He comes to the disciples on the road to Emmaus and asks them this astonishing question: "Ought not Christ to suffer these things and so enter into his glory?"

What can it all mean? What is the meaning of suffering?

Suffering is the result of sin; poverty, pain, sickness, death and all the torments of the mind, all are the result of sin.

When Christ was born, the world was already full of suffering. He did not bring the cross into the world, it was there already. The cross was a dead weight, it was the result of sin, and it punished sin, it offered no hope. Suffering was not a punishment planned, so to speak, by God. "God desires not the death of a sinner." God so loved the world, that man had made for himself the misery which was his punishment.

When Christ became man, He uplifted man's nature together with all its vital activities. He changed man's suffering into His passion. Man's suffering became redemptive.

By himself, no man can atone for sin, not all the united suffering of the world could atone for one small venial sin, because sin is against God, and so only God can atone for sin. But because Christ is God and He has given His own life to be man's life, man's sorrow has become Christ's sorrow and everything is reversed.

Now the cross, which was a dead weight, bears flower! The world's tears, which were cold and sterile, are changed to strong, life-giving wine, like the water of Cana. And now, one small

suffering of the most insignificant human creature can atone
for sin.

When Christ's earthly life ended and He ascended into
Heaven, He did not remove His life from man. He left Himself
on earth, in the sacred Host, and in the heart of man. Man's
sorrows continued to be Christ's sorrows, Christ's passion. They
continue to atone for sin. All the suffering we see today, all the
suffering we know in our own lives, is the passion of Christ. If
Christ had not changed our suffering to His passion, we should
still have suffered, but suffering would have been futile, destructive, useless.

Christ was not content simply to redeem us. He did more, He
became one with us. He took our lives and made them His life.
There is only one explanation possible—love. Love asks and
wants union, it wants nothing else. Real love can stop at nothing else, it desires not only to share in the life of the loved one,
but to live it, not to be with the other, but to be the other. If
anyone denies this, the answer is simple; he has never loved.

The whole meaning of our Catholic faith is union, union
with Christ, and through Him, union with one another. This
oneness is not a unity of ideas or ambitions or acts or circumstances, it is not a unity such as one finds in a society or group,
it is an organic wholeness. It is oneness like the oneness of the
various parts of the human body. Because this is so, no Christian
can be separated from any other Christian by anything whatever, we are one with our sinners.

This oneness gives our suffering an added value. It means
that, whatever of good one Christian does, all Christians share.
So, we can act for one another; if one Christian sins, another
can be holy for him; if one Christian dies for his faith, all those
who tremble share in his glory. And any Christian child in the
schoolroom can go into the white snows of Siberia and give
courage to the heroic bishops there.

Because all men's sorrows are Christ's sorrows, we can always find Christ on earth. "If you did it to the least of these little ones, you did it to me." The healing and service given to each other is given to Christ; we can clothe Him and feed Him and amuse Him and love Him in each other. What we refuse to each other we refuse to Christ. We may not know it, but every stir of pity, of compassion, of generosity, of tenderness, is the fruit of the Passion.

As Christ grows in the Christian soul, and as she comes to see with His vision, it is in others that she sees Him, for she is looking out, not in, and as He did, she has compassion on the multitude. She sees them with all the marks and effects of sin covering them, but *in* them the innocent Christ, needing her help. In the hospitals, she sees Him helpless in swaddling bands. In the refugees flying from their ruined cities and homes, she sees Him flying from Herod; in the dying she sees Him upon the cross.

This, then, is the essence of Catholic teaching about suffering. It is man's punishment, made by man, but changed by Christ to His redeeming sorrows. Through Christ, suffering has become, not an evil to be avoided at all costs, but a thing to be accepted willingly, even joyfully, as a means of sharing in the redemption of the world.

OF THE RESURRECTION OF CHRIST

Done is the battle on the Dragon black,
Our champion Christ confounded has his force;
The gates of Hell are broken with a crack,
The sign triumphal raised is of the Cross,
The devils tremble with hideous voice,
The souls are borrowed and to bliss can go,
Christ with his blood our ransom does endorse:
Surrexit Dominus de sepulchro.

Done in is the deadly Dragon Lucifer,
The cruel Serpent with the mortal sting;
The old Keen Tiger with his teeth ajar,
Which in await has lainé for so long,
Thinking to trip us in his clawés strong;
The merciful Lord would not that it were so;
He made him for to fail to get that thing:
Surrexit Dominus de sepulchro.

He for our sake that suffered to be slain,
And like a Lamb in sacrifice was dight,
Is like a lion risen up again
And as the sunlight flashes from his height;
Sprung is Aurora radiant and bright
On loft is gone the glorious Apollo,

The blissful day departed from the night:
Surrexit Dominus de sepulchro.

The great victor again is risen on height,
Who for our quarrel to the death was wounded;
The Son that waxed all pale now shines bright,
And darkness clears, our faith is now refounded
The knell of mercy from the heaven is sounded,
The Christians are delivered from their woe,
The Jewès and their error are confounded:
Surrexit Dominus de sepulchro.

The Foe is chased, the battle is done cease,
The prison broken, those jailers fled that dreamed,
The war is gone, confirmèd is the peace,
The fetters loosed, and blackening Hell unbeamed,
The ransom made, the prisoners redeemed;
The field is won, and overcome the Foe
Ungorged the goods for which the Dragon schemed:
Surrexit Dominus de sepulchro.

THE RESURRECTION

➤ FEW SCEPTICS would dispute the patent fact that the disciples of Jesus collapsed when he was arrested. Men do not readily confess to cowardice, and the story that the disciples twice fell asleep when they should have been keeping watch, and "all forsook him and fled" when Jesus was arrested, is not the sort of thing which the Evangelists would be expected to invent. . . .

Seven weeks later we find these timid, broken men risking imprisonment, persecution and death in the name of one whom they had forsaken in despair. How can we explain this psychological revolution?

There is only one explanation which fits the facts—the explanation given by St. Peter: "This Jesus hath God raised up, whereof we are all witnesses."

It is impossible to attribute such appearances after the crucifixion to collective hallucination.

People who mistake a polysyllabic and quasi-scientific phrase for an explanation may perhaps accept "collective hallucination" as the clue to this problem. But the scientist will ask whether there is any objective evidence of collective hallucination on this scale. Alienists, who should know, are sceptical on this subject. Normal people under abnormal conditions and abnormal people under normal conditions suffer from isolated hallucinations, but there is no record in science of normal people, not once but several times, and not under abnormal but under normal conditions, being collectively affected by the same persistent hallucinations.

I can speak with some personal experience on this point. Many years ago my friend, Claude Elliott, who is now Headmaster of Eton, and I devoted a long and dreadful day to the exploration of a Pyrenean peak on which a friend of ours had been killed. We were very tired, for we had left London at short notice, and had started our search the night of our arrival in the Pyrenees. Every time we turned a corner we expected to find our friend. Before long we began to see and to hear things; to see his body stretched out on the rocks, and to hear other members of the party shouting that they had found him. A vulture hovering near the cliff, as vultures will hover for days before attacking a dead body, provided a macabre touch which reinforced the illusion. These hallucinations were amazingly vivid while they lasted, but they never lasted for more than a second or two before reality broke in. I know of no case in which a hallucination affecting normal people has lasted for hours at a time.

Also note this difference. We were expecting to find our friend, and we mistook rocks for the friend whom we were expecting to find. The disciples were not expecting to see Christ. And on two occasions Christ was not recognized by those to whom he appeared.

In the case of Christ's appearances to the apostles there was no background of exhaustion, strain or terror. After a hard day's work in the open air the disciples meet together for the evening meal and Christ appears among them. The "hallucination" breaks bread, eats a bit of broiled fish and distributes the remains among them. An odd kind of "hallucination."

I do not know of any case of a sane man being gradually hallucinated against the steady resistance of a strong negative conviction. St. Thomas insisted on experimental proof before he would believe; he yielded gradually to the evidence of stubborn fact.

The alleged discrepancies in the accounts given in the Gospels of the appearances of the risen Christ present no difficulty.

"The usual characteristic of human testimony," writes Paley, "is substantial truth under circumstantial variety. That is what the daily experience of the courts of justice teaches us." And Paley mentions the fact that whereas Clarendon tells us that the Marquis of Argyll was condemned and hanged on Tuesday, other contemporary historians assure us that he was condemned on the Saturday and beheaded, not hanged, on a Tuesday. Yet nobody would deny the fact that his execution took place.

It was the appearance of Christ which transformed the Apostles; no other explanation is adequate to explain the transformation of these men from a broken and dispirited group into the triumphant missionaries who returned to Jerusalem. Had their faith been corroded by the least suspicion that the appearances of Christ were not objective, they would certainly have elected to preach the Gospel in the comparative seclusion of Galilee; they would never have dared to return to Jerusalem, the headquarters of the powerful party which had engineered the crucifixion, and of the Roman procurator who sent Christ to the Cross. They knew that imprisonment and death awaited them, and yet these men who had fled at the approach of danger launched their crusade in the very stronghold of the enemy. There is a mistaken impression that our ancestors objected less than we do to death and to pain. Subconsciously we are inclined to believe that the apostles and martyrs were men who did not understand the meaning of fear. But St. Mark makes it clear that the disciples were not naturally heroic men; their conduct in Gethsemane was, on the contrary, base and cowardly. Nothing but a conviction, overpowering in its force, nothing but a conviction coercive in its evidence of objective reality, could have wrought this amazing transformation. "Somehow the rugged fisherman Peter," writes Mr. Morrison in that excellent book, *Who Moved the Stone?*, "and his brother Andrew, the characteristically doubting Thomas, the seasoned and not too sensitive tax-gatherer Matthew, the rather dull Philip, intensely loyal but a little slow of apprehension, do not fit easily into the conditions required for an absolutely unshakable, collective hallucination. And if it is not both collective and unshakable, it is of no use to us. The terrors and the persecutions which these men ultimately had to face, and did face unflinchingly, do not admit of a half-hearted adhesion secretly honeycombed with doubt. The belief has to be unconditional and of adamantine strength to satisfy the conditions. Sooner or later, too, if the belief was to spread, it had to bite its way into the corporate consciousness by convincing argument and attempted proof."

The heterogeneous collection of Galilean peasants invaded Jerusalem, "the most keenly intellectual centre of Judea," and pitted their faith against "the ablest dialecticians of the day, and in the face of every impediment which a brilliant and highly organized camarilla could devise." *And they won.* Within twenty years they had threatened the peace of the Roman Empire. . . .

It is always tempting to take the past for granted, but when we think of the triumph of Christianity we must remember the contempt which the Roman felt for the Jews, and the disdain with which an educated Roman would sweep aside the grotesque creed which had discovered God in a common criminal executed by a Roman procurator. . . .

If the disciples of a Mahdi, executed in the Sudan by a British Court Martial, believed that he had risen from the dead and succeeded in converting the British Empire to their Creed, if the new gospel were preached in St. Paul's, and if strange African ceremonies replaced High Mass at Westminster Cathedral—if some such religious cataclysm as this took place, it would be no more amazing than the capture of Rome by the disciples of the Galilean. . . .

And he who attributes the transformation of the disciples to a subjective illusion has still to explain the objective fact that the tomb was empty on Easter Sunday.

In the most primitive accounts of the trial there is the assertion that the whole case against Jesus turned upon a sentence containing the words "in three days." There is every reason to believe that the Priests did, as St. Matthew tells us, take precautions against the disciples faking a resurrection by stealing the body from the tomb. And there is every reason to accept the recorded fact that the Priests sealed the sepulchre and placed a guard.

How did the body of Jesus escape from the tomb? The theory that Jesus did not die on the Cross and recovered in the tomb still leaves unexplained his exit from a closely guarded sepulchre. And it is impossible, as Strauss points out, that a man crippled by that terrible ordeal, even if he could have survived, could "have given to the disciples the impression that he was a conqueror over death and the grave, the Prince of Life; an impression which lay at the bottom of their future ministry."

Even more grotesque is the suggestion that Joseph of Arimathea removed the body. No motive has ever been suggested for such an action, and once again you are faced by the difficulty of evading the guard and by the further difficulty that the new tomb of Jesus would probably have become a shrine, and would certainly have killed stone dead the story of the Resurrection.

The disciples returned to Jerusalem and preached the Resurrection. Clearly, if the tomb had not been empty, the Priests would have triumphantly produced the body. And it was only because the disciples knew that no writ of *habeas corpus* could be served on one who had ascended into Heaven that they were able to prosecute their campaign with complete confidence and triumphant success.

In all the literature of the period there is no suggestion that the emptiness of the tomb was disputed. The only controversy which is recorded turns on the question as to whether the disciples had stolen the body. The vacancy of the tomb was common ground to the Christians and to their enemies.

There are, therefore, only two explanations which we need to consider. First, the orthodox explanation, that Christ rose from the dead, and secondly, the explanation advanced by the Pharisees that the disciples stole the body of Jesus from the tomb.

If the disciples had stolen the body, they would have had the best of reasons for knowing that Jesus had not fulfilled his promise to rise from the dead, and that he had died the death of a deluded fanatic upon the Cross. Knowing this, as they must have done, why should they have formed a conspiracy to impose upon the world a new religion in which they themselves did not believe? It is conceivable that these twelve men would have persisted to the end in maintaining an elaborate conspiracy of falsehood? Surely one or other would have broken away from so foolish and so pointless a conspiracy. For what had they to gain by this deceit? They were cutting themselves off from their countrymen, their friends and their relations; they were inviting persecution and martyrdom—for what? For a lie which they knew to be a lie. Is it conceivable that conscious deceit should have supplied the dynamics for a mission which transformed the world? Is it conceivable that men should have faced death with radiant courage in their efforts to propagate a doctrine which they knew to be false?

"I readily believe," writes Pascal, "those stories whose writers get their throats cut."

EASTER DAY

RISE, Heir of fresh Eternity,
  From thy Virgin Tomb:
Rise mighty man of wonders, and thy world with thee
  Thy Tomb, the universal East,
  Nature's new womb,
Thy Tomb, faire Immortalitie's perfumed Nest.

Of all the Glories make Noone gay
  This is the Morn.
This rock buds forth the fountain of the streames of Day.
  In joyes white Annals live this hour,
  When life was borne,
No cloud scowl on his radiant lids no tempest lower.

Life, by this light's Nativity
  All creatures have.
Death onely by this Day's just Doom is forc't to Die;
  Nor is Death forc't; for may he lie
  Thron'd in thy Grave;
Death will on this condition be content to Die.

THE ASCENSION

CHRISTIAN THOUGHT and piety have not gone very deeply into the study and understanding of the Ascension, though it is a mystery of immense richness. One is particularly struck by certain texts from St. Paul in which he studies it in connection with the expansion of the Mystical Body.

We find, to begin with, two very notable texts in the Epistle to the Ephesians:

> I, hearing of your faith in the Lord Jesus, and of your love towards all the saints, cease not to give thanks for you, making commemoration of you in my prayers, that the God of our Lord Jesus Christ, the Father of glory, may give unto you the spirit of wisdom and of revelation, in the knowledge of him: the eyes of your heart enlightened, that you may know what the hope is of his calling and what are the riches of the glory of his inheritance in the saints. And what is the exceeding greatness of his power towards us who believe, according to the might of the operation of his power which he wrought in Christ, raising him up from the dead, and setting him on his right hand in the heavenly places, above all principality and power and virtue and dominion, and every name that is named, not only in this world, but also in that which is to come. And he hath subjected all things under his feet, and hath made him head over all the Church which

is his Body, and the fulness of him who is filled all in all
(i, 15–23).

All the grace in the Church, then, all the gifts of the Holy
Spirit and the riches of eternal glory awaiting the saints, all
this is the result of the victorious strength of Christ as shown
in his Ascension. That is what St. Paul is pointing to in those
mysterious phrases, "above all . . . power," etc; and when he
says, "every name that is named," he is opening up to us vistas
of infinite spiritual worlds. On Ascension day the Father established Christ, the Incarnate Word, in His glory as supreme
Head of the Church. On that day Christ became Head of the
Mystical Body, and the Mystical Body is essentially a communication of the glory of the risen Christ to all mankind incorporated in it. The mystery of the Mystical Body was instituted
at the Ascension, to be brought fully into effect at Pentecost.

In another text from this Epistle the Ascension is even more
clearly indicated. It is one of the richest and most mysterious
passages in St. Paul, a text one could never weary of meditating
and discussing: "Ascending on high, he led captivity captive;
he gave gifts to men" (Eph. iv, 8). Christ has ascended on high
—that is the Ascension. He led captivity captive, setting man
free from the powers of evil to whom he was captive, and hence-
forward God's gifts are showered plentifully on the world, grace
begins to flow within the Mystical Body through the sacramental
life. It is because Christ is present in the glory of the Father
that the grace which is a sharing in His glory is continuously
communicated to all of mankind incorporated with Him. Christ
dwells within the Mystical Body as a living and lasting source
of grace and holiness.

St. Paul goes on: "Now that he ascended, what is it but
because he also descended first into the lower parts of the earth?"
What does the Passion mean but that Christ went down into
the realm of death? This is a point that is seldom explained,

and therefore we often fail to understand the significance of Christ's Passion for the whole world. Death is an evil power which, in company with sin, dominates mankind. Sin and death are two names for the same thing: death of the soul, and, resulting from it, death of the body. What was Christ doing in His Passion? Christ went down into death. He went where death is master. He put Himself into death's hands. The lower parts of the earth—the phrase does not simply mean the tomb, but also the lower regions, and in Greek theology the Resurrection was not simply Christ coming out of the tomb, but Christ coming up from the underworld. The notion is not the same—and the theological implications are far deeper. Christ went down into the domain of death, to that manhood which was under death's dominion, and there was a moment when death could cry "I am the victor". To which St. Paul gave that magnificent answer: "Oh death, where is thy victory?" Death, whose name is Satan, thought on Good Friday to be forever victorious, for Christ Himself was its prisoner. And then, on Easter morning, the gates burst, the prisons of death were opened up: "O Death, where is thy victory?"

Christ could not conquer death in this particular way without first becoming its prisoner. He fell into its power to set mankind free. And this gives His death an incomparable realism, and an incomparable grandeur, and gives the word *Redemption* its fullest meaning. It was not simply a buying back, the squaring of an account between Christ and Satan, but Christ's struggle against the powers of evil, and His victory over them all and over the dominion of death. This explains the rites of baptism as practised in the Early Church. The descent into the baptismal pool, which St. Paul connects with the burial of Christ, symbolized this going down into death. The newly baptized were incorporated into Christ's death before emerging victorious with Him. That victory of Christ's holds good for all men. Every man should reproduce in himself the whole mys-

tery of Christ—His Passion, Resurrection, and Ascension—and
baptism is a symbol of that conformity with Christ which is to
be carried on throughout life. Christ's victory over the powers
of evil is completed in us through mortification and the final
liberation it brings.

St. Paul continues, "He that descended is the same also that
ascended above all the heavens, that he might fill all things."
Christ has gone up above all the heavens, that is above every
creature. You realize that to the Fathers of the Church the
heavens and the angels were one and the same thing. When
you meet either word, *coeli* or *angeli*, it may be replaced by the
other. The heavens lend the angels their vastness; that is why
it is quite wrong to picture angels as beings with wings, for
they are immense spiritual worlds. To be raised above the angels
is to be raised above that mysterious spiritual creation which
surrounds us on all sides. We are immersed in the world of
spiritual powers, both the bad, those princes of this world with
whom St. Paul tells us we are always in combat, and the good,
those angels who surround the altar during Mass, whose
presence is so profound and so real a thing that our human
drama will always be played out in the background of this great
spiritual drama. The Ascension also means that Christ's manhood was raised above the whole spiritual creation. It is an
extraordinary thing that our needy human nature should be,
in Christ, raised up above the angels who by nature are so much
higher. One aspect of the mystery of the Ascension is the wonder
of the angels at adoring the God-Man. According to certain
Fathers of the Church, the sin of the fallen angels was refusing
to accept the Incarnation of the Word, because it raised mankind
above them, which they found humiliating.

We must try not to picture Christ going up to heaven between
two little angels. There were, of course, two angels who came
to console the Apostles after the Ascension. "Two men stood by
them in white garments. Who also said, Ye men of Galilee, why

stand you looking up to heaven? This Jesus who is taken up from you into heaven, shall so come as you have seen him going into heaven." But the presence of these two was simply a visible manifestation of the legions of angels surrounding Christ, who watched Him in wonder as He went past their ranks to be raised to the glory of the Father, to lift mankind above all the spiritual worlds to that glory.

St. Gregory of Nyssa gives us a most extraordinary description of Christ rising through the spheres of angels on the day of His Ascension, and the angels not recognizing Him. *Quis est iste?* —Who is that?—they ask. . . . And the angels who are with Christ answer: *Rex gloriae ipse est, rex gloriae*—Yes, He is indeed the King of glory. The angels do not recognize the Word of God in this man with the traces of His Passion still upon Him. It is, however, the same King of glory they saw descending to earth when the Word took flesh, returning clothed with the same humanity but this time bruised by death, still bearing the wounds of the Cross. This dialogue is the prelude to a heavenly liturgy of extraordinary grandeur, which expresses the central meaning of the Ascension, and St. Paul orchestrates all its themes most admirably. He goes on to show us what follows from the mystery: "He has ascended above all the heavens that he might fill all things." Another extraordinary statement. It is only in so far as Christ has ascended above the heavens that He can fill all things. In other words, the grace which is in Him can, when He is lifted up above all creation, spread out to fill all creation. It fills human creation first of all, inasmuch as Christ is now the source of growth in the Mystical Body. But it also fills angelic creation, so that, as St. Paul tells us, He may be first in all things, King of men, but also King of angels, *Rex angelorum*, so that the Word may rule a truly universal Kingdom. His kingship was instituted when He entered into glory; it will be established forever on the Last Day when Christ comes to take visible possession of His kingdom. Till then, His victory is still going on in mankind, and also in the world of angels, where God is working mysteriously to "fill all things."

St. Paul at once goes on to touch on another theme that concerns the apostolate: "And he gave some apostles, and some prophets, and other some evangelists, and other some pastors and doctors, for the perfecting of the saints, for the work of the ministry, for the edifying of the body of Christ." The fruit, therefore, of Christ's entry into His glory, is the *mission*, that is, the fact that men are chosen and called in Christ and in the Holy Spirit to do the work of evangelizing, as apostles, prophets, pastors or doctors, so as to build up the body of Christ. It seems odd that St. Paul does not speak of Pentecost—he goes straight from the Ascension to the mission—for we know that it was at Pentecost that the *charismata* were given, the spiritual gifts which turned some into prophets, others into apostles, or evangelists, because these are things effected by the working of the Holy Spirit. But what St. Paul wants to make clear is that the Ascension was the cause of Pentecost. It was from the moment when Christ entered into the glory of the Father that His action became life-giving within the Church, and that He began to teach the Church through the Apostles, through those who gave themselves to Him to work for His Kingdom.

Let us now look at the descriptions of the Ascension in the Gospels: we shall see that St. Paul's text gives them their fullest meaning. Christ said: "Go ye into the whole world, and preach the gospel to every creature . . . And the Lord Jesus, after he had spoken to them, was taken up into heaven, and sitteth on the right hand of God; but they, going forth, preached everywhere; the Lord working withal, and confirming the word with signs that followed" (Mark xvi, 15, 19–20).

Here, as in the Epistle to the Ephesians, the Apostles' mission is bound up with the Ascension. In St. Mark's Gospel one might get the impression simply of two facts stated side by side; St.

Paul shows their organic relationship: it is Christ, risen into the glory of the Father, who becomes the Source and the Head of the Mystical Body and orders its development: "the Lord working withal"—Christ acting in the Church as source of the Apostolate. At the beginning of the *Acts of the Apostles* we have a further description of the Ascension which sets up the same bond between it and the preaching of the kingdom: it was after Jesus had said to His Apostles: "You are witnesses of these things," that He was lifted up from their sight. St. John expresses the same mystery in a different way. During the discourse after the Last Supper Christ explained that it was necessary for Him to go to the Father, so that the Holy Spirit might come— "If I go not the Paraclete will not come to you" (John xvi, 7).

In the Epistle to the Hebrews we find another text about the Ascension, in a new perspective, that of the priesthood. The Epistle to the Hebrews is centred upon priesthood and sacrifice, showing sin as essentially man's refusal to recognize God's rule, and sacrifice as a recognition of it and therefore a means of returning to God's favour. By the Son's sacrifice mankind was brought back into communion with the Father. And the author expresses this in a text bearing directly on the Ascension: "Christ, being come an High Priest of the good things to come, by a greater and more perfect tabernacle, not made with hands, that is not of this creation: neither by the blood of goats, or of calves, but by his own blood, entered once into the holy of holies, having obtained eternal redemption" (Heb. ix, 11 ff.). It was at the Ascension that Christ entered into the true sanctuary, of which the Holy of Holies in the Temple was merely a figure, that is to say, into the Glory of the Father, having set man free from slavery of sin and of death.

To the extent that the mystery of the Ascension is bound up with the idea of priesthood and sacrifice, it also is contained in the sacrifice of the Eucharist. After the consecration, the priest recalls not only the blessed Passion and Resurrection of Our

Lord "but also his glorious Ascension"—*sed et in caelos gloriosae Ascensionis.* The whole mystery of Christ is there in the Mass, so the Ascension must be present. For a sacrifice to be complete, the victim must be offered—it must be accepted. The Old Testament tells us of sacrifices that were not accepted, or at least not fully accepted, by God. The Ascension was Christ's sacrifice being accepted by the Father. It is by union with this sacrifice that ours is made effective, that God looks upon it with benevolence, that by it we are really in communion with God; that is the meaning of the Mass. The Ascension is actually represented, too, in the liturgy of the Mass, for it is the nature of a sacrament that the reality should be not merely signified but present. The priest prays to the Father that Christ should be presented by the hands of His Holy angel on His altar on high: *in sublime altare tuum.* The Ascension is wonderfully evoked there. The Victim offered on the altar on high is Christ presenting Himself before His Father in heaven, bearing the wounds of His Passion and thereby drawing down the good pleasure of the Father on mankind.

In one of the most tremendous scenes in the Apocalypse the same mystery is again shown to us. St. John sees a sealed book, whose seal cannot be broken, and the mystery is set before the whole heavenly world.

> And I saw a strong angel, proclaiming with a loud voice: Who is worthy to open the book and to loose the seals thereof? And no man was able, neither in heaven, nor on earth, nor under the earth, to open the book, nor to look on it. . . . And one of the ancients said to me: Weep not; behold the lion of the tribe of Juda, the root of David, hath prevailed to open the book . . . And I saw, and behold in the midst of the throne, and of the four living creatures, and in the midst of the ancients, a Lamb standing, as it were slain (Apoc. v, 2–6).

How curious: a lion is announced, and it is a lamb that appears, and a lamb slain in sacrifice. The picture is overwhelming. Christ's victory is the victory not of a lion but of a lamb. Christ won the victory by sacrifice, and the vision of the Lamb breaking the seals signifies the Ascension. All creation, St. Paul tells us, awaits redemption by the Son of God. To St. Gregory of Nyssa, the whole angelic creation was in expectation, too. They are there, around God's throne, waiting until the book is at last unsealed—until the gates of death are burst open, and this cannot happen until the Lamb that was slain returns from the dead and receives from the right hand of Him who sits on the throne the book containing the names of the elect.

THE POET PRAYS TO THE CROSS

I PRAYED then to the beam,   blithe in mood,
with hearty will,   when I was alone
and few near me.   Then was my heart's thought
urged on its far way,   oft it had borne
times of weary longing.   I have hope of life now,
that I shall go seek   the victory tree;
more often now   than all other men
I honour it well.   My will is bent to it,
strong in my heart,   and my hope of safety
goes straight to the cross.   I have now but few
friends on earth,   but they are gone hence
from the world's joys,   seeking the King of glory.
They live now in Heaven   with the High Father;
they dwell in light,   and I lingering
long for that day   when the Lord's rood
which here on earth   I once gazed upon
will come to fetch me   from this fleeting life,
and bring me there   where is great bliss,
joy in heaven,   where the Lord's folk
sit feasting   in bliss unending,
and set me there   where I may forever
dwell in glory,   safe with the holy ones,
and taste their blessedness.   May the Lord be my friend
who once suffered   here on earth

on the gallows tree　　for men's sins.
He sets us free　　and gave us life,
a heavenly home.　　Hope was made new
with blossoms and with bliss　　where He bore burning pain.
The Son was victory-fast　　in His far-going,
mighty and enriched　　when He came with many,
a spirit-army,　　into God's kingdom,
The Almighty Lone-Wielder　　was bliss to the angels
and all holy ones　　who ere in heaven
dwelt in glory,　　when their Ruler came,
Almighty God,　　where His homeland was.

From *The Dream of the Rood.*

THE UPPER ROOM

⚑ FOR ONE SET of people in history, one particular room must have had vivid and crowded associations. Those people were the apostles and the first Christians, a hundred and twenty in all, who were gathered in the Upper Room on the day of Pentecost. They could remember how they first came into it. Six weeks back, their spirits already overcast with tragedy. Almost immediately, their Master warned them that one of their own number would betray him. There is nothing more unsettling to man's whole being than the sudden discovery of treachery in his fellow man. And worse still was the terrible whisper of doubt in each heart, "Lord, is it I?" And then the washing of the feet, and the Sacramental Meal.

In that room they reassembled, an hour later, panic-stricken fugitives. They, who boasted that they could drink the chalice of the last ordeal, meet there, in hiding. The only sorry boast of their party is Simon Peter . . . and then the door opens, and he, too, joins them, his face furrowed with tears. The apostasy is complete.

In the same room they met again, three nights afterwards. Through the twilight of their doubt came flashes of hope. The Tomb has been found empty; there are stories of a re-appearance. There will be trouble over this with the rulers; best keep the doors locked. And suddenly, through those locked doors, he whom they had abandoned returns, gives them his peace and his pardon.

A room haunted with memories; through that door, Judas crept out into the night; on that table the consecrated chalice reposed; through that window they listened to the shouts of "Crucify Him!"; that stone on the floor has been trodden by impassible feet. It was in these surroundings that the Holy Ghost came. The inspiration he brought was to be something altogether new in the world's history, yet it was to be based upon, and rooted in, memories of the past: "When he, the Spirit of truth is come, he will bring all things to your remembrance." The scene of their inspiration for the future was to be a scene enriched by past experience.

Inspiration and experience, how seldom they go hand in hand! *Si jeunesse savait, si vieillesse pouvait.* . . . So it is with the religions of the world. There are Eastern religions with an immemorial antiquity, which have no instinct to urge them forward, no vital power of self-adaptation. There are new religions in the West, which begin their careers full of an intoxicating initiative, but they have no roots in experience, and they do not last. With the Church it is otherwise. In those six weeks before Pentecost, the Apostles had already lived through, as it were, the whole cycle of Church history; there was nothing callow, nothing tentative, about their earliest *démarches*. And because she was born old, the Church remains ever young. She retains the memory of the Cenacle and the Catacombs, yet for her Pentecost is continually repeating itself, making all things new.

PENTECOST

◈ IF THE FATHER is power, the source of all, the creator by whom all things are made, the Son, the Logos, is wisdom, through whom all things are made and from whom all the order and beauty, the pattern and rhythm, of the universe are derived. Let us limit ourselves here to the consideration of that particular order and beauty which is the pattern of redemption, the work of the Word made flesh, a work which reveals and explains to us the pity of God, and which, by showing us the meaning of the Word in human terms, makes it easier for us to see what our own response to it should be.

He emptied himself of his glory, we are told: emptied himself, first, by shrouding the majesty of divinity in human lowliness; secondly, by setting aside, in the dereliction of Passion and Cross, even the human rights that belonged to him, and becoming a castaway for our sakes. All this is a part of the sacrifice which restores life to humanity because it restores humanity to God: a part but only a part. Colloquially we use the word sacrifice to mean only some hard and painful self-deprivation, as when we give up having or doing something for the sake of somebody else. But in sacrifice there are always two elements; there is first the offering, and for fallen man in his selfishness that is indeed something hard and costing; but the sacrifice does not end there, it is meant to lead on to something further. So in primitive sacrifices the animal is slain or the wine is poured out, but it is in the hope that the god may accept the sacrifice and enter into it, and so the offerers, through communicating in the victim, may themselves receive the divine life. First the offering, the destruction; but then the apotheosis of the victim, its divinisation; and then finally the sharing by the people in that glory. So in this sacrifice which fulfils all partial sacrifice: the divine Victim is first offered and done to death; but there follows the apotheosis of resurrection and ascension, and then the sharing by all the faithful in the divine life thus poured out: the Cross ends, not in the tomb or even in the glory given to the Son at the right hand of the Father in heaven, but in the flowing back of divine life into the world of men at Pentecost.

God's mercy calls us to be not only his children but his friends; he asks of us not only the surrender of our lives into his hands but the maturity and intimacy of friendship, the sharing of the sacrifice of his Son. But still there is something more. I tell you the truth, our Lord said to his disciples: it is expedient to you that I go. For if I go not, the Paraclete will not come to you: but if I go, I will send him to you. These are at first sight baffling words: what is it that the Paraclete will do for humanity which our Lord himself, apparently, cannot do? And why, in any case, must our Lord first go, that the Paraclete may come? In the answer to these questions we shall be able to see what remains to complete our picture of man's response to the Trinity.

How are we to try to think of this third Person of the Trinity who is called the Spirit? With the second Person we felt ourselves to be on safer, because homelier, ground, for the Word was made flesh and dwelt amongst us, and it is as the God-Man that in practice we think of him and worship him. Yet we must not exaggerate the incomprehensibility for us of the Spirit of Love: we know what we mean when we speak of the spirit of a family, a school; we know what it means to be wrapped about in

another human being's love; and when we speak of someone as
showing great spirit we think of him as infused with an energy
which so fills him that it pours out from him in greatness. And
historically our first glimpse of what the Spirit of God may be
is given us in the story of Pentecost: when the Apostles, from
being frightened men in hiding in an upper room, become
transformed, and transformed quite obviously from within, God
coming to them now not outwardly in human form but inwardly
as an infusion of divine energy—mighty wind, fire—so that they
rush forth, new men, to preach the wonderful works of God.

Inwardness: it is this that gives us the clue to our Lord's
meaning. Earlier he had told them: He that believeth in me,
as the Scripture saith, Out of his belly shall flow rivers of living
water; and St. John goes on to explain. Now this he said of the
Spirit which they should receive who believed in him: for as
yet the Spirit was not given, because Jesus was not yet glorified.
The third Person is called the Spirit of Truth, the Spirit of
Love: the two things go together. The Church prays: O God
who dost instruct the *hearts* of the faithful by the light of the
holy Spirit . . . God comes first into the world as man: and in
that first mission it is his humanity which determines the mode
of all that is done. He comes to raise and heal humanity through
the Cross; he comes to teach humanity, but as a man can teach
men, through the medium of the word, the voice, the external
sign. But that proposal of the truth to the ears and minds of
men is not enough to transform them, not enough to make a
new earth. There have been men who became entirely convinced intellectually of the truth of Christianity but still could
not go on at once to the final acceptance, because still the truth
had not taken possession of their hearts. The apostles were told
not to fear when they should be brought before the magistrates:
they would not have to think out painfully what they should
say: it would be given them in that hour what they should say,
it would pour out from within them. There is all the difference

in the world between having to argue for a position which you believe to be right but about which you do not *feel* strongly, so that you have to cast about in mind or memory for the right line of argument; and arguing over something about which you feel so strongly that it has become as it were a part of you: and you do not need to think out an argument, it pours out irresistibly from you because in expressing it you are expressing yourself.

So God comes to the world the second time not as man but as Spirit, not proposing the truth from without but instilling it into the heart, teaching the heart to become what the mind has apprehended, so that it is now a question, not of the mind possessing the truth, but of the truth taking possession of the heart.

And why must Christ first go in order that the Spirit may come? Because this coming is, as we have seen, the completion of the sacrifice of the Son, the immediate consequence of the glory of the Son. As yet the Spirit was not given, because Jesus was not yet glorified. So it is that, once the sacrifice is consummated and the Son is in glory with the Father, the Father and Son together send their Love to humanity, to be the inner sense of truth, the inner energy of love, in the heart of humanity, that then that indwelling Spirit, working through humanity, may transform and renew the face of the earth.

So the re-creation of man is completed. We have thought of the driving out of Mammon by faith in God's fatherhood; of the driving out of the flesh through hope in the Son; now we are shown the driving out of the devil through love in the Spirit. At the same time we are shown what our third and final response must be if we are to be fully Christians. God grants us and asks of us the filial love of a child towards its father, the more intimate love and communion of friend with friend; but now the third thing, the deepest thing of all, the most incredible to created and sinful minds: the love of the lover for the beloved, the deep and wholly inward union—one could almost say, in Donne's phrase, the interinanimation—of two beings becoming one in knowledge and love. To this, sonship is the obvious and essential preliminary; friendship, with its deepening communion in the life of prayer, brings it about; but here you have the fulfilment of the words of the hymn, Come, take possession of our souls: you are concerned not so much with communion as with union; the man in whom these things are really achieved can really say, I live now not I but Christ liveth in me. So Catherine of Siena said that Christ had taken away her heart and given her his own: God taking full possession of the personality is able, unimpeded, to act through it; and through those different modes of divinely inspired activity which we call the gifts of the Holy Ghost the personality sees and understands and judges as though with the eye and mind of God, and in external activity wields the power and fulfills the purposes of God. My Me is God, said St. Catherine of Genoa; it was this total possession and union which yet, so far from destroying personal identity, raises it to its highest power, that she was expressing.

REDEMPTION

ADAM, THE FIRST MAN, called to share by grace in the divine life, represented in God's eyes the whole of mankind. Adam's fall was the fall of mankind. Detached from its original supernatural goal, mankind then, like some planet detached from its sun, revolved only in crazy gyration round itself. Its own self became the centre of its striving and yearning. Man came to feel God, the very source of his spiritual life, as a burden. The first "autonomous" man in the ethico-religious sense was Adam, when he took the fruit of the tree of life. And so man no longer had any source whence he might renew his strength, except his own small self. He had abandoned the eternal source of living water, and dug himself a poor cistern in his own self. And the waters of this cistern were soon exhausted. Man fell sick and died. His self was his sickness and his self was his death. And all mankind died with him. Then, according to the eternal decision of God's love, the New Man came, the man of the new, permanent and indissoluble union with God, Christ the Lord. In Him erring mankind, man radically cut off from the divine source of his life, was finally reunited to God, to the Life of all lives, to the Fount of all power, truth and love. Mankind—not merely this man and that, not you and I only, but the whole of mankind, the unity of all men—was brought home again from its terrible diaspora, from its dispersion, back to the living God. The whole man came once more into being, permanently united with God, and so effectively united that he could never more, as the unity of mankind, be for any fault cut off from the divine source of his life. Therefore Christ, as the God-man, is the new humanity, the new beginning, the whole man in the full meaning of the phrase.

LOVE WE AS BROTHERS

FOR WE ARE ALL Christ's creatures, and by his coffer are we
    wealthy,
And brothers of one blood, beggars and nobles.
Christ's blood on Calvary is the spring of Christendom,
And we became blood brethren there, recovered by one body,
As *quasi modo geniti*,[1] and gentle without exception,
None base or a beggar, but when sin cause it.
Qui facit peccatum, servus est peccati.[2]

In the Old Law, as Holywrit tells us,
Men were men's sons, mentioned always
As issue of Adam and of Eve, until the god-man was crucified,
And after his resurrection *Redemptor* was his title,
And we his brethren, bought through him, both rich and poor
    men.
Therefore love we as lief brothers, each laughing with the other,
And each give what he can spare as his goods are needed.
Let each man help the other, for we shall all go hence.

[1] As though of one family.
[2] "Whosoever committeth sin is the servant of sin" (John viii, 34).

THE REDEMPTION

I

꧁ THE VERY HEART of the doctrine of the Redemption is that the human acts of Christ were the acts of a Person Who was divine.

Everything that Christ did and suffered and experienced must be seen as done and suffered and experienced by God. God grew to manhood, God was a carpenter, God rejoiced, God sorrowed, God suffered, God died. It is the last two phrases that force us really to face the mystery and test our realization of it. Yet if God did not suffer and die, then no one did, for there was but the one person in Christ; that is, there was no suffering, no dying: no sacrifice, no redemption. The phrase "God died" gives us at first the greater shock, but afterwards is less profoundly mysterious than the phrase "God suffered." The whole created universe, with everything in it from archangel down to electron, or any lower thing there may be, is held in existence from instant to instant solely by the continuing Will of God to hold it so. And the words God died seem to carry annihilation to all things that thus depend upon God. But it is by the operation of His divine nature that God sustains all things in being, and it is not in His divine nature that God the Son died but only in His human nature, the most glorious of created things, but a created thing for all that. Death is a separation of soul and body. The phrase God died means that for that three days' space God's soul was separated from God's Body: it was a real death but it left the divine nature totally unaffected.

But what are we to make of the phrase God suffered? Again the suffering was not in the divine nature, but in the human. Christ's suffering, the fear and agony in the Garden for instance, was real suffering, that is to say someone really suffered it. And that someone was God the Son. How this can be, what indeed it means, we cannot fully know, indeed we can hardly feel that we know at all. The mind seems able to make no statement here. Yet it is literally true that, even if we cannot *say* it, there are momentary flashes of light, glimpses and glances, in which we half *see* it; and there is no measuring the fruitfulness of even this momentary half-seeing for sanctity; and not for sanctity only but for plain human consolation.

Summarizing this relation of nature and person in Christ's atoning act, we see that because He was man with a true human nature He could offer a true human act in expiation of human sin, an act of total love to balance humanity's self-love; and because He was God, the human act He offered was of infinite value and so could satisfy and more than satisfy for the sins of men. But stating it thus, we see another question. Any act of Christ must be of infinite value, since the person who does the act is God. Why then does Christ offer His death, when some lesser act would have been of infinite value and therefore totally sufficient? Might He not have offered His thirst when He sat weary from His journey by Jacob's Well in Samaria? Or His patience under insult? Or any one of a thousand other things? Why did it have to be His death?

In one sense the answer is clear. He had come into the world to teach the truth—about Himself as God, for instance, about Himself as Messias, about the Kingdom which was to be in the world but not of it, about the Gentiles who would come into it, about the failure of the leaders of Israel to grasp the essentials of their own religion. His execution was the natural consequence. Only a miraculous intervention of the divine power could have prevented it. Given that He was to die, it is hard to think of His offering some lesser thing than His death as the sacrifice that should save mankind.

But all things are in the power of God. God could have intervened to prevent His death. Or He might have chosen a way of life that meant no such direct challenge to the rulers. Why, we may ask in all reverence, did the divine plan include the death of the Redeemer?

The two answers that instantly spring to mind are that nothing could show the love of God so overpoweringly as His willingness to die for us, and nothing could show the horror of sin so clearly as that it needed His death to expiate it. Now it is true that Calvary is a proof both of the awfulness of sin and of the love of God, but it would not be so unless there was something in the nature of sin that required Calvary. If the sin could as well have been expiated by some act of Christ less than His death, then Calvary would not show the horror of sin but would in fact exaggerate it. The same line of argument would not so obviously apply to Calvary as a proof of God's love, yet there would be something profoundly unsatisfying in the notion of God's showing His love for us by a needless death. A moment's reflection will show that there was something *in what Our Lord had to do* which made His dying the best way to do it. It is true that on the side of the Person who made the offering any act in the human nature, however small in itself, would have sufficed. But on the side of the nature in which the offering was made, can we feel that any act however small would have sufficed?

Obviously no. The sacrifice was a true act of human virtue offered in reparation for a human act of rejection of God. It is true that no act of human nature could by itself have sufficed to expiate, and that it was the divinity of His Person which gave the act of Christ's human nature the efficacy which by itself it could not have had. But that is no reason for reducing the human element in the sacrifice to a mere token. For if it were so, we should be left with a sense of an unreal transaction in which God makes an offering to God. It was human nature's offering, though it took a Divine Person to make it. The God who made the offering was man, too, and it was in His manhood that He made it. Human nature could not do all: yet it must do all that it could, leaving the divinity of the Person to supply for the remainder. In the profoundest sense humanity would want this. Expiation is something required not only by the nature of God but by the nature of man. There is something in man, which when his intellect is clear and his will right, longs to make expiation rather than merely have his sin forgiven out of hand. It belongs to human dignity that a man should want to pay his debt rather than have it written off. And if he cannot pay the whole of it, as in this supreme instance, he yet wants to pay all that he can. Had Our Lord's offering been by way of some human act of little cost, then one would feel that humanity's part in the expiation was barely more than a fiction. In fact Christ's humanity gave all it had to give, for a man has not more to give than his life. What divinity gave was only what humanity could not give.

But all this discussion is academic. To discuss what the Redeemer might have done gives us certain lights upon the problem of our redemption. But they are as nothing to the light that floods out from what He did do. He gave all that He had upon Calvary: martyrs since have died in the strength of His death, knowing that even humanly speaking He gave more than they. He died: if He had not, we should not have had the Resurrection. By baptism we are buried with Him in His death, and rise with Him in His Resurrection. Only God knows what splendours might have been associated with some other way of Redemption; but we have seen the splendour of this.

II

The sacrifice of Christ was totally effective. It could not be otherwise, given that He Who offered it was God. But it is im-

portant to grasp *what* it effected. Whatever it was meant to
effect, it did effect. But what was it?

At the moment of His death on Calvary, Christ Our Lord
said, "It is consummated." Something was completed. But something was beginning, too, and the something that was beginning
was not simply the paradisial enjoyment by men—either by all
men or by an elect or even by Christ Himself—of what He had
achieved by His sacrifice, but something with vast labour and
anguish and the possibility of failure in it for men, and with
work still for Christ to do. Something was completed. But, at
the right hand of the Father, Christ Himself continues His work
of intercession for us (Heb. vii, 25); and we have seen His last
days upon earth filled with the preparation of His apostles to
continue His work among men until the end of time.

The thing that was completed was the Redemption of the
race. The race had sinned in its representative man and as a
result was no longer at one with God: so that Heaven was
closed to it; bound up with the severed relationship of the race
with God there was a mysterious subjection to the Devil: by
his victory over Adam the Devil had secured some kind of
princedom over Adam's race, so that he is called the Prince of
this World. His princedom carried no legal rights but vast
power: in the decree *Firmiter,* Pope Eugenius IV says "no one
has merit of the Mediator." The primary effect of Our Lord's
sacrifice was the undoing of Adam's sin. The princedom of the
Devil was destroyed. And the breach between the race and God
was healed, so that Heaven was opened to the members of the
race. This fundamentally *is* the Redemption.

Let us consider these two results in turn. "If the Son of God
was revealed to us," says St. John, "it was so that he might undo
what the devil had done" (I John iii, 8). It is foreign to our
habits of thought to attach any real importance to the Devil,
that strange intervening third in the relations between man
and God. But this is a defect in our mental habits. It can never

be intelligent to take lightly anything that God takes seriously. And God takes the Devil very seriously indeed. It will be remembered that when, after the fall of man, God had foretold Redemption, He had not only foretold *it* to the Devil, but had expressed it in terms of a victory *over* the Devil: the seed of the woman was to crush his head.

When the hour of the Redemption came, Our Lord was intensely preoccupied with this aspect of it as the struggle between Himself and the Devil issuing in victory for Himself over the Devil. Early in Passion Week He cried out: "Now is the judgment of the world: now shall the prince of this world be cast out" (John xii, 31). At the Last Supper He returns to the theme twice: "The prince of this world cometh; and in me he hath not anything" (John xiv, 30); and again "The prince of this world is already judged" (John xvi, 11). Why was Our Lord so preoccupied with Satan? It may be because He was restoring the order of reality against which Satan is the great protest, so that Satan's power was ranged against Him at the peak of intensity. What is interesting is that the Devil so little understood the nature of Our Lord's mission, that he rushed upon his own defeat. For as St. Luke and St. John both tell us it was Satan who entered into Judas to cause him to betray Christ into the hands of His enemies, thus precipitating Christ's redemptive sacrifice. It is some consolation to us to know that an enemy of intellect so powerful is not always well informed.

But the overthrow of Satan's princedom is only incidental to the healing of the breach between the race and God, by which Heaven is opened to the race of men. Let us repeat that this was something done *for the race*. John the Baptist had hailed Our Lord: "Behold the Lamb of God. Behold him who taketh away *the sin of the world*" (John i, 29). There was a sin of the world, and Christ died to destroy it. "Now once, at the end of ages, he hath appeared for the destruction of sin by the sacrifice of himself" (Heb. ix, 26). As a result, Heaven was once more opened to men. A man was enthroned there where no man had yet been, a man who had gone there to prepare a place for us. As the Roman Missal has it, in one of the prayers of Easter Week: "He unlocked for us the gates of eternity."

Thus the sin of the race in the representative man, Adam, was taken away by the new representative man, Christ. "A man had brought us death, and a man should bring us resurrection from the dead; just as all have died with Adam, so with Christ all will be brought to life" (I Cor. xv, 21). It is magnificent, and the soul rejoices. Yet the intellect, trying to comprehend, may be faintly troubled. At first glance there seems something arbitrary and almost capricious in it. Adam falls, and we are informed that Adam represented us and we have all fallen in him. Christ atones, and we are informed that Christ represents us and we are all redeemed in Him. Where, we might wonder, do we really come in? Who and what are these representatives? Above all, why?

But there is nothing arbitrary. Each is our representative because of a real relation of us to him. We have already seen that this is so of Adam. There is a solidarity of the human race, linking us physically to one another, and to the first man from whom we all come: and because of it our fate was involved in his. Christ is entitled to act for us by a double title: first on the side of His Divinity, He is the God by whom and in whose image man was created; second on the side of His humanity, He is the perfect man, so that where Adam was the first man in time, Christ is the first man in value, Christ is the moral head of the race as Adam the physical. Adam represents humanity in that all of us come from him, Christ in that there is no element of humanity in any of us (Adam included) that is not better and richer and completer in Him. So that His act in compensation of Adam's is available for all men (Adam again included). The barrier erected by man's sin between the race and God is down. There is no longer a sin of the race to stand between us and sonship of God, between us and entry into Heaven.

But our different relationships to Adam and to Christ involve a difference in the way of our sharing in the result of their acts. We fell in Adam inasmuch as we are united with him: we are restored in Christ inasmuch as we are united with Him. Adam's act becomes ours because we are (as we cannot help being) one with him. Christ's act becomes ours only when we become (as we may unhappily fail to become) one with Him.

We are incorporated with Adam by the mere fact of being born; for incorporation with Christ, we must be re-born. "The man who came first came from earth, fashioned of dust, the man who came afterwards came from heaven, and his fashion is heavenly. The nature of that earth-born man is shared by his earthly sons, the nature of the heaven-born man, by his heavenly sons; and it remains for us, who once bore the stamp of earth, to bear the stamp of heaven" (I Cor. xv, 47). We fell as members of humanity stemming from Adam; we are restored as members of a new humanity stemming from Christ.

We may now look again at what was completed by Our Lord's sacrifice on Calvary. Satisfaction was made, complete satisfaction, for the sin of the human race: the breach between God and the race was healed. That work was done, done completely, done once for all, because Christ had offered complete satisfaction for the sin of the race. He had not only satisfied but more than satisfied: He had merited for men restoration to the sonship of God, the supernatural life in which that sonship consists, the life by which we can look upon the face of God in Heaven. Heaven was once more open to men.

III

But the opening of Heaven does not mean that every man will get there. Some will fail: the defeat of Satan in his effort to hold the race does not mean that he will have no more victories over individuals. In other words the Salvation of the individual does not follow automatically upon the Redemption of the race. It is a further problem, involving a further warfare. In plain words, though no man enters Heaven save because Christ offered the atoning sacrifice, no man enters Heaven simply because Christ offered the atoning sacrifice. His sacrifice availed both for the Redemption of the race—satisfying for sin and meriting restoration—and for the Salvation of the individual, but in different ways: it effected the Redemption of the race, it made possible the Salvation of the individual.

It is worth our while to pause for a moment on the distinction here made between Redemption and Salvation. Obviously, of course, there can be no hard and fast allocation of the word Redemption to what Our Lord did for the race and Salvation to what He does for the individual; He was the saviour of the race as well as of the individual; by redeeming the race, He redeemed the individual. Yet I think there is a tendency in Scripture to use the words more often in the way here suggested.

However this may be, let us repeat that the sacrifice on Calvary was a propitiation not only for the representative sin of the race but for the personal sins of all members of the race: "He is the propitiation for our sins; and not for ours only, but also for those of the whole world" (I John ii, 2). "He hath washed us from our sins in his own blood" (Apoc. i, 5). But whereas the Redemption of the race was entirely His work and therefore wholly achieved, the Salvation of the individual depends upon our cooperation with His work, and some of us may fail. This is the reason for a variation of phrasing in Scripture— Christ being said at one time to have died for all and at another time to have died for some—which at first seems puzzling. The first phrase means that He excluded none from the reach of the sacrifice, the second that some have excluded themselves and so are not reached by it. "Being consummated, he became, *to all that obey him,* the cause of eternal salvation" (Heb. v, 9). But nothing must dim our realization of the truth that He died for all without exception: "Such prayer is our duty, it is what God, our Saviour, expects of us, since it is His will that all men should be saved, and be led to recognize the truth; there is only one God, and only one Mediator between God and men, Jesus Christ, who is a man, like them, and gave himself as a ransom for them all" (I Tim. ii, 5).

Christ died for all. "But though He died for all, yet not all receive the benefit of His death, but those only unto whom the merit of His passion is communicated" (Council of Trent VI:2). Salvation depends upon our receiving the supernatural life by which we become sons of God and having this life in our souls when we die. Christ merited it for all men. But, as we have already seen, we do not receive it automatically merely by being born (for by birth we are one with Adam in whom we fell) but by being re-born in Christ, made one with Him in such a way that in Him we are restored. If we do not receive the life, or if we receive it but lose it and die without it, then we shall not be saved. Christ dying made our salvation possible, Christ living still operates to make it actual.

How? Christ works for us in Heaven in His own Person, upon earth through His Church. In the final section we shall consider Christ still working on earth. Here let us consider Christ in Heaven. We have seen that He is at the right hand of the Father in the whole of His reality, body and soul and divinity. We have also seen that He continues to make intercession for us: "Jesus continues for ever, and His priestly office is unchanging; that is why He can give eternal salvation to those who through Him make their way to God, He lives on still to make intercession on our behalf" (Heb. vii, 25). As St. Thomas says (S. T. III, q. 54): "interceding for us, He ever shows the Father what kind of death He bore for man." In other words Christ Our Lord is ever in the presence of His Father in that sacred

humanity which He offered once for all upon Calvary: and by
that continuing presence before God of that which was offered
for us, our own continuance in the way of salvation is made
possible. "He sits now at the right hand of God, annihilating
death, to make us heirs of eternal life" (I Peter iii, 22).

IV

To The End of Time

"Behold I am with you all days, to the consummation of the world."

(Matthew xxviii, 20)

NARRATIVE

At the Last Supper, Our Lord said to these men who were just about to desert Him almost in a body: "I do not speak of you any more as my servants; a servant is one who does not understand what his master is about, whereas I have made known to you all that My Father has told me; and so I have called you my friends. It was not you that chose me, It was I that chose you. The task I have appointed you is to go out and bear fruit, fruit which will endure" (John xvi, 15–16). Clearly He was preparing them for some great thing, and clearly we shall not understand His plan for mankind unless we see their place in it.

In that plan for mankind there are many elements, but as His teaching proceeds two emerge as dominant. One is the coming of the Kingdom, the other the spiritual shaping of men's souls by the gifts of truth and the life He brings. Take the teaching on the Kingdom first. The angel who announced to Mary that she was to be His mother said of Him: "His kingdom shall never have an end"; and it was on His claim to found a kingdom that the Jews framed the charge upon which Pilate sentenced Him to death. But Our Lord made it clear that His kingdom was not the kind of kingdom the Jews wanted, nor the kind of kingdom that Pilate would have thought worthy of drastic preventive action. The interchange between Our Lord and Pilate, indeed, is worth noting. Our Lord had said, "My kingdom is not of this world." Pilate asks: "Thou art a king then?

Our Lord answers: It is thy own lips that have called me a king. What I was born for, what I came into the world for, is to bear witness of the truth." Here as elsewhere we see that Our Lord's kingdom is bound up with the spiritual gifts He had come to bring. He was founding a kingdom in which those who believed in Him should receive truth and life.

Just as the kingdom and the gifts were two sides of the one reality, so we find the thing for which He was preparing the Apostles stated sometimes in terms of the Kingdom and sometimes in terms of the gifts. Thus at the Last Supper Our Lord told them: "I dispose to you as My Father has disposed to me a kingdom." The key words here are "as my Father has disposed to me." We are all meant to enter the kingdom, but as citizens of the kingdom. Our Lord was set over the kingdom as ruler by His Father; and now we know that the Apostles are to be rulers in the kingdom, and not merely citizens. In that kingdom the ruler must be not only one who commands but one who serves: Christ serves supremely; but in their measure the Apostles likewise must serve. His service we have already analyzed as opening the Way to Heaven by the sacrifice He offered, and giving the Truth and the Life that men need to tread the Way. He equips the Apostles to continue to serve in all those same ways. They may, in the religious sphere, require obedience to their commands, for without that there would be no unity and very soon no society. But this is simply the background to service. They are to dispense the gifts of Truth and Life, for these cannot be given once for all, but each new generation born into the world, each new person born into the world, must receive them. This continuance of the gifts of Truth and Life must strike us as obvious once we grasp what the gifts are. But there is another continuance too—the sacrifice is in some way to continue upon earth. At the Last Supper, Our Lord makes His Apostles not only teachers and ministers of the sacraments but priests, too, offerers of sacrifice. For there was to be sacrifice in the kingdom. St. John says in the Apocalypse: "Thou wast slain in sacrifice—Thou hast ransomed us with thy blood and given us to God. Thou hast made us a royal race of priests to serve God" (v, 9).

Our Lord sees His kingdom and speaks of His kingdom with great precision of detail. Just before His Ascension He said to His Apostles: "Go ye and teach all nations; baptizing them in the name of the Father and of the Son and of the Holy Ghost, teaching them to observe all things whatsoever I have commanded you, and lo, I am with you all days, even to the consummation of the world" (Matt. xxviii, 19–20) . . . The mission Our Lord gave the Apostles was to last till the end of the world, so that He was speaking to them not as themselves only, but as officials in His kingdom who should have successors until the end of time. They were to teach, that is they were to communicate truth; and they were to baptize, that is they were to communicate life. He who is the Way and the Truth and the Life sends these men out to bring to the world His gifts of truth and life: and to bring men to the Way, too, for in finding them we find Him. Where they are He is—"I am with you all days, even to the consummation of the world." This continuous presence of Christ with His Apostles gives us a double guarantee; first, the certainty that the truth and the life we receive from them we are actually receiving from Him, so that they are true truth and living life, *His* gifts to us not their gifts to us; second, and even more vital, the certainty that in contact with them we are in contact with Him.

That the Kingdom should have teachers and ministers of the sacraments is obviously necessary; for till the end of time men will need Christ's gifts of truth and life, and He has chosen to dispense them through men. Why the Kingdom should have priests may not be at first so obvious. For Christ, our High Priest, has offered the totally effective sacrifice and it cannot be added to. Yet priests there are and a continuance of sacrifice. Clearly if there are priests and a sacrifice they will be men through whom Christ is offering sacrifice, just as it is He Who is teaching through the teachers and giving life through the ministers of the sacraments. The teachers of the Church are not adding to His teaching; the ministers are dispensing no life but His; the priests are offering no new sacrifice.

This then was the provision that Our Lord made for the souls of men that they might come to Him, be united with Him, and receive His gifts till the end of time. His kingdom would grow as it moved outwards and onwards towards its two limiting points—all the nations of the earth and the end of time—and there would be some increase of complexity in its structure to meet new needs created by its growth. But it would all be within the living framework He established upon earth—one kingdom, with a smaller body of officials serving the great body of plain citizens, and among the officials one who is head over the rest and the servant of all. So the kingdom was, when the Holy Ghost descended upon it at Pentecost. So it still is. So till the end of the world it will be. And at the end of the world Christ will come again.

RETURN TO THE CHURCH

The Soul speaks:

I

I have fallen on the law of your Faith as on a naked sword.

Its sharpness went through my understanding, straight through the light of my reason.

Never again shall I walk under the star of my eyes and on the staff of my strength.

You have torn away my shores, you have done violence to the earth under my feet.

My ships are drifting out to sea, you have cut all their moorings.

The chains of my thoughts are broken, they hang wild over the deep.

I flutter like a bird about my father's house, to find a crack that will let your strange light through.

But there is none on earth save the wound in my spirit—

I have fallen on the Law of your Faith as on a naked sword.

II

But strength still goes out from your thorns, and from your abysses the sound of music.

Your shadows lie on my heart like roses and your nights are like strong wine.

I will love you even when my love of you is ended.

I will desire you even when I desire you no more.

Where I myself begin, there will I cease, and where I cease
there I will forever remain.

Where my feet refuse to take me, there will I kneel down.

And where my hands fail me, there I will fold them.

I will become a breath in the autumn of pride, and snow in the
winter of doubt.

Even as in graves of snow shall all fear sleep in me.

I will become dust before the rock of your teaching and ashes in
the flame of your commandments.

I will break my arms if I may clasp you with their shadow.

The Church answers:

What I break is not broken and what I bend down to the dust
that I raise up.

I have been without grace to you because of grace, and out of
compassion I have been pitiless.

I have dazzled and blinded you till your borders are effaced.

I have overshadowed you that you may no longer find your
defences.

As an island is swallowed by the sea so have I engulfed you that
I might float you into eternity.

I have become a mock to your understanding and a violence
to your nature,

That I might bolt and bar you like a prison and drag you before
the gates of your spirit.

For where your inmost thirst would take you, the fountains of
earth have ceased to flow,

Where your last nostalgia fades blue, all the clocks of time are
stopped.

See, I carry on my wings the white shadows of otherness,

And my forehead feels the breath of another shore.

It is for this that I must be a wilderness to your reason, and a
nothingness on your lips,

But to your soul I am the start and the way home, I am the rainbow of her peace with God above the clouds.

THE CHURCH THE MYSTICAL BODY

I

THE WORK of Redemption and Revelation was accomplished through Human Nature assumed into union with the Divine—God did not, so to speak, act merely in virtue of His Deity, but through Humanity as well. First a nation, then a tribe, then a family and then a person, were successively drawn from the world as a whole—Israel, Judah, the line of David, and, finally, Mary—and then, by an unique act of the power of the Holy Ghost, a created substance was produced so perfect and so pure as to be worthy, in a sense, of becoming the vehicle of the Deity: this substance was then assumed into union with God and used for His Divine purposes—in short, the Sacred Humanity of Jesus Christ, by which He lived and suffered and died as man, was the instrument of both Revelation and Redemption; by a human voice He spoke, His human hands were raised to bless, a human heart loved and agonized, these human hands, heart and voice —broken, pierced and silenced as they were—were the heart, hands and voice of Very God. Consider that claim carefully. Though the Person was the Person of God, the nature by which He was accessible and energetic was the nature of man. It is by union with that Humanity that Christians believe themselves redeemed. Thus in that last emphatic act of the life of His Humiliation He took Bread, and cried, not Here is my Essential Self, but "This is my *Body* which is given for you," since that

Body was the instrument of redemption. And this act was but a continuation (though in another sense) of that first act known as the Incarnation. He who leaned over the Bread at that "last sad supper with His own" had, in another but similar manner, leaned over Mary herself with similar words upon His lips. God, according to the Christian belief, used in both actions alike a material substance for His Divine Purpose.

II

Up to this point practically all those known as "orthodox Christians" are more or less agreed. Catholics go a step further—a step in a certain sense parallel to, though not identical with, the act of the Incarnation—and believe that He further takes into union with Himself the Human Nature of His disciples, and through the Body thus formed, acts, lives and speaks. Let us sum it up in one sentence. Catholics believe that as Jesus Christ lived His natural life on earth two thousand years ago in a Body drawn from Mary, so He lives His mystical Life today in a Body drawn from the human race in general—called the Catholic Church—that her words are His, her actions His, her life His (with certain exceptions and restrictions) as surely as were the words, actions and life recorded in the Gospels: it is for this reason that they give to the Church the assent of their faith, believing that in so doing they are rendering it to God Himself. She is not merely His viceregent on earth, not merely His representative, not merely even His Bride: in a real sense she is Himself. That in this manner,[1] as well as in another which is not our business at present, He fulfills His promise to be with His disciples all days, even to the consummation of the world. To express the whole position once more under another aspect, in order to make clear what is the position on which I purpose to enlarge, it may be said that God expressed Himself in terms of a single life in the Gospels, and of a corporate life in the Church.

[1] His Real Presence in the Blessed Sacrament.

The written Gospel is the record of a past life; the Church is the living Gospel and record of a present life. Here He "looks through the lattice," visible to all who have eyes; here He reproduces, in century after century and country after country, the events and crises of the life lived in Judea. Here He works out and fills up, on the canvas of the world's history, that outline laid down two thousand years ago: He is born here, lives, suffers, dies, and eternally rises again on the third day. Jesus Christ is the same yesterday, today and forever.

Before passing on to consider the possibility of this position, as well as a very startling analogy supplied to us by recent scientific research, it is suggestive to consider how extraordinarily strong is the support given by the Scriptures to the Catholic claim that the idea which I have described was the idea of Jesus Christ Himself and of His contemporary disciples.

For example, the position could hardly be put more explicitly than in the words "I am the Vine, you the branches," or "He that heareth you, heareth me: He that despiseth you, despiseth me," or "As my Father sent me, even so send I you."

For the only distinction possible to draw between the Vine and the branches lies in saying that the Vine stands for the whole and the branches for its parts. The branches are not an imitation of the Vine, or representatives of the Vine; they are not merely attached to it, as candles to a Christmas tree; they are its expression, its result and sharers of its life. The two are in the most direct sense identical. The Vine gives unity to the branches, the branches give expression and effectiveness to the energy of the Vine; they are nothing without it; it remains merely a Divine Idea without them. You cannot, that is, apprehend the Vine at all in any real sense *as vine* except through the branches. So, again, in passage after passage of St. Paul's writings, phrases are used that are practically meaningless, or at the best wild and furious exaggerations, unless this identity of Christ and His Church is assumed to have been in the writer's

mind. Again and again souls living in union with Christ are
named His body considered as a whole, or as members considered separately; they are said to possess the "Mind of Christ";
they are described in a mysterious phrase, lucid only on the
Catholic interpretation, as filling up what is "wanting of the
sufferings of Christ"—carrying out, that is to say, on the stage
of the world's history, the agony and death recorded in the
Gospels, extending before the eyes of the world today—and indeed, in every period of history—the bloody sweat, the nails and
the scourge seen in Gethsemane and Calvary. The instruments
of the martyr's passion are the instruments of His. It is impossible, I think, for those who at any rate regard the New Testament as an adequate record of the intentions and words of
Christ and His friends, to deny that the idea which I have attempted to describe was the idea of the Founder of Christianity
as understood by those who heard Him speak.

III

Now what has been said up to this point may well be regarded
by some critics as being nothing more than a rather forced and
metaphorical statement of what is really an impossible position
to maintain literally—a presentation, possibly rather picturesque,
but hopelessly idealistic, of a mere illustration. I mean, however, a great deal more than that.

Every organic body—the body, let us say, of a man or a dog—
may be regarded under two aspects. First, it possesses one single
and unique life, that may properly be called the life of the body,
beginning before birth and ending at that moment called death.
Yet, sheltering, so to speak, under this unity—in fact, contribut-
ing to it—are lives whose number is beyond computation—viz:
the lives of the innumerable "cells" that compose the body.
These cells are continually coming into being, living each its
life, and finally dying and passing away with the destruction of
the tissues, yet in no sense interrupting by these changes the

one continuous life of the body as a whole. The body of a full-grown man has no single cell, at any given moment, which it possessed at the time of its birth; yet his body, we say, has lived continuously from his birth up to that given moment. The cells are indeed individuals, but they are a great deal more, in virtue of their mystical cohesion.

Now this physical illustration may perhaps appear a little forced; yet surely the analogy is too remarkable to be passed over. We considered just now whether it was possible to speak of the Life of the Church as identical with the Life of Christ—of the identity, that is, of the myriad consciousnesses of Catholic Christians with that Divine consciousness of Christ; and we see that recent research supplies us with a parallel, exact, so far as we have seen it, with the entire Catholic claim on the point. We see how it is not only possible, but essential, for an organic body—that is, for the highest form of physical life with which we are acquainted—that it should consist from one point of view of a myriad infinitesimal lives that lose themselves, and yet save themselves, in the unity of the whole, and that the unity of the whole, while it transcends the sum of the individual cell-lives, is at once dependent upon them and apart. If this is true of physical life, literally and actually, it is surely not unreasonable to expect that it should be true also of spiritual life; and the coincidence is the more remarkable when we remember that the science of cell-life is of very recent date.

Jesus Christ still lives upon earth as surely, though in another and what must be called a "mystical" sense, as He lived two thousand years ago. For He has a Body in which He lives, a Voice with which He speaks. As two thousand years ago He assumed one kind of Body by which to accomplish His purposes, so He has assumed now another kind of Body in which to continue them; and that Body consists of a unity of myriad cells—each cell a living soul complete in itself—transcending the sum of the cells and yet expressing itself through them. Christianity, then, is not merely an individual matter—though it is that, also, as surely as the cell has individual relations with the main life of the body. But it is far more: It is corporate and transcendent. The Catholic does not merely as a self-contained unit suck out grace through this or that sacramental channel; the priest to him is not just a viceregent who represents or may misrepresent his Master; a spiritual life is not merely an individual existence on a spiritual plane. But all things are expanded, enlarged and supernaturalized by an amazing fact: He is not merely an imitator of Christ, or a disciple of Christ, not merely even a lover of Christ; but he is actually a cell of that very Body which is Christ's, and his life in Christ is, as a matter of fact, so far more real and significant than his individual existence, that he is able to take upon his lips without exaggeration or metaphor the words of St. Paul—"I live—yet it is no longer I that live; it is Christ that liveth in me"; he is able to appreciate as no separatist in religion can appreciate, that saying of Christ Himself, that unless a man lose his life, he cannot save it. Still there moves on earth that amazing Figure whose mere painted portrait in the Gospels has driven men—artists, seers and philanthropists—mad with love and longing—and we are part of it. There still sounds on the air the very voice that comforted the Magdalene and pardoned the thief; the same Divine energy that healed the sick and raised the dead is still active on earth, not transmitted merely from some Majesty on high, but working now, as then, through a Human Nature that can be touched and felt.

I see through her eyes, the Eyes of God to shine, and through her lips I hear His words. In each of her hands, as she raises them to bless, I see the wounds that dripped on Calvary, and her feet upon her Altar stairs are signed with the same marks as those which the Magdalene kissed. As she comforts me in the confessional I hear the voice that bade the sinner go and sin no more; and as she rebukes or pierces me with blame I shrink aside trembling with those who went out one by one, beginning with the eldest, till Jesus and the penitent were left alone. As she cries her invitation through the world, I hear the same ringing claim as that which called, "Come unto me and find rest for your souls"; as she drives those who profess to serve her from her service I see the same flame of wrath that scourged the changers of money from the temple courts.

As I watch her in the midst of her people, applauded by the mob shouting always for the rising sun, I see the palm branches about her head, and the City and Kingdom of God, it would seem, scarcely a stone's throw away, yet across the valley of the Kedron and the garden of Gethsemane; and as I watch her pelted with mud, spurned, spat at and disgraced, I read in her eyes the message that we should weep not for her but for ourselves and for our children, since she is immortal and we but mortal after all. As I look on her white body, dead and drained of blood, I smell once more the odor of the ointments and the trampled grass of that garden near to the place where He was crucified, and hear the tramp of the soldiers who came to seal the stone and set the watch. And, at last, as I see her moving once more in the dawn light of each new day, or in the revelation of evening, as the sun of this or that dynasty rises and sets, I understand that He who was dead has come forth once more with healing in His wings, to comfort those that mourn and to bind up the brokenhearted; and that His coming is not with observation, but in the depth of night as His enemies slept and His lovers woke for sorrow.

Yet even as I see this, I understand that Easter is but Bethlehem once again; that the cycle runs round again to its beginning and that the conflict is all to fight again; for they will not be persuaded, though One rises daily from the dead.

CORPUS CHRISTI MYSTICUM

And we see you come toward us with golden brow in the
  returning light of our joy.
For He from whom we went forth has come after us, and He
  from whom we scattered has gathered us into Himself.
He has found us in the lap of our wretchedness and has put on
  humility in our hands.
He dwells in the wine of your chalices and in the white bread
  of your altars.
You lay Him on our longing, you place Him on our hungering
  lips.
You lay Him deeply into the heart of our solitude, and it opens
  like gates unbarred:
The dust of atoms blows together, for the stillness of eternity is
  mightier than a storm:
We are of one flesh and of one blood.
We are the flame of one soul-birth—
You are the true form of the world!

THE MYSTICAL BODY IN HEAVEN

HOSTS OF THE REDEEMED are continually passing into
heaven, whether directly, or mediately by the road of purification in the Suffering Church. They pass into the presence
of the Lamb and of Him who sits upon the throne, in order
face to face—and no longer in mere similitude and image—to
contemplate the Trinity, in whose bosom are all possibilities
and all realities, the unborn God from out of whose eternal
well-spring of life all beings drink existence and strength, motion
and beauty, truth and love. There is none there who has not
been brought home by God's mercy alone. All are redeemed,
from the highest saint to the new-born child just sealed by the
grace of baptism as it left the world. Delivered from all selfish
limitations and raised above all earthly anxieties, they live,
within that sphere of love which their life on earth has traced
out for them, the great life of God. It is true life, no idle stag-
nation, but a continual activity of sense and mind and will. It
is true that they can merit no longer, nor bear fruit now for
the Kingdom of Heaven. For the Kingdom of Heaven is established and grace has finished its work. But the life of glory is
richer far than the life of grace. The infinite spaces of the Being
of God, in all Its width and depth, provide a source in which
the soul seeks and finds the satisfaction of its most intimate
yearnings. New possibilities continually reveal themselves, new
vistas of truth, new springs of joy. Being incorporated in the

most sacred Humanity of Jesus, the soul is joined in most mysterious intimacy to the Godhead Itself. It hears the heart-beats of God and feels the deep life that pulsates within the Divinity. The soul is set and lives at the centre of all being, whence the sources of all life flow, where the meaning of all existence shines forth in the Triune God, where all power and all beauty, all peace and all blessedness, are become pure actuality and purest present, are made an eternal now.

This life of the saints, in its superabundant and inexhaustible fruitfulness, is at the same time a life of the richest variety and fulness. The one Spirit of Jesus, their Head and Mediator, is manifested in His saints in all the rich variety of their individual lives, and according to the various measures in which every single soul, with its own special gifts and its own special call, has received and employed the grace of God. The one conception of the saintly man, of the servant of Christ, is embodied in an infinite variety of forms. The Litany of the Saints takes us rapidly through this "celestial hierarchy." Beginning at the throne of the most holy Trinity and passing thence to Mary, the Mother of God, and then through the hosts of the angelic choirs to the solitary penance of the great Precursor, St. John the Baptist, it leads us to St. Joseph, the foster-father of the Lord, the man of quiet dutifulness and simplicity of soul. Next to them tower the figures of the Patriarchs and Prophets, primitive and sometimes strange figures, but men of strong faith, of sacred constancy, of ardent desire. Sharply contrasted with them are the witnesses of the fulfillment, the apostles and disciples of the Lord: Peter, Paul, Andrew, James and the rest. And while every name denotes a special gift, a special character, a special life, yet all are united in one only love and in one gospel of joy and gladness. And around and about these outstanding figures what a harvest and rich crop of infinite colour and in infinitely diverse fields! All holy martyrs—All holy bishops and confessors—All holy doctors—All holy priests and levites—All holy monks and

hermits—All holy virgins and widows—All saints of God. It is
that "great multitude which no man can number, of all nations,
and tribes, and peoples, and tongues: standing before the throne
and in sight of the Lamb, clothed with white robes, and palms
in their hands" (Apoc. vii, 9).

But however wondrously glorious all these holy figures are,
each in his own way, yet all are outshone by one, by the Queen
of all angels and saints, Mary, the Mother of God. Like every
creature in heaven and on earth, she too was called into existence
out of nothingness. An infinite distance separates her from the
Infinite, from Father, Son and Holy Ghost. And she has no
grace, no virtue, no privilege, which she does not owe to the
divine Mediator. Both in her natural and in her supernatural
being, she is wholly the gift of God, "full of grace." . . . There is
but one God, the Triune God, and every created thing lives in
awe of His mystery. But this one God is a God of life and of
love. So great, so superabundant is this love, that it not only
raises man to its own image and likeness by the natural gifts
of reason and will, but also, by the precious gift of sanctifying
grace, summons him from his state of isolation to an unparalleled
participation in the Divine Nature and in Its blessings, to a sort
of active co-operation in the work of God, to effective initiative
in the establishment of the Kingdom of God. It is the profoundest meaning and the amazing generosity of the redemption, that
it raises the rational creature from the infinite remoteness of
its impotence and from the abysmal ruin of its sins into the
Divine Life, and thereby makes it apt—while preserving its
creaturely limitations—to co-operate in the work of redemption.
The Scriptures tell us that the angels in their measure shared
in the work of creation, and that they gave the Law to Moses
(Gal. iii, 19; Hebr. ii, 2), thus co-operating effectively in the
establishment of the Old Covenant. The new creation also and
the New Covenant are not perfected without the co-operation
of secondary causes, the blessed angels and men. So the whole

of redeemed humanity enters in its measure into the circle of the Divine Life. To that extent it is not only the object of the divine work of salvation, but also subject and agent in that work, although the creature, of course, remains always a creature and can co-operate in the work of salvation only through God's power. Yet, looking at the matter as a whole, the true Kingdom, whence comes all blessing, is not God alone, not the divine "One" alone, but the "One and all," or rather the totality of all the members whom Christ, their Head, introduces into the divine life of God, who is fruitful in His saints. . . .

Our God is the transcendent, absolute God, who became Man for us in His Son, and therefore no solitary God, but the God of angels and saints, the God of fruitfulness and abundance, the God who with a veritable divine folly by the incomprehensible decree of His most free will takes up into Himself the whole creation that culminates in human nature, and in a new, un-heard-of supernatural manner, "lives in it," "moves" in it, and in it "is" (cf. Acts xvii, 28). . . . The saints are not mere exalted patterns of behaviour, but living members and even constructive powers of the Body of Christ. They possess, therefore, not merely a moral, but also a religious significance. Like the apostles and prophets, upon whom they are founded (Eph. ii, 20), they are essentially and forever the fellow-workers of Christ (II Cor. vi, 1), His servants (Matt. x, 24) and marriage guests (Matt. ix, 15), His friends (John xv, 14) and His glory (II Cor. viii, 23). They have all an abiding inward relation, a real and vital connexion with the whole Christ (*totus Christus*), and their importance for the welfare of the whole Body depends upon the special function which they have to fulfil within its organism.

That which is valid of the saints in general, holds in the highest measure of the Queen of all saints, Mary the Mother of God. The mystery of Mary's divine Motherhood does not merely comprise the bare fact that the Word took flesh and blood, our human nature, in her womb. The Catholic is not content merely to repeat with gladness the words of the inspired woman in the Gospel: "Blessed is the womb that bore thee, and the paps that gave thee suck." He listens with a far deeper attention to our Lord's answer: "Blessed are they that hear the word of God and keep it" (Luke xi, 28). Mary's importance in the work of salvation does not lie chiefly in the purely bodily sphere of morality and religion. It consists in this, that Mary, so far as lay in her, gave the best of herself, even her whole being, to the service of God, and that, however infinitely small all human doing and suffering are in comparison with the Divine Perfection, she surrendered this infinitely small without limitation or stint to the visitation of Divine Grace, and so prepared herself to be the sublime instrument of the divine redemption. We know little or nothing of her early life; but from the moment that she appears upon the stage of history, Mary is irradiated with light: "Hail, full of grace, the Lord is with thee, blessed art thou amongst women" (Luke i, 28). No angel has ever spoken a greater or holier word than that of man or woman. For centuries now the Church has pondered this angelic salutation, prayerfully and lovingly, and has discovered continually in it new glories of Mary. And yet her mystery is still unexhausted. In the light of the same Gospel story we see her as one who in the deep consciousness of her lowliness (Luke i, 48, 52, 53) is full of ecstatic joy and rejoices in God her Saviour and in Him alone (i, 46), and in the ardour of her maiden surrender and overmastering inspiration foresees and proclaims the amazing truth: "Behold, from henceforth, all generations shall call me blessed" (i, 48). None other grasped as she did, at once and at the very beginnings of the Gospel, its revolutionary and triumphant power, and therefore the Church calls her "Queen of Prophets." We know further that her whole subsequent life was lowliness and simplicity on the one hand, and on the other strong and joyful faith. Bethlehem and Golgotha are the two termini of a way of sharpest renunciation, of heroic resignation, of complete "self-emptying," such a way as our Lord Himself travelled (Phil. ii, 7). The sword foretold by Simeon (Luke ii, 35) pierced ever more sharply into her soul as the process of her self-abnegation advanced.

First it was at that scene in the temple when she listened to Simeon's prophecy (Luke ii, 34–35), and then at the marriage feast of Cana (John ii, 4) and at that meeting in Capharnaum (Mark iii, 33; Matt. xii, 48; Luke viii, 21) when her Son said, "Woman, what is it to me and to thee?" and, "Who is my mother?" and then, finally, beneath the Cross. In all these experiences of her life, with ever deeper sorrow and comprehension, she disengaged her divine Son from her heart and surrendered Him to the Father: "Queen of Martyrs." But her faith was as strong as her humility. She "kept all these words," which were spoken of her Son, "pondering them in her heart" (Luke ii, 19, 51). And so she became the precious and pure source of that history of His infancy, the faithful evangelist: "Queen of Evangelists." It was his mother's faith that produced the miracle of Cana, the first manifestation of our Lord's glory among men (John ii, 1). And Mary was a blessed witness also of His last revelation of His glory, in the fiery tongues of Pentecost (Acts ii, 3). No apostle learnt the mystery of Jesus so fully and so profoundly, or preserved his experience so faithfully, as did the "Queen of Apostles." It is this radiant image of Mary, as portrayed by St. Luke and St. John, which our Lord had in mind when He directed the woman in the Gospel from the bodily motherhood of Mary to her spiritual sublimity: "Blessed are they who hear the word of God and keep it" (Luke xi, 28). This gives the scene its illuminating character and its importance in the history of our salvation. But all the sublimity of Mary's moral personality, all the depth of her virginal devotion, and all the strength of her faith culminate in the word which she spoke to the angel: "Behold the handmaid of the Lord, be it done unto me according to thy word." These were no common, everyday

words; no words such as fall from men in the changing circum-
stance and casual course of life. They were words out of the
depths and recesses of a soul that was pure and noble beyond
all earthly measure, words that were her being, her expression,
her achievement. By them of a truth, she consecrated her body
to a "reasonable service" (cf Rom. xii, 1 ff.), and that is the
source of her blessedness. The "Blessed" with which our Lord
corrects that woman's praise, rings then like a conscious reference
to the angel's "Blessed" in the same Gospel. "Blessed art thou
that hast believed that those things shall be accomplished that
were spoken to thee by the Lord" (i, 45). The gladness of redeemed humanity resounds in those words of St. Elizabeth.
They are the first jubilee of the Gospel. And they are true of
Mary beyond all others, for she by her "Be it done unto me"
preceded all others along the way of redemption, yes even helped
to prepare that way. Without her consent there had been no
redemption, and therefore is she for us all the "Gate of heaven."

And so the wonderful fact that God is not alone in the work
of redemption but that creatures too, in their measure, truly
share in that work, is illustrated nowhere more clearly than in
Mary. It is true that the fact that Mary had such privilege was
due to Grace alone, that she was called from eternity to be the
Mother of God and was from the beginning immersed in Christ's
redeeming grace, so that she was conceived Immaculate, without
stain of original sin. It was grace too, and grace alone, which
gave her heart its ardent and complete devotion to the Saviour
and its maiden resolution, so that she "knew no man" (Luke i,
34) and as "Virgin of virgins" was that closed door "through
which no man shall pass, because the Lord of God of Israel hath
entered in by it" (cf. Ezech. xliv, 2). Yet the grace of God does
not offer violence, but would be freely accepted. And therefore,
however infinitely small Mary's own activity may appear in
comparison with the activity of God, there remains a human
strand in the divine robe of our salvation, the "Be it done unto

me" of Mary. And the Catholic exalts Mary above all angels and saints (*hyperdulia*), because it has pleased God to give her decisive words this effective position in the work of redemption. The Fathers from the time of St. Justin Martyr continually urge this importance of Mary in the history of salvation, and contrast it with the sin of the first woman. Just as Eve's consent to the serpent's temptation brought sin and ruin, so did Mary's consent to the angel's message introduce redemption. So Mary possesses not only a personal relation to the Son of God and her personal salvation, but also a relation to the "many" who are redeemed by her Son. She is mother not of the Redeemer alone, but also of the redeemed; and so she is the mother of the faithful. The Catholic acknowledges in heaven not only a Father, but also a mother. Though by her human nature she is infinitely distant from the Father, yet her special graces have raised her to a wonderful nearness to God, and as mother of the Redeemer she reflects God's goodness and bounty with an inwardness and a truth that are possible to no other creature. When the Catholic speaks of his Heavenly Mother, his heart is full with all the strength of feeling that is contained in that word. Mary is as it were a gracious revelation of certain ineffable and ultimate traits in the nature of God, which are too fine and too delicate to be grasped otherwise than as reflected in the mirror of a mother. Ave Maria!

TE MARTYRUM CANDIDATUS

AH, SEE THE FAIR CHIVALRY come, the companions of Christ!
White Horsemen, who ride on white horses, the Knights of God!
They, for their Lord and their lover who sacrificed
All, save the sweetness of treading where He first trod!

These through the darkness of death, the dominion of night,
Swept, and they woke in white places at morning tide:
They saw with their eyes, and sang for joy of the sight,
They saw with their eyes the Eyes of the Crucified.

Now, whithersoever He goeth, with Him they go:
White Horsemen, who ride on white horses, oh fair to see!
They ride, where the Rivers of Paradise flash and flow,
White Horsemen, with Christ their Captain: for ever He!

MASS FOR THE PEOPLE

⚑ Fr. O'Grady looked at his watch, the server was late. He checked a feeling of irritability, and was shocked by the difficulty he felt in checking it.

Was sanctity within *his* reach after all, he asked; could his great hands lay hold of it, he who never knew the sweetness of the complete act of love, the unbroken prayer, the whole hour of meditation, the work accomplished, the sensible sweetness of the sacramental word spoken, even one hour out of the twenty-four, unbroken, for his personal delight!

Could he who never knew that completeness in his soul, that inward closed circle of light, be a Saint?

Could his day of fragments be a day in a Saint's life?

And the answer came to him paralysing in its beauty, this broken life of his was the breaking of the bread, that in the broken bread, the whole Christ be given to his people. Soon, in a few minutes now, his people would be at the altar rails, opening their mouths like sparrows for their crumb of Life, and in their crumb of Life they would receive all Life, whole.

Father O'Grady paced up and down, rubbing his hands together to keep warm—"Break *me*, dear Lord, but in the breaking of the Bread, be whole in Your Body upon earth!"

Lately, he had asked himself as he trudged home from the parish visits, what is the meaning of the lives of these unknown,

insignificant people, who yet must somehow fulfill the strange
prophecy, "And there are some of whom there is no memorial:
who are perished as if they had never been born, and their
children with them. But they were men of mercy, whose godly
deeds had not failed."

The priest was on the side of life, he had no other work, no
other raison d'être but to give life, and the life he gave could
not be killed. He was not outside of the world's love because he
was a priest and alone, he was the heart of the world's love, its
core, because the Life of the World is born every day in his
hands at Mass. He looked at his watch again. How late the boy
was! He tried to say the acts of Faith, Hope and Charity, to
fill his mind with the words of the prayers to dismiss his distrac-
tions. But it was no use. This morning, distraction got the better
of him, do what he would.

At last a clatter outside proclaimed the arrival of the little
server. How often Fr. O'Grady had tried to impress upon this
boy that he represented all the Christians in the world before
the Altar of God, when he answered Mass, and how well the
Christianity of the world should brush its hair and clean its
shoes and wash its hands, to enter the Holy of Holies and offer
the heart of mankind! To-day he was even more dishevelled
than usual, tousled, smeary, his bootlace undone, and it was
apparent that the World had overslept and tumbled straight
out of bed, and would to-day be even more than usually absent-
minded and clumsy—yet Fr. O'Grady looked at the urchin ten-
derly, all his irritability passed. After all the world *is* like that,
late, distracted, grimy, but with a good if unstable will to serve;
and might not this sudden new tenderness in the priest's heart
be a reflection from aeons and aeons away, of the tenderness of
the Eternal Father, waiting from eternity for the scruffy, sniff-
ing, unconcentrated, often unwashed, imperfect, weak and loving Christian world, to come to Him.

"Tie your shoelace," he said, "and damp down your hair—
and here flick your face with this wet towel, and hurry now,
put on your cotta and light the candles."

And the dishevelled Christian world, transformed, in a smooth
white cotta, with a wet golden curl, and nothing of "the old
man" left but the huge boots jabbing out from his cassock,
walked out with the expression of a Botticelli angel, to light the
candles for Mass.

Even during the few steps that he walked from the sacristy
to the sanctuary, the humiliation of being himself left Father
O'Grady, the emptiness, the dryness of his soul, ceased to matter
at all.

He had only to give himself now, to give himself to the
words and the movements of the Mass, to give his body, his
hands, his tongue, to give his whole being, easily, unresistingly,
to move through the groove trodden out for him, to move in it
like water flowing in the deep groove in the rock, worn through
the heart of the world by generations of the adoration of men.

At the entrance to the sanctuary, he turned to the congrega-
tion and said: "This Mass is offered for the people of the
parish."

There were only a few people present, the little server, a
handful of old women, an Irish sailor, and a very old man.
But since Christ was present in them, the whole Christian
world was there.

So all the people of the parish, for whom Mass was offered,
were there. The dockers already loading and unloading the big
ships; the sailors who had just put out to sea, and the sailors
ploughing their way home; the factory girls on their way to
work, making the streets gay with their bright skimpy finery;
the women scrubbing the steps with their arms up to their
elbows in soapy water; the mothers washing up the menfolk's
early breakfast before waking the children; the children sleeping
the warm, woolly sleep of early morning; the marketers setting

up their stalls; the flower women in their shawls, and their gents' straw boaters, carrying their great baskets of bronze and red and yellow flowers; the patients in the hospitals, newly washed and smoothed in cool white wards; the night nurses, pale and craving for strong tea and sleep; the day nurses pinning their starched caps, and wondering if it would be fried bread and bacon, or only fried bread for breakfast; the old folk in the workhouse, sitting quietly on their wooden benches; the prisoners in the gaol, looking up at the slit of silver sky, through the high, narrow windows of their cells; all were there, at the Mass that was being offered for them, the people of the parish.

Father O'Grady made the Sign of the Cross.

"In the name of the Father and of the Son and of the Holy Ghost. Amen," and bowed down under the burden of the sins of the whole world. His own sins were a heavy enough load, and now he bowed under the weight of all sin. But when he straightened himself up from the Confiteor, the burden of the whole world's sin, and his own with it, had fallen from his back, and his shoulders were strong. For it was Christ who rose up and went up to the altar—Christ who had seen evil naked, face to face, Christ who had been brought down to the ground, under the world's sin to sweat His blood into the dust, and Christ who has overcome the world.

The Mass moved forward with beautiful precision.

"Kyrie Eleison."

"Christe Eleison."

Sharp, urgent little knocks at the door of Heaven.

"Gloria in Excelsis Deo. . . . "

The angels' carillon swung into motion by the beating of a man's heart, and onward, hurrying forward with urgency of a lovers' meeting. The bright, short prayers sparkling over the priest's mind, bringing him swiftly to the Offertory.

He lifted the unconsecrated Host, light as a petal on its thin golden paten, and with it lifted the simple bread of humanity, threshed and sifted by poverty and suffering. He offered the broken fragments of their love, made into one loaf.

He lifted the wine and water mixed in the Chalice, and with it offered the blood and the tears of his people to God.

And God accepted the offering, the fragments of love were gathered up into the wholeness of Love and nothing was wasted. The Mass moved swiftly, hurrying forward as if the longing of generations had set its urgent pace towards the climax. But now the pace grew slower, charged with so immense a momentum of Mystery that it could only move forward in larger, fuller, slower gestures. The wonder rising like the rising of a tide to the flood. And as the Miracle came closer and closer time ceased to be at all. Simply, effortlessly, directly the Mass moved, not backward or forward in time, but into the eternal *now* of the Last Supper. Into the stillness of the Upper Room, where the voice of Christ fell upon the souls of His Apostles, like summer rain falling upon the sown earth.

Slowly, exactly, Father O'Grady repeated the words of Consecration, his hands moved in Christ's hands, his voice spoke in Christ's voice, his words were Christ's words, his heart beat in Christ's heart.

"Who the day before He suffered, took bread in His holy and venerable hands, and lifting His eyes to Heaven towards Thee O God, His all powerful Father, giving thanks to Thee, blessed and broke and gave to His disciples, saying TAKE AND EAT YE ALL OF THIS, FOR THIS IS MY BODY."

Fr. O'Grady lifted up the consecrated Host in his short, chapped hands, the server rang a little bell, the sailor, the handful of old women and the very old man bowed down whispering "My Lord and my God" and the breath of their adoration was warm on their cold fingers.

Father O'Grady was lifting up God.

A cry arose from all over the world, "Come down from the

Cross if you are the Son of God!" "Save yourself and us too if
you are the Christ."

But Christ remained on the Cross. His fingers closed on the
nails. He would not come down from the Cross. He would not
dethrone the children, he would not discrown the poor, he would
not scatter the fragments of the bread of love. He would not
break faith with sinners or fail the failing. He would not for-
sake the young men coming up to die His death.

"Come down from the Cross! come down! come down! save
yourself and us!"

But Christ remained on the Cross. His fingers closed on the
nails. The Crown of Thorns was in flower, the five ribs like
the five fingers of the world's pain gripped His heart, and His
heart broke open and the river of the world's life flowed out of it.
A crimson flood sweeping His heart and brain and flowing out
into the tips of His fingers, swept through His Mystical Body.
Through the eternal heart of Rome, through the lonely mind
of her august Shepherd, out into the least and lowliest of men,
and the last little infant howling at the touch of the waters of
Baptism, the blood of the world's life flowed into the finger
tips, which stretched out on the Cross, measuring the reach and
stretch and extremity and ultimate possibility of love.

"Come down from the Cross if you be the Son of God!"

"Save yourself and us too if you are the Christ."

The world strained at the nails, wrenched and dragged, the
Cross was shaken in the earth, bent like a tree in the storm,
dragged earthward by the weight of man's body, but it was
rooted in rock, and the Cross was built to the shape of man,
not man to the shape of the Cross. The world's suffering
was built and fitted to the size of each man, and the Cross
stood.

"Come down, come down, come down!"

But Christ would not come down from the Cross.

The life of Riverside went on, the day's work had begun, a

ship was coming in from the sea, another putting out. An old man was dying, and a child was being born.

The little server rang his silver bell.

The people bowed down low.

Time stopped.

Fr. O'Grady was lifting up God in his large, chapped hands. Christ remained on the Cross.

The blood and sweat and tears of the world were on His face. He smiled, the smile of infinite peace, the ineffable bliss of consummated love.

THE CRUCIFIXION
Michelozzo

THROUGH THY CROSS AND PASSION

O Christ my Lord which for my sins didst hang upon a tree,
grant that thy grace in me poor wretch may still ingrafted be.

Grant that thy naked hanging there, may kill in me all pride
and care of wealth, sith thou didst then in such poor state abide.

Grant that thy Crown of pricking thorns which thou for me
    didst wear,
may make me willing for thy sake all shame and pain to bear.

Grant that those scorns and taunts which thou didst on the cross
    endure,
may humble me, and in my heart all patience still procure.

Grant that thy praying for thy foes may plant within my breast
such charity as from my heart I malice may detest.

Grant that thy piercéd hands which did of nothing all things
    frame,
may move me to lift up my hands, and ever praise thy name.

Grant that thy wounded feet whose steps were perfect evermore,

may learn my feet to tread those paths which thou hast gone
before.

Grant that thy bitter gall which did thy empty body fill,
may teach me to subdue myself, and to perform thy will.

Grant that thy wounds may cure the sores which sin in me hath
wrought,
grant that thy death may save the soul which with thy blood
was bought.

Grant that those drops of blood which ran out from thy heart
amain
may meek my heart into salt tears to see thy grievous pain.

Grant that thy blessed grave wherein thy body lay awhile,
may bury all such vain delights as may my mind defile.

Grant that thy going down to them which did thy sight desire,
may keep my soul when I am dead, clean from the purging fire.

Grant that thy rising up from death, may raise my thoughts from
sin,
Grant that thy parting from this earth, from earth my heart
may win.

Grant Lord that thy ascending then, may lift my mind to thee,
that there my heart and joy may rest, though here in flesh I be.

THE BLESSED EUCHARIST

᭝ CHRIST'S LOVE for us compels Him to enter into ever closer union with human souls, to be even nearer to them than He was when He moved on earth and conversed with those about Him. During His mortal life He spoke and His words sank into His hearers' hearts and stirred them strangely. But in Holy Communion His contact with us is much more intimate and vital than it then was with those who thronged His footsteps along the Galilean highways. It is also much more active and life-giving. Our Lord's love is of a Divine Purity, and it is therefore divinely disinterested. It is solely in view of our interest that He desires to enter into this close relation with us in which His soul is united with ours. It is we, not He, that derive advantage from this spiritual union.

On two distinct occasions God His Father in Heaven proclaimed that the Child of Mary was His beloved Son in Whom He was well pleased. The significance of this testimony lies in this: there is no being in whom God can find His pleasure, and to whom therefore He can extend His love, unless it be Jesus Christ or one who bears a resemblance to Him. No other form of human life can please God except His, or one that takes its pattern from His. Hence St. Peter says: "Be it known to you all, and to all the people of Israel, that by the name of Our Lord Jesus Christ of Nazareth, whom you crucified . . . this man standeth here whole; neither is there salvation in any other. For there is no other name under heaven given to men, whereby we must be saved." Unless we are pleasing to God we cannot be saved, we cannot realise the purpose of our divine adoption. We cannot please God unless we resemble Jesus Christ, and the Blessed Sacrament is instituted for the very object of perfecting in us this likeness. Bodily food is transformed into the flesh of him that receives it; this heavenly food, the food of our souls, which is the Body and Blood of Jesus Christ, has the directly opposite effect; it changes him who receives it into Itself. It must not be forgotten that the presence in us which follows the reception of Holy Communion is a living, active presence. Our Lord is more present with us than is a person with whom we are speaking. As He influenced whilst on earth those who allowed themselves to fall under the charm of His Personality, so He exercises a profound effect on the soul of the communicant, if that soul wishes to submit to His action. We cannot be in the society of one who is good without being incited to goodness; we cannot be with Our Lord—and we are as close to Him as our desires extend—without receiving the effects of His virtue and without being stirred to become as He was, without being drawn, in a mystical sense to become one with Him, to become "Christified."

He lived through human life in all its stages and conditions. In this He accumulated a vast store of merits and graces for His Mystical members. As Head of the Mystical Body He can communicate to each cell of the body the graces appropriate, and the activities proper to its state. No matter what be the age, function or condition in life of any of His members, He can communicate to that member a holiness which works in it a resemblance to Jesus Himself. Priests, religious, school children, all receive the same spiritual food. To the priest it imparts the grace to comport himself as Our Lord Himself did in His work of teaching and sanctifying men. At the Holy Table the religious sister draws from the fountain of all grace the Christlike pru-

dence, wisdom and patience that she needs to train and instruct
in truth the youth committed to her care. Children, in their
turn, learn from contact with Our Lord that candour, docility
and supernatural obedience that distinguished Him during the
period of His boyhood. In short, each receives from Holy Communion that form of sanctity that his life requires in order to
have that life formed on the pattern of the corresponding stage
in the life of Jesus. As with the manna in the desert, each finds
in it the savour that he relishes, desires and needs.

In a word, the Holy Communion has as its distinct effect to
form in us the mind and heart of Christ. The motive force of
His Life was Divine Charity, that is, love of God, zeal for His
Glory and an ardent desire to translate that Love into the activity
of His daily life. The Blessed Sacrament is called the Sacrament
of Love. It was the supreme expression of the love of Jesus for
us. It was the uttermost point to which love could go, even
having omnipotence at its service. Its virtue is to *provoke on our
part* a corresponding charity. St. Thomas tells us that. It does
not merely give us the habit of charity, it gives us charity in act—
it excites to the act of charity. Every action on the part of Jesus
as boy, as youth, as man, was inspired, animated, and informed
by love of God. Holy Communion has its direct, special and
connatural effect to enable us to perform the acts of the state
of life in which we are, in a similar disposition of charity.

But if the Holy Eucharist produces such wonderful things in
our souls, why is it that so frequently those who communicate
show so few signs of becoming better? This is a common objec-
tion. Men are always prone to judge by what appears. The
Saviour Himself commented on this tendency on more than one
occasion. The subtle effects of transformation that take place in
the depths of a Christian's soul are visible only to God. That the
changes effected by Holy Communion are imperceptible does not
mean that they are not real. The operation of the Blessed Sacrament may be likened to the invisible, slow and mysterious work-

ing of the seedling in the earth, of which the Lord speaks on
another occasion. . . . But in spite of the hiddenness of the working of the Holy Eucharist in souls "there are moments when we
get transient glimpses within us of what the habitual presence
of the Blessed Sacrament has done for us. We perceive that it
has not only done something to each virtue and grace God may
have given us, but it has changed us, it has done a work in our
nature; we perceive that it has impregnated us with feelings and
instincts which are not of this world and that it has called up or
created new faculties to which we cannot give a name, nor divine
their functions." We think that the effect of each communion
is small because we do not understand what immense opposition
to His transforming charity Our Lord finds in the soul of each of
us. The less opposition to Him, the greater the effect—hence the
efficacy of the Holy Eucharist, normally speaking, is proportioned to the perfection of the dispositions we bring to Its reception. The more perfect our dispositions, the greater benefit we
shall ordinarily derive from our communions.

What are these dispositions? The first is Faith. We should
approach the Holy Table with a firm belief that under these
appearances of bread and quite close to us is the same Jesus
Christ who was born of Mary, lived on earth, and died on the
Cross to expiate our sins. We should stir up our minds and
hearts to a vivid realisation that when we receive Jesus Christ
we are receiving God the Son, the Second Person of the Blessed
Trinity, Who comes to us hypostatically united with the Sacred
Humanity and prepared to use it as an instrument of His Divine
Power to effect a wonderful change in us. And we should
ardently desire that the same God and Saviour should by His
presence penetrate into our souls, sanctify them, expel from them
everything impure, and fashion them to the resemblance of His
Own. Since this is the Sacrament of Charity we should excite
ourselves to a great love of Him Who gives Himself to us.
And since this love would be false, did we not include in it

those who are His members, those who partake with us of the
same spiritual food, those who receive the same supernatural
gift as ourselves, we must bring to the Holy Table a spirit of
forbearance and love, free from all deliberate feelings of jealousy,
envy or dislike of our fellow Christians. And finally, since there
are only two loves which can dispute the possession of our
hearts—the love of God and the love of ourselves—and as it is
the latter that alone is an obstacle to the Creator's taking complete possession of our souls, let us give up all self-love. If our
communions are to produce a deep, transforming effect on our
souls, we must aim at desiring God as our only Good, and not the
satisfaction of our own desires. We should yearn to be made,
through the Bread of Life, more and more like to God and more
and more removed from the form of our evil self. The final disposition, and perhaps the most practically important, is that we
should long to have developed in us through an intimate contact
with the Saviour in the Holy Communion, a docility of heart
and mind like to His. Life presents great difficulties to all. Some
Christians, when faced with them, approach the Lord to expos-
tulate with Him about them. Others, more enlightened, come
to Him for light, encouragement and strength to bear up against
their difficulties after the example of the Saviour. These latter
necessarily derive more benefit from their Communions than
the former. It is much better to use our contact with the Lord
for the purpose of drawing spiritual development out of our
trials than of seeking to evade them. We take our natural food
in order to be able to live and work, not to evade life's burdens.
We should nourish ourselves spiritually with a view to acquiring
the strength to bear the Cross—that is, the lifework that is ours,
as elevated to the supernatural order. The Holy Liturgy speaks
of the Blessed Sacrament as "a sacred banquet in which is given
us a pledge of future glory." St. Thomas tells us that It, in-
directly, diminishes the force of the concupiscence of the flesh
and gives us power to resist the corrupt desires of our senses and

is a most powerful aid to the cultivation of Holy Purity. The Fathers love to call it the Seed of Virgins.

. . . . There is one important aspect in which the Blessed Eucharist differs from the other sacraments. These latter are signs of a supernatural effect on the soul; the Blessed Eucharist is a sign of an abiding presence under the Sacred Species of the Source of all grace—of Jesus Christ Himself. Wherever is the White Host, there is present Our Lord in all his reality, with the same understanding, the same affection, the same divine power and the same profound sympathy with everything human as He had during those days on earth. . . . The going to visit Our Lord is just as real and just as effective, or rather more real and effective, than it would be were we living with Him when He passed His days at Nazareth. We think that were we alive then we should never have wearied of returning to the Holy House to converse with Him and His Mother and Joseph. Perhaps! If we had a very strong and deep faith—yes. But if we had only the faith that we actually possess, our visits would have had that measure of frequency and spontaneity that they now have— that, and no more. To be attracted and drawn to the side of Jesus in a way that affects our spiritualization is to be drawn by the Divinity that is in Him. Other attractions will not transform us. That divinity is just as "visible" now as it was then, when He stood by His carpenter's bench. If we "sense" it now, we would have "sensed" it then. If we are not attracted now we could not have been attracted then. It is always "the same Jesus Christ, yesterday and today, and the same for ever." All vital contact with the Reality that He is is on a supernatural level. To sense and reason He is always hidden. If we were to enter Joseph's workshop and look on Jesus, we should see with our eyes only a man like ourselves, simple and upright and a pains-taking workman. Nothing more; that is what all His fellow-townsmen saw. Their gaze could not penetrate deeper because of the imperfections of the dispositions of their hearts. I suspect

that the visits of the ordinary good people of the village, drawn
to the Holy House by supernatural interests, were just as occasional as those of ordinary good people in the present day to the
Blessed Sacrament. No more than that.

One who thinks that were he at Nazareth he would desire
to go very often to see Our Lord, and who does not desire to go
often to the church where the same Lord dwells, is labouring
under a delusion. He is simply wanting in faith. It is the same
loving Saviour, with the same kind heart, the same majesty, the
same holiness and the same zeal for our good, who once abode
in Nazareth and now abides in the tabernacle.

PASSION

🍃 *The Church speaks:*

I will sing a Gloria that shall fill the top of my towers with the
   clangour of their bells.

Praise the Lord all sorrow of the earth!

Let the impoverished praise Him, and those who are in exile, let
   the disappointed praise Him, and the disinherited, let Him
   be praised by all whom nothing satisfies.

Be He praised by the bright torment of the spirit, and by the
   dark torment of nature.

Be He praised by the holy torment of love.

Be He praised by the solitude of the soul and by the soul's captivity.

Be He praised by the sorrow of sin and by the woe that all things
   perish,

Be He praised also by the bitter anguish of death.

See, I strip my altars of all adornment, all their fine linen must
   fade like the loveliness of flowering fields.

All the images on them must hide their faces.

I will take away my last consolation, I will remove the Lord's
   Body, that my soul may become deep night,

For the sorrow of the world has become blessed, because it has
   been loved.

Behold the wood of the Cross on which hung the Salvation of
   the world.

LOVE EXPRESSING ITSELF IN PAIN

❧ THE PROBLEM of Suffering is the one problem of all ages. Every age produces a new solution. It was once thought, with extreme simplicity, that it was merely a matter of accurate reward and punishment—"Be virtuous; and you will be immune from suffering"—that God fought not with the largest battalions but with the most pious. And, again and again, the theory broke down. "In spite of my beautiful theories," cries David, "I see the wicked flourishing like green bay-trees. They come into no misfortune like other folk, neither are they plagued like other men. Then thought I to understand this; but it was too hard for me. Until"—but the rest comes later.

Or again, men have sought to solve the problem by suggesting that interior consolations always compensated for the exterior sufferings of the virtuous; that they really felt happy, in spite of appearances to the contrary. This lasted tolerably well as a theory until men really began to know their own souls; and then they found that interior sufferings were just as real, and even more poignant, than exterior. They found, moreover, that it was actually the good who suffered in this way more than the bad; that the sensitive, delicate conscience and perceptions were tormented in a manner of which the superficial animal knew nothing; that suffering was not just a question of external scourge and nails, but of a Gethsemane agony so acute that the soul herself sweated blood. So they were driven from this stronghold, too.

Finally, it has been suggested by one of the most recent and prosperous of the sects that the problem of pain is no problem, because there is no pain!

Now, I need hardly say that I do not propose to suggest another solution of my own; but I think it is worth while to point out the solution that Jesus Christ offers. His solution of suffering is to suffer.

Indeed, this is not so fatuous as it sounds, if it will be remembered that the intellect is only one department, and that a very small one, of our being. When Christ was before Herod, Herod's mistake was that he tried to compress the question before him into the single point of sensation or emotion. He did not judge Christ with the whole of his being, but with a part only. He condemned Him because He did not satisfy an arbitrary emotional test. Now, it is just as foolish to judge the problem of Pain by an intellectual test. If pain were a mere matter of the intellect, it might be reasonable; but pain affects the whole of our personality at once—physical, mental, emotional and spiritual. Pain, therefore, like Religion itself, is a thing that has to be judged by the whole of our personality. In a word, it has to be experienced; and somewhere in this total experience, not in any mere intellectual explanation, the solution lies.

Now this was the solution of Jesus Christ. "He learned obedience," says St. Paul, "by the things that He suffered." He solved pain by enduring it. He opened every fibre and nerve of His Human Nature to pain; there was no whole spot in Body or Soul. Physical and spiritual thirst were alike parts of His experience. "I thirst! . . . Why hast Thou forsaken Me? . . . My soul is athirst for the living God." He experienced solitude—the solitude of failure. "Of the people there was none with Me." "He came to His own, and His own received Him not." He was obedient unto death: He tasted Death, and therefore He

conquered it. But the great point of it all is that with His Will
He did all these things. "I lay down My life of Myself." He did
not merely bear the Cross, He took it up—first, interiorly in
Gethsemane; then exteriorly at the steps of the Praetorium.

He did not, therefore, argue about pain; for you can no more
compress pain into mere argument than you can compress Religion, or exactly analyze Love. These really great things must be
experienced; you have not all the data of the problem of pain,
until you have suffered all of it. And is it not, after all, a solid
fact that it is not the sufferer who is most perplexed by the problem of pain, but the people who look on—in fact, the people who
regard it merely intellectually? You can no more solve the problem of pain by the intellect alone, than you can explain the
beauty of a sunlit sea or the augustness of a thunderstorm by
chemical analysis of sun and sea-water and electricity. Men do
not say "I will not believe a sonata by Beethoven is beautiful
unless I can smell it. I will not consent that theft is a crime
unless I can taste it to be so." Yet people do have the effrontery
to say "Unless I see I will not believe," or "Unless I understand
I will not believe." Or, "Unless I can intellectually apprehend
the meaning of pain I will not submit to it without a protest."
The actual sufferer, therefore, if only he will not try to be too
clever—which is another word for trying to be narrow-minded
—the actual sufferer is not nearly so much puzzled by pain as
his friend who looks on; and the *willing* sufferer—he who actually cooperates with and welcomes pain—is not puzzled at all.
He cannot explain it; he cannot, that is, throw the experiences
of his whole personality into terms of a part of it; but he is no
longer puzzled. He knows. It is like a man in love: he cannot
put it into words; he bursts out in sonnets, it may be, or sere-
nades; he will talk about it for hours together; but he will also
end by saying that words and music are no good, that you must
experience it to understand it. It is much bigger than any analysis
that can be made of it. That is why lovers, and contemplative

monks who scourge themselves for joy, are considered the monu-
mental fools of the world. It is because they cannot put into
words what is actually incapable of being put into words—because they grow incoherent and ecstatic, as they are bound to
do—because they cannot translate into terms which the poor
narrow-minded world seems to think are the only terms worth
using—because they cannot write down with pen and ink—what
all the blood of the human heart cannot describe. It needs the
Blood of God, forced from Him in Gethsemane, torn with
scourges from Him in the Praetorium, sucked from Him by
nails and thorns, and finally tapped by the spear, to its very last
drops, from a Sacred Heart—it needs this Blood, offered willingly, adequately to experience and to show what is the solution
of the problem of pain—*which is, in fact, the very same thing
as the problem of Love.*

The Gospel is a record of Love expressing itself in Pain. Here
is One who yearns for sacrifice—not on behalf of merely this or
that person—but for all persons. "How am I straitened," cried
Jesus Christ. "How am I compressed and confined, until this be
accomplished! How am I held back and restrained until I am
set at liberty by the fettering nails of the Cross—until I can
empty Myself wholly and entirely of every drop of blood, of
every spiritual consolation—until I am, indeed, in My Humanity, so utterly dry and wrung out that indeed I may be said
to thirst—until I am so utterly lonely, in so appalling a solitude,
that I have bidden even My mother farewell, have been forsaken of all My friends . . . I am not truly possessed by My
friends, until I have ceased to possess them." In one sentence,
Christ could not be said to have succeeded in His object, until
He had, down to the very last detail of His plan, completely
failed. With Him, and Him alone, nothing succeeds like
Failure.

Now, this identity of what the world calls failure and what
God calls success is illustrated by many of Christ's deeper say-

ings, and lies luminous in the very heart of the darkness of
Calvary. It is this surely that reconciles ultimately such paradoxes as—"Except a man lose his life, he cannot save it." "Blessed
are they that hunger and thirst, for they shall be comforted."
"Except a man hate his father and mother He cannot be My
disciple," and "Except a man take up his cross"—reach, that is,
the very lowest disgrace and failure that this world can conceive
—"he cannot be My disciple." It seems, as we regard it, almost
painfully obvious that, as I said just now, Divine Love cannot
be said to have won any victory—cannot, that is, have fully
expressed its own nature of Sacrifice, until it has undergone
what the world reckons failure in every point. For Love must
have pain—more, it must become Pain—or else it dies indeed.
Here, too, is the reconciliation of that most mysterious saying
of all—"He that believeth in Me, shall never die"—that is, "He
that is really united with Me, finds Death to be the ultimate
satisfaction of Love—and this is Life." As we turn, then, from
the record of Christ's life in the Gospel to His Life in the
Church, we find precisely the same phenomenon repeated over
and over again.

Here is St. Paul first, crying in an ecstasy of Love—"I die
daily"; "As dying, yet behold we live"; "I live, yet not I, but
Christ liveth in me"; and above all, that phrase so often quoted
before—"I fill up . . . what is lacking of the sufferings of Christ."

As we regard the Church, then, as the Body in which Jesus
Christ leads a mystical life, a thousand difficulties are explained:

First, what is that strange passion known only among Catholics as a wholesome and recognized instinct, by which men and
women—even boys and girls—in the very height of vitality and
strength, think that the one thing worth doing is to immure
themselves in a cell, in order to suffer? What is the instinct that
makes the Carmelite hang an empty cross in her cell, to remind
herself that she must take the place of the absent figure on it—
and yet keeps the Carmelite the most radiantly happy of all

women? The joy of a woman—I might say the gaiety of a woman
—over her first child is but a shadow of the solemn joy of a
Carmelite, the irrepressible gaiety of a Poor Clare—women, that
is, who have sacrificed every single thing that the world thinks
worth having. Certainly it is not the same as Oriental asceticism,
for the object of the Oriental is to escape from being, to be
released from the Wheel of Life—and the object of the Catholic
ascetic is to be bound to it more closely, to realize and express
himself more fully—at least that kind of self-expression that is
called self-sacrifice.

The thing is simply inexplicable except on that one hypothesis—that that the unique thirst of Jesus upon the Cross is communicated to His members, that His ambition to suffer is perpetuated continually in that Mystical Body in which He reenacts
the history of His passion—that these are the cells of that Body,
which, like His Hands and Feet, are more especially pierced by
nails, and who rejoice to know that they are called to this august
vocation, by which the Redemption wrought on Calvary is perpetually reenacted on earth; who "fill up what is lacking of the
sufferings of Christ," who are lambs of God whose blood mingles
with the Blood of Calvary, victims whose sacrifice is accepted as
united with His.

Again, as has been hinted before—this conception of the
Church as the Body of Christ is surely the one hypothesis which
makes the sufferings of *individuals* tolerable to contemplate. I
have attempted to indicate how, as it appears to me, the problem of suffering in general will be ultimately solved—by arguing
that Pain always is the expression of Love, that it is only an evil
to those who do not love, and that it is a positive joy to those
who, by love, accept and welcome it; and that Failure, as the
world calls it, again and again corresponds to the overlapping
of the human by the Divine. But all this does not touch really the
suffering of the individual who has not learned how to welcome

it. There still remains the problem of the little crippled child, and of the innocent girl who goes mad with melancholia.

Now if you treat those cases as individual—if you regard the child as merely a complete entity in himself—the thing is and always must be inexplicable. Again and again we find ourselves asking, why should *he* suffer! He is not a Carmelite who understands; he is not a sinner to be reformed by discipline.

But if you reflect that Humanity as a whole is a great organism, used by God as the Body of His passion: and that in the sufferings of this Body He carries out, on the mystical plane, His Redemption, and satisfies His Divine thirst for pain; and that this child is one cell of the Body of pain; you are no more intellectually puzzled as to why this child should suffer in particular, than you are intellectually puzzled as to why your finger should ache, instead of yourself. Your finger does not ache instead of yourself; you ache in your finger. This child does not suffer instead of Humanity; but Humanity suffers in him, and Christ therefore in him. If, in short, you will insist upon treating each unit only as a unit, you will never be satisfied; but if you understand that these units are more than units—they are cells in a Body; and if, further, you understand that it is Jesus Christ who lives and acts in this Body, that He truly, therefore, identifies Himself with every one of His members, a host of difficulties become luminous.

"Inasmuch as ye do it, or do it not, unto one of the least of these—you do it, or do it not, to Me."

ALTER CHRISTUS
Poem written in a Mental Home.

Lord, for the pain I cursed You for last night
I do most gladly offer thanks today . . .
For, not with pride but deep humility
In me, and by me, and through me, I find—You!
In my stripped loneliness, Your own imprisonment—
My bruises mark Your scourging; and the same
Rude jests ring in my ears that rang in Yours—
And round my aching head I seem to feel
Even today, the racking crown of thorns . . .
I too was bound—and, though I never died,
I was like You—my *spirit* crucified.

THE MARKS OF CHRIST

We may define the lack of order in the personality of a neurotic as, objectively, a departure from the sanity of Christ, since in Christ we see the harmony and order which should be in humanity. Now departure from the sanity of Christ does not mean departure from the sanctity of Christ. In other words, it is possible for a neurotic person to be closer to Christ than a healthy one.

In order that this may be understood it is necessary to remind the reader that the causes of neurosis are generally multiple. Among the causes leading to it we have been considering one—the spiritual and important one—of a man's personal need for God seen in his desire for a Final End and for happiness. Even this, as we have seen, can to a certain extent, cease to have meaning. People can be neurotic for other reasons. All neurotics can benefit from the Sacraments, but even those who use the Sacraments and pursue a Final End can still be neurotic. What we have written concerns those who are mentally disordered because they have no sacramental life and no purpose to give meaning to life, and no happiness because they have failed successfully to desublimate the natural love the soul has for its God. There is no strict correlation between the presence of neurosis and the absence of Christian life. There may be, but not necessarily. Some of the crooks of history have been free from neurosis. The rich man whose soul was required by God went to bed with animal contentment in his soul. This is no doubt shared today by the equally sane and godless sharks one meets occasionally on the stock-exchange. On the other hand there is no strict correlation between the presence of Christian life and the absence of neurosis. People may be neurotic through physical causes and through heredity, though there are generally psychological causes as well. Good people have suffered from scruples; saints have suffered from melancholia. Above all, people may be saintly and good in spite of, and even because of, neurosis.

Considered in its subjective aspects, neurosis is mental pain and suffering of the mind. In the mind of God all men are seen through the mirror of the humanity of Christ. Christ is a suffering One, and He suffered by human instruments, because when sin came, so did death, and the Model of humanity chose death as the consummation of Atonement for the sin which had lost us our sonship. Christ came in suffering for Atonement. He is a suffering King, and His subjects are suffering subjects. But remember it was His subjects who crowned the King with thorns.

All humanity, then, suffers as the King of men suffered upon earth. This happens whether you are a follower of the King or not. Jew and Gentile, black and white, they all suffer. They carry the mark of the seal whether they know it or not. In each the Passion of Christ reappears.

The Christian has a supreme advantage, however, because, enlightened by grace, he not only knows this truth but can be convinced of its value. The Christian is one who is identified by the Sacraments with Christ. He is called to be the Son of God by grace, as Christ is the son of God by nature. In the eyes of God Christ is a suffering One. He carried the wounds of Calvary. Now the Christian can carry his wounds—and his neuroses—as a witness of his sonship before the Father.

Of all the wounds a man can carry perhaps the wounds of

the mind are hardest to bear. Christ shed His blood on Calvary; but He sweated blood in the Garden of Gethsemane when the weight of the world's evil pressed upon His mind. You remember how, on the night before His crucifixion, He went with His apostles to Gethsemane. And there, as St. Matthew and St. Mark relate, He said to them: "My soul is sorrowful, even unto death." Here is St. Luke's description of what followed: "And he was withdrawn from them a stone's cast: and kneeling down he prayed, saying: Father if thou wilt, remove this chalice from me: but yet not my will but thine be done. And there appeared to him an angel, strengthening him. And being in an agony, he prayed longer. And his sweat became as drops of blood trickling down upon the ground." The neurotic is called to accompany Christ, not so much on the road to Calvary as on the road to Gethsemane.

We all meet neurotics. We pity them. We may feel superior to them because they cannot stand on their own feet. We see ourselves in them, caricatured and magnified as if in a convex mirror. That is the root of it. We see humanity, raw and quivering, and there is no urge to pour in oil and wine; we do not like travesties of ourselves. But let us pause, as Francis paused before the leper. Like him, we will discover Christ. In the neurotic, even in the psychotic, the manic depressive, we see the torture of the mind of Christ. In that twilight of the human spirit is the answering echo to the call of Christ to His Father in Gethsemane to let the chalice pass from Him, and in the darkness of the soul Christ calls, as He called on Calvary: "My God, my God, why hast thou forsaken me?" The pain of the Christ mind turns to God in the pain of the human mind. The neurotic carries the mental stigmata of Christ.

This is credible, but, for some, not palatable. Only the flame of faith will carry conviction of it, and even the flame may scorch while yet it heals.

To any neurotic who may read this, let us add that only the

nearest friends of Christ, the chosen apostles, were invited to Gethsemane. They were healthy and slept. Perhaps only the sick of mind can really keep the vigil. The supernatural limit to pain is martyrdom. Martyr, of course, is a word which means witness. The neurotic is called to martyrdom within. He is the witness of Gethsemane.

TENEBRAE

"O vos omnes
Qui transitis per viam
Attendite et videte
Si est dolor
Sicut dolor meus . . ."

For the waters have indeed
Come unto my soul.
And not the wildly fair
Tumultuous singing cataracts of spring . . .
No, nor the leaping, lashing, foam-head waves
Of the unconquered ocean;
No, nor yet
The grandeur of the rivers to the sea . . .
The waveless lake—the everflowing spring . . .
The rock-battalioned gem of deep-sea pool . . .
No—but the dark and slowly-rolling tides
Foamless and silent—deadly still and cold,
Of that vast ocean without bound . . .
Despair.

For; "I am the man
Who see my poverty

By the rod of His indignation . . .
He has led me into darkness,
And not into light . . .

Attendite, et videte
Si est dolor sicut dolor meus."

SITIO: THE THIRST OF CHRIST

He said, as he hung on the Cross, I thirst; and it was first of all an expression of his physical suffering. But when the Word makes use of words it is like those mountain masses where range succeeds range beyond the eye's reach. I thirst: there is meaning upon meaning; and we can think of the words as expressing too the unquenchable thirst of God for the love of man, the endless pursuit of man by the love of the Hound of Heaven. It was that thirst which was part of the agony of the Cross, but which also had led to the Cross. Beyond the physical thirst there is the sad longing of Christ's human heart; and beyond that again the deep mystery of the Godhead which the human longing expresses: the deep mystery of which Angelus Silesius spoke in bold and terrible words: the mystery of divine love becoming a beggar at the door of humanity.

God is described for us as a jealous God. We must not interpret the words in a crude sense, as though it were the petty human emotion we were speaking of, as though God were jealous of the love we might give his other creatures. To love him is necessarily to love the other things that are his handiwork and the objects of his love—though indeed to love them in the right way, the way we sometimes find very hard, to love them precisely as his, so that our love of them is part of our love of him. But he is a jealous God because his love is a burning and consuming fire: it demands a total response; and it will burn and consume the human heart in order to obtain it.

The saints know the terror and joy of that fire, which burns away all the dross from their hearts and makes their own love perfect. The souls in purgatory—the crucible of fire—know it as they failed to know it in this world, and are made perfect in their turn. Indeed it is all too possible to escape the knowledge in this world; to live our lives on the surface, to serve God quite well, to persuade ourselves that we love him, but never really to discover what love means. It feels so much safer if we can tame love, domesticate it, keep it within modest bounds. Even with our human love we tend to do that: either to degrade it altogether and make it a matter merely of glamour, of unreal romance; or to think of it as a small and placid thing, not big enough or fierce enough to interfere with the equable tempo of our lives, forgetting that this love too can be strong as death, and that many waters cannot quench it, and that it is a love of that kind that makes human beings really live. And so it is too with the love of God and our response to it; we try to substitute for the raging fury and terror and loveliness of a forest fire a neat little stove in our sitting-rooms. And of course we can, if we will, thus escape the violence, the stark demands, the burning; because though Love pursues he does not force, precisely because the *redamatio,* the giving back of love to Love, must be a free gift or it will not be love at all. But to escape it all: that is far more terrifying than all that love can do to us, because it means in the end that we may be left out in the cold; we may miss life altogether; we may forge for ourselves the fate of those of whom the Apocalypse speaks, who being neither hot nor cold are worthy only of being spewed out of the mouth.

But if the thirst of God is an awful thing it is also a lovely thing; it is also the mystery of God's pity. I thirst: and it is a thirst to give life to men, and to give it in spite of their blindness and weakness and betrayals. Amen, I say to thee, this day shalt thou be with me in paradise: and the man was a criminal, and yet he was to be with Christ in paradise, and to be that day with Christ in paradise. Do we wonder where, in that case, is the justice of God? For us, we may think, if we are lucky, a long purgatory though we try to live fairly good lives; and yet for the thief an instant paradise. But it is what our Lord himself had said, that the publicans and sinners would enter the kingdom before the righteous—because it is better to be a sinner and yet be humble, yet be capable of love, than to be righteous and respectable and at the same time still deeply tained with self-love and self-esteem—and we know if we look into our hearts, how strong that self-love is in us. If the thief was to be taken at once to God it was because the personality of Christ, the sound of his voice or the glance of his eyes, had brought about a revolution in his heart, had shown him the meaning of the consuming fire, had caused that fire instantaneously to take possession of him; and so in spite of his crimes, in spite of all the past, the process was complete, his heart was ready.

At the end, we are told, we shall be judged on love. That is why the thirst of God is not only awful but lovely and consoling as well. If we try to be humble and to open our hearts to love, then we need not fear. We are weak and therefore we sin; and sometimes we sin in a far worse way, becoming hard and rebellious and giving ourselves deliberately to evil; but always there is forgiveness, even to seventy times seven, if we turn again to God in humility and love. How foolish to worry, as people sometimes do, lest they may suddenly one day commit grave sin, and suddenly die, and so be lost in spite of a lifetime of love and faithfulness: as though God were a harsh and malevolent Judge awaiting an opportunity to make convictions. This day shalt thou be with me in paradise: a life devoted to love would never in fact end suddenly in a grave sin, but the love of God is such that the opposite may be true, and has been true: that a life of sin can end in sudden glory.

This then is the love into which we are asked to throw our-selves; and if we hesitate at the paradox of a love which is at once so fierce and so gentle, so devouring and so patient, there is the figure of Christ on the Cross to keep us from shrinking from the fierceness, to re-assure us as again and again in the pages of the Gospel he re-assures us, Fear not, and to show us in the agony of his own body how the fire of divine love is a fire that first of all devours the heart of God.

And if we need further re-assurance we shall find it in those other words that he spoke from the Cross, the words in which he gave his mother to be a mother to John and to the whole race of men. We think of God as our Father, as he told us to do; but we must not allow ourselves to think that this means a limiting of God to those qualities we associate with fatherhood to the exclusion of the qualities of a mother. Our Lord tells us precisely the contrary in his likening of himself to the hen gathering her chickens under her wings; and that final tender-ness of divine love is expressed and proved for us in the delicacy of this parting gift from the Cross whereby the Son of Man bequeaths to us the mother who had borne and fed and nursed him, and who was there at the end to take his dead body into her arms.

How then can we fear the thirst of God? And yet we continue in fact to flee him down the arches of the years: why? Because in our blindness we prefer the labyrinthine ways of our own egoism: we know that to love is to give, to love totally is to give totally, and we fear the loss of our own self-hood: never more to be able to arrange things for ourselves (as though we ever could), never more to feel that we are the masters of our fate . . . And so we miss the fire, we miss the fullness of life, we miss the real freedom. That is why Good Friday is not just an event in the past but something that is to be done in us every day: that going down into the deep places where we see our-selves for what we really are, see reality as it is, that leaving of the conventional religious shallows to plunge into the ocean of love, that companionship of Christ on the Cross that teaches us to say with him his final word: *In manus tuas:* into thy hands. . . . That is the acceptance of reality; that is the gateway to life. Into thy hands, O Lord, I commend this joy, this sorrow, this problem, this decision; into thy hands I commend each moment as it comes, each event as thou sendest it to me; into thy hands I put this thing I have to do or suffer; into thy hands this love, this responsibility; into thy hands this weakness, this failure, this wrong thing that I have done; and so, finally, into thy hands I commend my life as a whole, all that I am: be it done to me according to thy word—that is the thing that is asked of us, and in the last resort that is the only thing that is asked of us. And if we are trying to do this we need not fear; and if in the end we can succeed in doing it wholly and gladly we shall have shared fully in the *In manus tuas* of Christ, and so we shall be able to share also in his *Consummatum est:* we shall have learnt fully the meaning of love, and so, with Christ in his glory, we shall have come home.

THE CRUCIFIXION

Oh, man's capacity
For spiritual sorrow, corporal pain!
Who has explored the deepmost of that sea,
With heavy links of a far-fathoming chain!

That melancholy lead,
Let down in guilty and in innocent hold,
Yet into childish hands deliverèd,
Leaves the sequestered floor unreached, untold.

One only has explored
The deepmost; but He did not die of it.
Not yet, not yet He died. Man's human Lord
Touched the extreme; it is not infinite.

But over the abyss
Of God's capacity for woe He stayed
One hesitating hour; what gulf was this?
Forsaken He went down, and was afraid.

CHRIST TO THE SUFFERER

"LAMENT NOT thy path of woe,   O loved man—
it is not unbearable.   I hold thee dear,
and will set my guard   in power about thee.
My might is above all   on this mid-earth,
victory speeds Me. . . .
See now the path   where thy blood poured down,
the road dark-stained   by thy bone-breaking
and thy body bruises.   No more may their blows
harm thee, who hast borne   their hard hate."
The beloved champion   looked backward then,
hearkening to the words   of the Glory-King;
he saw groves standing,   fair, green-blowing,
bright with blossoms   where his blood had fallen.

From the poem *Andreas*

LIFE VICTORIOUS

ꙮ CHRISTIANITY IS OFTEN reproached with being a religion of sorrow and life-slaying renunciation. The reaction against this is the secularist insistence on the things of this world, natural and bodily pleasures, the happiness of healthy activity amid beautiful scenes. And in fact Catholic devotion has for centuries emphasised too exclusively the aspect of suffering. Though every altar has fittingly its crucifix, and the church walls are almost covered with the Stations of the Cross, we seldom see representations of the triumphant Christ, the Resurrection and Ascension. Where they are depicted at all, they occupy a subordinate place as panels in a reredos or among the subjects in a stained glass window. The impression received is inevitably that the Passion and generally the sorrowful mysteries are the centre of the Christian religion.

In fact, the Liturgy, with its fifty days of Paschal alleluias as against a fortnight of Passiontide, shows the true proportion. The Cross is the way; the Resurrection the goal. The Cross is of time; the Resurrection for eternity. And the Cross itself is primarily not the suffering of death, but the victorious struggle of Life over and through death. Doctrinally and liturgically the central position of the Church is clear. She refuses to blink the fact of suffering and death, and their necessity in a sinful world —facts from which the modern world is trying desperately to turn away its eyes. Nor will she shrink from demanding renunci-

THE RESURRECTION
Piero della Francesca

ation, the taking of the Cross. But she does not, like many oriental cults, make renunciation an end in itself. She will not, perversely, value suffering for its own sake, or morbidly fall in love with death.

Keeping the *via media* between East and West, optimism and pessimism, the shirking and the cult of pain, she teaches, through her theology and her liturgy, that happiness is man's true good, not sorrow, that he is made, not to suffer but to be happy, and that eternal happiness may, if he will, be his. Also that death is evil, life good, and man destined to life, not death. For Christ came to give abundant life and everlasting life. Thus the Cross, while duly affirmed, is set in its right place in the scheme of salvation.

CARRION COMFORT

Not, I'll not, carrion comfort, Despair, not feast on thee;
Not untwist—slack they may be—these last strands of man
In me ór, most weary, cry *I can no more.* I can;
Can something, hope, wish day come, not choose not to be.
But ah, but O thou terrible, why wouldst thou rude on me
Thy wring-world right foot rock? Lay a lionlimb against me?
    scan
With darksome devouring eyes my bruisèd bones? and fan,
O in turns of tempest, me heaped there; me frantic to avoid
    thee and flee?

Why? That my chaff might fly; my grain lie, sheer and clear.
Nay in all that toil, that coil, since (seems) I kissed the rod,
Hand rather, my heart lo! lapped strength, stole joy, would
    laugh, chéer.
Cheer whom though? the hero whose heaven-handling flung me,
    fóot tród
Me? or me that fought him? O which one? is it each one? That
    night, that year
Of now done darkness I wretch lay wrestling with (my God!)
    my God.

THE RELIGION OF THE HEART

✑ JUNE IS THE PEAK MONTH of the flower-year; and visitors to our churches register disappointment when they find our best floral effects distributed round the Sacred Heart statue. Of all our statues, commonly, it has the least artistic merit; pose, features, and colouring indicate that the repository has gauged, all too accurately, the popular taste. The visitor, if he does not share our creed, is apt to exclaim, "How unevangelical! How un-English!"

He is wrong on both counts. "The Heart of Christ in Heaven towards sinners on earth, or, a Treatise demonstrating the gracious Disposition and Tender Affection of Christ in his humane Nature now in Glory, unto all his Members under all Sorts of Infirmities, either of Sin or Misery," was written by Thomas Goodwin, a Cambridge man, victim of the Laudian repression and chaplain to Oliver Cromwell.

There is nothing unevangelical about the devotion to the Sacred Heart. No, the question raised by Thomas Goodwin is, How far can Christian devotion legitimately go in the direction of the sentimental?

It is a kind of approach that scandalized at once the Jansenism of Port Royal and the robust Anglicanism of the Warburton school, and it was really a matter of good taste. Theologically, you cannot drive a wedge between the human and the Divine Nature in our Lord for the purposes of worship. But it is possible to concentrate on the Sacred Humanity with an intensity of imaginative affection which some critics will inevitably label sentimentalism.

"As sweetly as doves do converse with doves, sympathising and mourning each over other, so may we with Christ, for he thus sympathiseth with us"; that is Goodwin's claim, but there will always be a kind of up-stage Christianity which finds fault with such demonstrations. Who are we (it will be asked) that we should dare to feel *sorry* for the Crucified? And such minds will suspect that the bad art (for it is, mostly, bad art) springs naturally from a wrong fount of devotion.

Is there, quite apart from theological orthodoxy and unorthodoxy, a right and a wrong approach in such matters? Can we suppose there is good taste and bad taste in devotion, as in the arts? And if so, ought the views of those who have good taste be a canon, as in the arts, for those who lack it? I am unashamedly glad to be able to leave such questions unanswered.

LITANY FOR THE FEAST OF THE MOST SACRED HEART

❧ *The Church speaks:*

Now I will pray the ardour of the soul as a great litany is prayed.
Now I will raise the song of praise that is not sung but loved.
Blood-red secret of all that is:
Holy Heart, divine Heart, almighty Heart.
Be loved, Love, eternal Love, be thou eternally loved.

Hearth in the dark of the frozen world,
Be loved, Love!
Flame-shadow over all the false brightness of the world,
Be loved, Love!
Burning sign in all the false rest of the world;
Lonely Heart, flaming Heart, unquenchable Heart:
Be loved, everlasting Love.

Heart deep as the nights that have no face:
Be loved!
Heart strong as the waves that have no shores:
Be loved!
Heart tender as little children that have no bitterness:
Be everlastingly loved!

Rose from the flower-beds of the invisible,
Rose from the chalice of the humble maiden,
Blossoming rose-bush, in which heaven and earth are entwined:
Be loved, everlasting Love!

Royal Heart in the flowing mantle of Thy blood:
Be loved!
Brother-Heart in the wild mockery of the thorny crown:
Be loved!
Breaking Heart in the stark ornament of Thy death wounds:
Heart dethroned, Heart betrayed, Heart cruelly martyred:
Be loved, everlasting Love, be everlastingly loved.

Heart before whom the mighty find their knees,
We ask Thee for Thy love.
Heart before whom the careless find their tears:
We ask Thee for Thy love.
Heart in whom thieves and murderers yet find forgiveness,
Great Heart, Heart of mercy, Heart of glory,
We ask Thee for Thy love!

Red-thorn of our gladness,
Sorrow-thorn of our repentance,
Fair evening glow of our own setting,
We ask Thee for Thy love.
Crimson cloth that turns sin pale as death:
We ask Thee for Thy love.
Ruby stream after which the sick souls thirst:
We ask Thee for Thy love.
Whispering nearness in which parted friends may meet:
We ask Thee for Thy love.

Comforting lamp of the distressed,
Lighthouse of the persecuted and the disgraced,

Hidden chamber in which the gentle dead may yet breathe;
All-knowing Heart, all-guiding Heart, ultimate Heart:
We ask Thee for Thy love!

Heart that takes us all to itself,
Heart that strikes the centre of all our hearts,
Heart that breaks the proud hearts of us all:
We ask Thee for Thy love!

Heart that makes solitude into a great people:
We ask Thee for Thy love.
Heart that makes discord into an united people:
We ask Thee for Thy love.
Heart in which the whole world becomes Thy people:
We consecrate ourselves to Thy love.
Overflowing Heart, overflaming Heart, overstorming Heart:
Be loved, Love, everlasting Love, be everlastingly loved.

That Thy Dawn may break with kindling light,
We consecrate ourselves to Thy love.
That Thy day may bring fire to our hearts,
We consecrate ourselves to Thy love.
That Thy day may burn all our hearts into Thine,
We consecrate ourselves to Thy love,
Mighty Heart, ineluctable Heart, all-consuming Heart.

Fire! Fire! The angels' wings are burning, the swords of the
    seraphim are aflame!
The lights of heaven are burning, the depths of earth are burn-
    ing, rocks and yesterdays are all aflame!
The expectation of all creatures burns—the spirit burns in the
    darkness of high thought.
All has been taken from love, all must become love; sing "Holy,
    Holy, Holy!" rustling flames of the Seraphim!

Heart from which the heavens draw their glory,
Heart from which suns and constellations draw their beginning
    and their end,
Heart from which the souls of the blessed draw their blessedness.
World-ordering Heart, world-conquering Heart, Thou only
    Heart of hearts:
Amen. Amen. May the day of Thine infinite love come quickly.

CHRIST THE KING

⟩ THE KINGSHIP OF CHRIST is not constitutional. It is absolute.
God is absolute. Christ is that strange Representative who *is*
that which He represents. No one of us contributes directly to
the rights of Christ over us. He possesses them of His own
nature.

These rights are not departmental merely. Christ came to
save, because He loved, the whole man. Therefore, His loving-
kindness extends to that body which in part we are. His tender
miracles of healing were not *only* "signs," meant to startle men
into attending to spiritual truths, or to prove a point. He loved
the little child He took into His arms: He liked it to be there.
He really was sorry for Martha and for Mary: He was truly
solicitous for the hungry unshepherded thousands: the pain of
the sick was His. Therefore we are right, in His Name, to spend
ourselves even for the physical well-being of our fellowmen:
all those corporal works of mercy, as we name them, whatever
shape they take—welfare work, the finding a job for the prisoner,
scouting, summer camps for children—are indeed as that cup of
water which shall not lose its Christian reward, since it has
cooled the lips of Christ, whom in the least of His little ones
we serve in our small ways. To decry such tasks—with all their
laborious modern complications, such as co-operation with gov-
ernmental enterprise—as we have sometimes heard them decried,
is foolish, cruel, and all-but heretical. But never shall we make

that body, to which He wishes well, our ultimate care, as though there were naught else to which He should wish better. We have seen Christ triumph perhaps most splendidly in those sick whom He does not cure, in those sad whom He consoles, but the source of whose sorrow He does not dry up. Nor shall we forget that *Himself* would He never favouritize. With Himself He was not gentle. He rose; and we shall rise. But from the Crucifixion He sought no exemption, nor shall we ask ourselves to be exempted. We dare to say: It is always the ascetic who has won. History has justified the Cross. The Law then of our King is Tenderness unlimited, but tenderness unselfish. There need be no fear that our pity may degenerate into complaisance, if it be a pity so unselfish as to deny to itself even the recompense of gratitude.

Christ is then King, too, even of minds and wills. He is to bring all intelligences into subordination to Himself. Not that He shuts us off from other truths that we might, apart from Him, acquire; but He is perfect truth, and in His Light we see all other lights. He who is not a Christian must work laboriously up from such scattered evidence, such stammered hints, as the observation of human nature and of history may supply to him. To some temporary, partial, hypothetical interpretation of the world, solution of its problems, method of approach, he may tentatively reach. We have our short cut—a short cut for once legitimate. We, as Christians, have the duty and the privilege of looking forthwith at Christ, and seeing forthwith Truth, and descending thence to judge of all things else. The short cut is no easy option. For to many a sacrifice will it lead us. But the sacrifice will not be left too hard. Magnificent was the French king's motto: "I need no hope, in order to begin; no success need I, in order to persevere." But those hopes, that success, which he could do without, were subordinate and secondary things. With the ultimate hope, the indefectible assurance, we, in our infinite task, cannot dispense, dare not try to do so. We need them, even to know fully what we are aiming at: we need them, if we are to fight to the finish. I know few more tragic spectacles than that of the man who, without any certain hope, with only a guessed-at aim, yet nobly and toilsomely devotes himself to what he surmises may prove the welfare of his fellows, grinding his heart against that granite that the world, at one time, seems, panting his soul out in that vacuum which at other times it is—that ultimate illusion within which his own self expires and vanishes. Not thus need we be; of us this is not asked. Even if it be asked of our impatience only that we should wait—wait in the dark, and impotent: well, "the darkness is not dark with Thee, but the night is as clear as the day."

But since society is a real thing, and men do not live as nomads, Christ, King universally, has His absolute rights thereto. We dare not undertake a transaction that involves our fellow-men—and which does not?—without consulting His law. That law were gladly consulted, I am convinced, far more than it is, even by men of our generation, were it but allowed. I do not believe that there is more than the tiniest percentage among us who actually want the memorials of our dead to be those squat pyramids, those blunted columns, that imply nothing whatsoever unless it be that memory alone, and neither hope nor help, is all we can contribute to those who have served and died. The cenotaph itself would be a mockery to me, a mere crossless bulk, indeed, a deliberate academic propagandist impertinence, did I not know that by now it is wholly enveloped in a cloud of prayer for the souls of those fallen, and that the Cross it does not carry has been signed on a million hearts as men pass it by and do on its occasion what it does not ask. No arch that they are building, to support the tottering fabric of Europe, will hold even its poor self up, if the builders still reject that stone which is its key.

Hence even in economics, even in your problems of housing,

wages, dividends, there is no doubt at all but that the Christian must see what Christ has to say about them: even in politics, where the Church takes no side, any more than Christ did, where no principle is involved, there *can* indeed not only be principles involved—and then no such question is alien to Christ's rule—but there can be tendencies or preferences, so that a man may be acting more according to Christ's mind, or less. Seek even here what Christ would suggest, even where He does not command: where He commands, the well-being of individual, family, group or nation is dependent on that command. . . .

We see then Our Lord Jesus Christ crowned with many crowns—King, because of His Nature: one with the Lord of Heaven and Earth: true God from true God, and King necessarily of all creation, since in Him were all things made, who is the Archetype, and in Him all things hold together; and since unto Him, no less, are all things made, who is the Omega no less than the Alpha of that all-inclusive series that contains all words. King, further, in His Mission, since through Him, no less than into Him are all things to be "recapitulated," brought to a head, receive their explanation: if St. Paul so often speaks of the Consummation of the ages, that is not because he foresees an intolerable series of years, at last finding their exhausted end, but, because he sees past, as future, building itself up, conspiring, aspiring, towards the perfect Christ. The crowded scroll of the world's history remains ever sealed with its seven seals, nor can heaven or earth or hell unroll it or read its secret, unless the Lamb be sent forth from God's Throne, who looses the seals, and reads the book, since Himself is not only Solver, but Solution. King finally in His actual work, since whatsoever earthly things are just, whatsoever things are pure and fair, are seen to find their full meaning and reality, co-ordination and perfection, and their only sanction in the Truth and Law of Christ—and King in that vast work of the supernaturalization of our souls, which without Him could not so much as begin, whereas with Him and through Him, "in His divinity we are made partakers, who in our humanity did not disdain to share."

And lo, having His head thus crowned with many crowns, He lays them, far as He may, aside. Being rich, He becomes poor. Master of all, He is among us not as one with servants, but as one who serves. Being in origin and by nature God, He deems not the being treated as God's equal a thing at all costs to be held on to, but empties Himself, taking upon Himself the nature of a slave, and is found, to human eyes, just what mere man is. And He humbles himself yet further, subordinating Himself even unto death, and that, a death upon a cross. *"That,"* cries St. Paul, exultant, "is why God hath utterly exalted Him, so that at the Name of Jesus every knee should kneel"—and we kneel, as a man may kneel, because he loves. King, to be obeyed: King, rejoicingly served; and King, because loved. For the sake of that uncrowning, we love Him and thereby better than recrown Him. The little son of Mary: the working-lad: the labouring man of Nazareth. The man who walked hungry amid the waving corn: who sank exhausted in the patch of shade beside the ancient well: who slept in the cabin of the little boat, "His head upon a pillow." Terrified, heart-sick, in Gethsemane: heart-broken on the Cross: sending Magdalen to be His messenger: known, at Emmaus, when He broke the bread. And the vast duty of our subjecthood almost narrows itself to this—try, when you can remember, to do some action of your day simply that it may please Him—for no other reason than that! What will not be the response of His royal Heart? and seek what He has made so easy, His humble Court, His modest audiences, at those altar-rails: there will you meet Him, whom having not seen, you love: in whom, though now you see Him not, yet believing, you are filled with joy unspeakable and full of glory. If thus you add this tiny ray or that to His new crown, that we bestow on Him, the full splendour of that crown turns back towards you, envelops you wholly, and crowns you in your turn.

THE HUMAN RACE COMES TO BE JUDGED

So TO SION'S HILL   there come up together
a host, great, mighty,   true to their Maker,
bright and blithe;   blessedness is their share.
Then from the four   far corners of earth,
the uttermost ends   of the world's kingdom,
angels all-shining   together blow
their clamorous trumpets;   mid-earth trembles
beneath men's feet.   They sound together
strongly, gloriously,   in the star's pathway;
they sing and run out   from the south and the north,
from the east and west   over all creation.
They wake from the dead   the sons of men,
all mankind   to the grim judgment,
aghast from the old earth;   they bid them stand up
straightway from their fast sleep.   There the sorrowing folk
are heard, sad-hearted,   hard-beset,
lamenting their grief   for deeds while living,
sore afraid.   This is the great fore-sign
of all the portents   which ever yet
were shown to men.   For there, mingling,
is the mighty host   of angels and devils,
the brightest and darkest;   both are there,

the fair and the swart,   and a home is shaped for them,
but far unlike   for angels and devils.
Then swiftly   on Sion's hill
from the south-east   a gleam of sunlight
comes from the Creator,   shining more radiantly
than any man   may dream in his heart,
bright-gleaming.   Then God's Son
through the arches of heaven   comes ever onward,
and Christ's face   is gloriously seen,
the King's presence   from the eastern sky.
He is sweet to hearts   of His own folk,
bitter to the baleful,   varied wondrously,
far unlike   to the happy and wretched.
The deep places din.   Before Him there sweeps down
a great fire whelming   over the wide ground.
Strong and bright   are the stars falling.
Then will the sun   be changed to swartness,
to blood's hue,   which before shone bright
over the old world   of the children of men
and the moon herself   who once in the night
gave light to mankind   shall fall low.
And all the stars   shall be shaken through heaven
on strong winds   storm-beaten. . . .
Then a mighty army,   forever young,
fares onward   before the All-Wielder.
They, called by name,   must needs obey,
bear their breast-hoard   before God's Bairn,
their spirit's treasure.

From the poem *Christ*.

THE LAST JUDGMENT

❧ MEN DIE and go to bliss or woe. Meanwhile the world goes on. Christ died at the hands of sinners and rose again in victory over sin and death. But sin and death go on. The victory, complete in Christ, is progressive in men: its completion lies somewhere in the future. Satan is dethroned, but not driven from the field. He has lost the human race, but may still win individuals, and go close to winning many more, and trouble many whom he does not even go close to winning. It was after Our Lord's Resurrection and Ascension that St. Paul wrote to the Ephesians (vi, 11): "You must wear all the weapons in God's armoury, if you would find strength to resist the cunning of the devil. It is not against flesh and blood that we enter the lists; we have to do with princedoms and powers, with those who have mastery of the world in these dark days, with malign influences in an order higher than ours."

The world is filled with the turbulence of men. The writer of the *Book of Wisdom* would not have to soften a line in his harsh picture: the proportions may be different, the world makes certain advances, but all these things are still here—"They neither keep life nor marriage undefiled: but one kills another by envy or grieves him by adultery. And all things are mingled together, blood, murder, theft and dissimulation, corruption and unfaithfulness, tumults and perjury, disquieting of the good;

forgetfulness of God, defiling of souls, changing of nature, disorder in marriage, and the irregularity of adultery and uncleanness."

But all this is only the colourful front face of things. This is humanity tormented by its own evil and by powers of evil greater than its own. Behind it and within it Christ is forming the new humanity, re-born and re-made in Him. The Mystical Body continues to grow. There are the millions who have died in Christ and are inbuilt into the Body forever, and there are the millions still on earth in whom His life principle is working, evidently or secretly. Behind all the turbulence, the building of the Mystical Body goes on ceaselessly, and it is humanity's real work, little as so many humans suspect it, perversely as so many work against it, tepidly as so many cooperate.

The building goes on ceaselessly, but not by mere addition of more and more. It is growing toward something. So St. Paul tells the Ephesians: "Far off or near, united in the same Spirit, we have access through him to the Father. You are no longer exiles, then, or aliens; the saints are your fellow-citizens, you belong to God's household. Apostles and prophets are the foundation on which you were built, and the chief corner-stone of it is Jesus Christ himself. In him the whole fabric is bound together, *as it grows in to a temple,* dedicated to the Lord" (ii, 18–21).

Here the Church is seen as a building growing into a temple. Two chapters later we see it as a Body growing to maturity. We have already seen the application of the verses that follow to the individual soul, but they apply equally to the Body as a whole: "So we shall reach perfect manhood, that maturity which is proportioned to the completed growth of Christ . . . We are to follow the truth, in a spirit of charity, and so grow up, in everything, into a due proportion with Christ, who is our head."

Both figures convey the same truth. The building of a temple is more than an endless heaping together of stones. It is an adding and an arrangement, and it has a term: a moment comes when the temple is built. Only God knows the shape and proportion of the temple He is building; only God knows how close the temple is to completion. So with a body: it is not merely an endless growing of new cells: it has a shape and proportion and grows towards a maturity. How close Christ's Mystical Body is to its maturity, He knows and we do not. But it is not fanciful to think that with the completion of the temple, the human race will cease to generate. To what purpose would new generations be born, when the Mystical Body of Christ is complete?

II

Of the coming of Jesus in power to judge the world Scripture tells us something. St. Paul writes: "That is for the day when the Lord Jesus appears from Heaven, with Angels to proclaim His power; with fire flaming about Him"—an echo of Our Lord's own phrase: "When the Son of Man comes, it will be like the lightning that springs up from the East and flashes across to the West." There will be the sound of a trumpet, and the dead will arise in their bodies. Thus Our Lord tells us: "Immediately after the distress of those days, the sun will be darkened, and the moon will refuse her light, and the stars will fall from heaven, and the powers of heaven will rock; and then the sign of the Son of Man will be seen in Heaven; then it is that all the tribes of the land will mourn, and they will see the Son of Man coming upon the clouds of heaven, with great power and glory; and he will send out his angels with a loud blast of the trumpet, to gather his elect from the four winds, from one end of heaven to the other" (Matt. xxiv, 29–32).

St. Paul gives a further detail concerning those who are still alive upon earth when that day comes: "It will happen in a moment, in the twinkling of an eye, when the last trumpet sounds; the trumpet will sound, and the dead will rise again, free from corruption, and we shall find ourselves changed; this corruptible nature of ours must be clothed with incorruptible life, this mortal nature with immortality" (I Cor. xv, 52–54).

It is not only the just who will rise again: "When the Son of Man comes in his glory, and all the angels with him, he will sit down upon the throne of his glory, and all nations will be gathered in his presence, where he will divide men one from the other, as the shepherd divides the sheep from the goats; he will set the sheep on his right, and the goats on his left. Then the King will say to those who are on his right hand, Come ye that have received a blessing from my Father, take possession of the kingdom which has been prepared for you since the foundation of the world. . . . Then he will say to those who are on his left hand, in their turn, Go far from me, you that are accursed, into that eternal fire which has been prepared for the devil and his angels. . . . And these shall pass on to eternal punishment and the just to eternal life" (Matt. xxv, 31–46).

Of the detail of the Judgment we are told little. In the passage just quoted, Our Lord makes the sentence depend upon works of charity done or refused by us to men, and therefore done or refused to Himself. It is the common teaching that these works of charity are used here as representative of the virtues in general. The Judgment will be a complete judgment, in which men will see their own actions in their true value, and in the whole of their context—that is to say, in relation to the actions of all other men, and these in relation to the overruling providence of God: so that in a sense there will be spread before the mind of man a picture of the whole created order and of the marvellous pattern of God's work in it and upon it. At last we shall see the shape and bearing of all things.

The Kingdom of God will then be established in its fulness. What will be the place of matter in it? Souls will once more be united with bodies, so that we shall be constituted in the completeness of our personality. Will these bodies have any connection with the bodies we now have? The answer is yes, but the detail is not clear. After all, while I have the same body now that I had twenty years ago, no single cell in it is the same: every cell I had then is gone and a new one has taken its place. Yet it is not mere verbalism to say that I have the same body. Clearly, apart from the cells there is an element which somehow persists and by persisting preserves the identity of my body. It would be beyond the scope of this book to set out the philosophic and scientific theories as to the nature of the persisting element. But it may be this element, whatever it is, that will be re-united with the soul in the resurrection of the body and constitute the identity of the new body with the old. Anyhow our resurrection bodies will be, in the theological phrase, glorified bodies: corruption will be clothed with incorruptible life, mortal nature with immortality. At last we shall know what it is to be a man, for the union of soul and body will exist with no rebellion or inertia on the body's part to diminish the union. In Christopher Dawson's phrase "Matter will be once more the extension of spirit, not its limit; the instrument of spirit, not the enemy."

What matter will be there, apart from the human body, or in what condition, we do not know very well. Scripture, both Old Testament and New, is filled with the promise of new heavens and a new earth. Here is St. Peter: "The day of the Lord is coming, and when it comes, it will be upon you like a thief. The heavens will vanish in a whirlwind, the elements will be scorched up and dissolve, earth and all earth's achievements, will burn away. . . . And meanwhile, we have new heavens and a new earth to look forward to, the dwelling place of holiness" (II Peter iii, 10, 13). The whole twenty-first chapter of the last book of the New Testament should be read. I quote here the opening verses:

"Then I saw a new heaven, and a new earth. The old heaven, the old earth had vanished, and there was no more sea. And I, John, saw in my vision that holy city which is the new Jerusalem, being sent down by God from heaven, all clothed in readiness, like a bride who has adorned herself to meet her husband. I heard, too, a voice which cried aloud from the throne, Here is God's tabernacle pitched among men; he will dwell with them, and they will be his own people, and he will be among them, their own God. He will wipe away every tear from their eyes, and there will be no more death, or mourning or cries of distress, no more sorrow; those old things have passed away. And he who sat on the throne said, Behold I make all things new."

That inanimate nature will in some way be involved in the kingdom that shall never end seems certain, however mysterious may be the detail. St. Paul writes much on this. Thus to the Romans (viii, 19–22): "If creation is full of expectancy, that is because it is waiting for the sons of God to be made known. Created nature has been condemned to frustration; not for some deliberate fault of its own, but for the sake of him who so condemned it, with a hope to look forward to; namely that nature in its turn will be set free from the tyranny of corruption, to share in the glorious freedom of God's sons."

This destiny of the material creation is bound up with the role of the Second Person of the Blessed Trinity in and through whom all things were created and who became man for the remaking of the design that man had spoiled. Consider two of the things St. Paul said. The first is to the Colossians (i, 15–20): "He is the true likeness of the God we cannot see; his is that first birth which precedes every act of creation. Yea, in him all created things took their being, heavenly and earthly, visible and invisible. . . . He takes precedence of all, and in him all subsist . . . it was God's good pleasure to let all completeness dwell in him, and through him to win back all things, whether on earth or in heaven, into union with himself, making peace with them through his blood, shed on the cross." And to the Ephesians (i, 8–10): "So rich is God's grace, that has overflowed upon us in a full stream of wisdom and discernment, to make known the hidden purpose of his will. It was his loving design, centered in Christ, to give history its fulfilment by resuming everything in him, all that is in heaven, all that is on earth," or, in the Douay version: "In the dispensation of the fulness of times to re-establish all things in Christ."

The essential of life in the Kingdom will be in this, that in union with Christ we shall gaze upon the face of God, our whole being uttering itself in knowledge and love of Him. But just as God's infinite knowledge and love of Himself does not exclude creatures but flows over into knowing and loving them, so our total knowledge and love of God likewise will not exclude creatures but will flow over into knowledge and love of them. And God will be all in all.

PRAYER TO CHRIST OUR LORD

Lo, the Day-Spring,   brightest Angel
sent to men   over this middle-earth,
soothfast beam   of the very Sun,
more bright than stars—   Thou Thyself
givest light forever   to time going by.
As Thou, God,   begotten of God,
true Son of the Father,   in sky's glory
without beginning   forever wert,
now in its need   Thine own handiwork
begs Thee boldly   that Thou bring upon us
that bright sun,   and come Thyself
to enlighten swiftly   those who long since
wrapped in mist   and in murk darkness,
sat through a long night,   sin-enfolded.

Sources of the Selections

F. J. Sheed's from *Theology and Sanity*, except the first section of the Prologue, which is from *A Map of Life*

Hilaire Belloc's "Nazareth" and "Capharnaum and the Lake" from *Places*; "Anno Domini" from *The Silence of the Sea*; "Noël" and "Sonnet" from *Sonnets and Verse*

Caryll Houselander's "The Bride of Life" from *The Reed of God*; "Philip Speaks" and "Matthew Speaks" from *The Flowering Tree*; "Gethsemane" from *Guilt*; "Suffering Redemptive" from *This War Is the Passion*; "Mass for the People" from *The Dry Wood*

Gertrud von Le Fort's from *Hymns to the Church*

Sister Maris Stella's from *Frost for St. Brigid*

Sigrid Undset's from *Christmas and Twelfth Night*

J. P. Arendzen's "Herod, the Magi and the Star" from *The Gospels: Fact, Myth or Legend?*; "Why Hast Thou Forsaken Me?" from *Whom Do You Say?*

G. K. Chesterton's from *The Everlasting Man*

Maisie Ward's from *The Splendor of the Rosary*

C. C. Martindale's "Our Lady of Egypt" from *Our Blessed Lady*; "A Carpenter's Son" and "True Son of Abraham" from *What Think Ye of Christ?*; "Life and the Food of Life" from *Creative Words of Christ*; "Christ the King" from *Christ the King*

Robert Farren's "Manchild" from *Time's Wall Asunder*; "Immolation" from *Selected Poems*

Léonce de Grandmaison's from *Jesus Christ*

Walter Farrell's from *A Companion to the Summa*

Karl Adam's "Perfect Man" and "God the Son" from *The Son of God*; "Redemption" and "The Mystical Body in Heaven" from *The Spirit of Catholicism*

Eileen Duggan's from *Over the Bent World*

Ronald Knox's "The Patience of Christ" from *A Retreat for Priests*; "Palm Sunday," "The Upper Room" and "The Religion of the Heart" from *Stimuli*

Alfred Noyes' from *The Unknown God*

P. R. Régamey's from *Poverty*

Edward Leen's "The Last Supper" and "The Blessed Eucharist" from *In the Likeness of Christ*

Margaret Harrington's from *Calvary and Community*

Charles O'Donnell's from *Over the Bent World*

Gerald Vann's from *The High Green Hill*

Vincent McNabb's from *A Life of Our Lord*

Arnold Lunn's from *Now I See*

Jean Daniélou's from *Advent*

Robert Hugh Benson's from *Christ in the Church*

Eithne Tabor's from *The Cliff's Edge*

Alan Keenan's from *Neuroses and Sacraments*

E. I. Watkin's from *The Catholic Centre*

Poems not included in the above list will be found in *Poetry and Life: an Anthology;* the translations of the old English poems on pp. 262, 281, 307, 393, 408, 417 are by Margaret Williams, R.S.C.J. They appear in her *Word-Hoard*. The Langland poems on pp. 199 and 318 are from Henry W. Wells' translation of *The Vision of Piers Plowman*.

We are grateful to all the authors who have given permission for the inclusion of their works, as also to

Longmans, Green & Co., Inc., for Sigrid Undset's "Mother and Child" from *Christmas and Twelfth Night*.

Miss Dorothy Collins and Dodd, Mead & Company, Inc., for "The God in the Cave" and "The Riddles of the Gospel"; reprinted by permission of Dodd, Mead & Company from *The Everlasting Man,* by G. K. Chesterton. Copyright 1925 by Dodd, Mead & Company, Inc.

The Macmillan Company for Karl Adam's "Redemption" and "The Mystical Body in Heaven" from *The Spirit of Catholicism,* copyright 1935 by The Macmillan Company; also for Eileen Duggan's "Nationality," from her *Poems,* copyright 1939 by The Macmillan Company.

Sir Francis Meynell for Alice Meynell's "The Crucifixion."

Oxford University Press for Gerard Manley Hopkins' "Carrion Comfort" from his *Poems*.